CW00968020

CRICKET CAULDRON

CRICKET CAULDRON

The Turbulent Politics of Sport in Pakistan

Shaharyar M. Khan

and

Ali Khan

Foreword by Imran Khan

Harper
Sport

An Imprint of HarperCollins*Publishers*

First published in the UK in 2013 by I.B. Tauris & Co. Ltd, London

First published in India in 2013 by Harper Sport
An Imprint of HarperCollins *Publishers* India

Copyright © Shaharyar M. Khan and Ali Khan 2013

ISBN: 978-93-5029-500-7

2 4 6 8 10 9 7 5 3 1

HarperCollins *Publishers*
A-53, Sector 57, NOIDA, Uttar Pradesh – 201301, India
77-85 Fulham Palace Road, London W6 8JB, United Kingdom
Hazelton Lanes, 55 Avenue Road, Suite 2900, Toronto, Ontario M5R 3L2
and 1995 Markham Road, Scarborough, Ontario M1B 5M8, Canada
25 Ryde Road, Pymble, Sydney, NSW 2073, Australia
31 View Road, Glenfield, Auckland 10, New Zealand
10 East 53rd Street, New York NY 10022, USA

Printed and bound at
Thomson Press (India) Ltd.

TABLE OF CONTENTS

ILLUSTRATIONS

FOREWORD

When I heard the verdict in the spot-fixing case against the three Pakistani cricketers – Salman Butt, Mohammad Asif and Mohammad Amir – I felt an intense sadness. A sadness borne of the realization that what had occurred – particularly in the case of the 19-year-old Amir – was an enormous waste of exceptional talent. Three careers had been cut short because corruption and dishonesty had eaten into the soul of Pakistan cricket. But as pointed out in this book, can we blame the three transgressors? Have they failed Pakistan? Or has Pakistan collectively failed them? What ails Pakistan cricket in specific terms ails Pakistan generally and across the board. Lack of accountability, corruption, dishonesty, a broken education system – these are the issues that Pakistan as a nation faces.

That is why *Cricket Cauldron* is such an important book. It touches on all these issues and not simply the cricketing ones. It surveys the political, social and cultural landscape in Pakistan as seen through a cricketing lens. As the authors have contended, cricket, more than any other sport, provides a mirror image of a nation and its people. *Cricket Cauldron* will therefore interest not only cricket lovers but also those who seek to understand Pakistan today – an often chaotic but vibrant nation that has great untapped potential.

The book reveals for the first time the behind-the-scenes developments during the 2006 Oval Test crisis and the player power that critically reared its head at the time. For instance, few people are aware of Geoff Boycott's stellar defence of the Pakistan team's stand against the ball-tampering accusation before the ICC Tribunal. The book assesses Bob Woolmer's impact on the national team and provides fascinating insights into the circumstances of his tragic death. It critically examines the organization of cricket in Pakistan from grass roots upward to national level, including the first step in promoting women's cricket, selection, coaching, umpiring, curator training and ground assistance. It provides an in-depth description of the historic Indian tour of Pakistan in 2004, which required diplomatic skills, minute logistic arrangements, security, media organization and the welcoming of 20,000 Indian fans that went back to India, in the words of the Indian High Commissioner, as '20,000 Pakistan Ambassadors to India'. These visitors included Nehru's great-granddaughter and great-grandson, Priyanka and Rahul Gandhi. That tour was a path-breaking success in Pakistan–India cricket relations and a remarkable achievement in people-to-people public relations. The suspicion and animosity created by border disputes and two full-scale wars between Pakistan and India have been a great burden on both countries, giving us an unfortunate point of convergence – widespread poverty and crippling defence spending. The 2001 tour was an eloquent expansion of the desire for peace and good neighbourly relations in the region, and *Cricket Cauldron* devotes considerable space to the use of cricket and sport as a means of bridging differences. In this, Shaharyar Khan's diplomatic skill and his insider experience of these issues provide a valuable insight into the organization and administration of Pakistan cricket.

Turning to Pakistan's political and social scene, as viewed through the prism of cricket, the authors have analysed issues that have led to massive corruption, spot-fixing, overt religiosity and lack of discipline, and that have so grievously damaged the image of Pakistan and its cricket. Included in the book are extracts of the ICC Tribunal's decision that led to the three players, Salman Butt, Mohammad Asif and Mohammad Amir, being found guilty of spot-fixing. This verdict was confirmed in a criminal case in a British high court. The socio-political factors that underpin the case and Pakistan's volatile cricket are looked at in some detail. All this makes the book a unique treatise on the political, cultural and social problems that Pakistan faces today.

I appreciate the authors asking me to write the Foreword to the book as a cricketer and as a political figure in Pakistan. I commend this book for the insider account of Pakistan cricket and for grasping the main political and social issues across the Pakistan spectrum as reflected in its current cricket landscape. For me, the story of Pakistan cricket and the story of Pakistan today are one and the same – it is a story of unfulfilled promise. Pakistan's cricket isolation is mirrored by a wider international isolation. In order to address this, Pakistan cricket and Pakistan as a nation need to tackle the very issues that are brought up in *Cricket Cauldron*.

Imran Khan

PREFACE

I began writing this book soon after Bob Woolmer's tragic death and the controversies that swirled around his unexpected passing, and their effect on the Pakistan team and Pakistan cricket. More than six years have passed since Bob Woolmer's untimely demise and Pakistan cricket has been overtaken by wave upon wave of controversies, such as drug abuse, ball tampering, excessive religiosity, player factionalism, and now, spot-fixing. These controversies have stirred Pakistan's volatile cricket cauldron and have brought forward the ugly face of Pakistan cricket. I therefore decided to change the orientation of the book to examine the cricketing and socio-political issues that mire Pakistan cricket in a morass of controversy. In this task, I have been aided by my son and co-author Dr Ali Khan, Associate Professor at Lahore University of Management Sciences (LUMS), a trained Social Anthropologist and also a cricket-playing student of the game.

The book attempts to deal with these issues, to which I bring to bear my insider account of Pakistan cricket in my nearly three years as Chairman of the Pakistan Cricket Board (PCB). Ali Khan has assessed the socio-political and cultural issues related to the game in Pakistan, much of which is based on in-depth interviews with players, administrators, knowledgeable cricket journalists and former stars. We hope the book will throw some light on the burning problems of Pakistan cricket.

The book is emphatically not aimed at a self-serving justification of my policies as Chairman of the PCB. It places the issues of cricket facing Pakistan squarely on the table. On one hand it outlines my failures, such as the emergence of player power so evident during the infamous 2006 Oval Test catastrophe and my unsuccessful attempt to have a new constitution for the PCB, and on the other hand it notes the successes like the upward graph of cricketing performance, significant improvement in the PCB's financial health, and the diplomatic and public relations triumphs at the international and bilateral level. Other issues, too, are assessed, always looking at both sides of the coin.

We need to acknowledge the invaluable assistance we have received from our publishers for their guidance and probing questions related to the manuscript. Credit is due to the superb editing commissioned by the publishers as also to the typists, notably Safina Joseph and Aqsa Asif of LUMS, my former PS Zafar and my daughter-in-law Mariyam Zaman. We are especially indebted to Ramchandra Guha for his seminal history of Indian cricket in his book *A Corner of the Foreign Field* (Picador, 2002). A special note of thanks to our energetic research assistant Hissan ur Rehman, who interviewed a vast cross-section of cricketing personalities and conducted intensive ethnographic research for this book, and to Ateeb Gul, who painstakingly compiled the index for this book.

INTRODUCTION

'What's bred in the marrow comes out in the batting. Do you agree?' This was the very first question fired at me during my viva voce examination for entry into the Pakistan Foreign Service in 1957. Clearly, the examiners had done their homework and seen from my biodata that I was deeply involved in cricket. The question took me aback but I managed a semi-coherent reply that eventually led to a 40-year career in the Pakistan Foreign Service. I ended up as Foreign Secretary (seniormost civil servant at the Foreign Office) after serving as Pakistan's Ambassador to Jordan, the United Kingdom and France. One of the sacrifices of a career in the Foreign Service was that my participation in cricket was relegated to a secondary pursuit, especially when serving in non-cricketing countries like Tunisia, Switzerland, Jordan or Rwanda. But that initial question kept gnawing at me. While I believed that what was bred in the marrow did indeed come out in the batting, I wondered whether this extended from the individual to the nation. Did cricket also reflect a nation's character – its history, its personality, its culture, its social make-up, its insecurities, its politics, its religious commitment?

This book aims to discern how far cricket reflects Pakistan's national ethos. Do the ingredients that are bred in Pakistan's marrow come out, metaphorically, in the batting? My insider account of

Pakistan cricket aims to provide a prism through which deeper currents of Pakistan's character and brief national history can be understood. How does the terror syndrome affect cricket? What are the challenges, both diplomatic and cricketing, that cricketers face in Pakistan–India matches? Is cricket a factor in establishing Pakistan's attempt to be treated as India's sovereign equal in all domains? How does history affect the Pakistani cricketer? Does he suffer the insecurity of a new state that was not on the world map in 1947 as against India's long historical and cultural tradition? Or does the cricketer inherit a certain superiority complex drawn from the Muslim military conquests of India and the knowledge that Pakistan was a country carved out of nothing and against all odds? How does the increasing sway of orthodox Islam in Pakistan affect the make-up and outlook of the national team? What factors draw the Pakistani cricketer towards criminality like drug abuse, match-fixing and corruption? Do Pakistani cricketers mirror the country's social make-up, such as the lack of education, or a feeling that the world, especially the developed world, is constantly conspiring against Pakistan?

As I wend my way, chronologically, through the three-year journey as Chairman of the PCB, I intend to answer the questions raised in the paragraph above through the prism of cricket. My co-author adds a deep ethnographic analysis to complement my insider account. The answers we come to are by no means conclusive. Many are speculative and personal, but every succeeding chapter analyses the issues as we travel across the cricketing landscape.

Over the last decade much has been written by writers and academics attempting to analyse the complexities of Pakistan's society, culture and politics. This has been done through an ethnographic lens (Magnus Marsden [2005], Naveeda Khan [2010]), a political science viewpoint (Anatol Lieven [2011], Humeria Iqtidar [2011]) and a historical perspective (Ayesha Jalal, Farzana Shaikh [2009][1]). There has also been a veritable explosion of fiction from Pakistani writers reflecting the socio-political preoccupations of the country (Mohsin Hamid, Daniyal Mueenuddin, M. Hanif, Kamila Shamsie[2]). But somewhat surprisingly, there has been no work looking to understand Pakistan through an analysis of sport and in particular of cricket. Few phenomena are as deeply ingrained in the psyche of the Pakistani people as cricket and as such few expressions of 'popular culture' are likely to reflect the inner workings of society as does cricket.

The idea that sport is reflective of society – that what is present in society (religion, ethnic divisions, class distinctions, nationalistic zeal) will find its way into sport – is not new. Ever since C. L. R. James's seminal account of cricket in the West Indies,[3] the idea that cricket imitates society has been in place. Cricket, more than any other game, reflects the political, social and economic environment of a country. The West Indians are aggressive – like gladiators – brash and immensely colourful. They reflect the huge talent and panache of the Caribbean people. The Australians are frank, truculent and open-hearted. The English are cautious, low-key and disciplined. India's image has changed along with its own global image. Once the epitome of the colonial gentleman – elegant, exotic but genial – the team has changed alongside India's rise as an economic powerhouse. From being a talented but almost timid team the new generation is self-assured, aggressive and untainted by their colonial baggage. This book looks at Pakistan and how its cricket has charted the country's journey through the decades following independence. A young, brash, new-kid-on-the-block – chaotic, undisciplined but endowed with immense natural talent. A team of rarely fulfilled promise.

Sir John Major, former British Prime Minister, has epitomized cricket's influence on a country and its people in his superb book, *More Than a Game*, in the following words. Writing about the power of cricket he states:

It can uplift whole communities – whole nations even – or cast them down. And because cricket is played largely in the mind, and reflects the society from which the cricketers spring, it can imprint the character of that nation indelibly upon the minds of those who watch the way in which a national team plays.[4]

This book looks to explore how cricket is an expression of wider socio-political processes. But like rituals, sport is not only reflexive but has other qualities as well. As a collective event of great emotional value, it draws attention to something, it provides explanations, it reinvigorates certain events, highlighting and stressing that event's importance. What happens on a cricket field makes a statement about what is important in life – defeating the colonial masters for the first time at the Oval in 1954, winning a series against India in India for the first time and making an impact on the international scene. These are events in Pakistan cricket that reverberate well beyond the sporting arena. The ritual or sport therefore is not simply reflective of something else. The ritual itself engages individuals; it collectivizes an experience and therefore is able to shape attitudes.

The idea that sport, seen here as a ritual activity, is 'reflective' of society is certainly true. But while this book looks at that aspect of the ritual, it must also be recognized that the ritual itself – in this case the sport of cricket itself – represents an unparalleled opportunity to examine how multiple meanings are assigned to this activity. The meanings so constructed by different actors will have the ability to be exported from the sporting event to interpretations of society more generally, thereby making the process not only reflective but also a two-way exchange.

CHAPTER 1

CRICKET'S ROLE IN THE BIRTH OF PAKISTAN

In the nineteenth century, as the British presence grew in India, they brought with them the sports that they had developed at home – cricket, hockey, tennis, football, squash, badminton and even polo.[1] In India, British civilian and military officers drawn mainly from British public schools began playing cricket matches among themselves and built tennis and squash courts, especially in the garrison towns. They developed hockey, football, polo and cricket fields across India and encouraged tennis and squash 'markers' (professionals) – invariably Pathans who are hardy, lithe, mountain people with remarkable hand-eye coordination – to give them practice and maintain the courts. Similarly, at cricket they needed net bowlers and soon these low-paid professionals began to master the intricacies of their chosen sport.

During the nineteenth century organized cricket began to take root in India, mainly in the port cities of Bombay, Karachi, Madras and Calcutta. Originally, cricket matches were played between English settlers, but by the middle of the century, the relatively affluent Parsi community, comprising traders, businessmen and technicians, began to form their own clubs or gymkhanas.[2] The Parsis, descended from the Persian Zoroastrians, were a small but influential community who took to cricket with enthusiasm. After a while, the Parsi clubs felt strong enough to challenge English

1

teams, and the Parsi community greeted their first success with elation. In 1895 and 1899, the Parsis sent teams to tour England but neither team set the Thames on fire. At the turn of the twentieth century, Hindu communities in these port cities started their own gymkhanas and began playing cricket, notably on the west coast of India. Soon the Hindus and Parsis were engaged in intense rivalry, their matches drawing fair crowds at the gymkhana grounds. The English still reigned supreme in the triangular contests but the communal gymkhanas were gaining ground on the British with every passing year. A decade or so later the Muslim community followed the Hindus by opening their own gymkhanas. The Muslims were encouraged to take to the sport by Sir Syed Ahmed Khan, the liberal Muslim educationist who had founded the Aligarh Muslim University, which produced a number of fine sportsmen. By the early 1920s, there were four separate communities playing organized cricket across India – the English, the Parsis, the Hindus and finally, the Muslims.

Cricket was given a significant fillip in India when Lord Harris – captain of England and the MCC – was appointed Governor of Bombay in 1890. Harris was a patrician who believed in demonstrating British supremacy in India through cricket. He invited his fellow county captain Lord Hawke to bring out an English team to India. Other English teams followed with stars like F. S. Jackson, Jack Hobbs and Wilfred Rhodes appearing for them. These teams successfully overcame the challenges of India's mainly communal teams. Later, another super imperialist and patrician, Douglas Jardine, led an MCC team to India in 1933 followed by Bryan Valentine's MCC squad in 1936. By then India was beginning to produce outstanding indigenous cricketers like C. K. Nayudu (Hindu), Wazir Ali (Muslim), Amar Singh (Hindu), Lala Amarnath (Hindu) and Mohammad Nisar (Muslim).

The communal quadrangular matches that sprouted up across India attracted large crowds and provided financial gains to their sponsors and the players. Though vociferous in their support for their respective communal teams, the matches were played before sporting crowds with no communal incidents. Initially the key matches were played between the English and their budding rivals, the Parsis. Then the rivalry encompassed the Hindu–Parsi competitions. Later the Muslims entered the fray and as the Hindu–Muslim debate in India heated up, grudge matches were played between the two major communities of India.

In the late nineteenth century, the British establishment encouraged the Indian princes – Britain's most loyal subjects in India – to take to cricket and promote the game. From their midst arose a genius – Ranjitsinhji – who almost set the Thames on fire. His batting exploits in England greatly romanticized the sport across the British Commonwealth. Ranji was followed a generation later by his nephew Prince Duleepsinhji and the Nawab of Pataudi, who toured Australia in 1932–3 as a member of Douglas Jardine's bodyline team. All these princes scored centuries on their Ashes debuts. The Indian princes took to cricket with great fervour and became willing sponsors and employers of the game.

At the turn of the century, cricket reflected in India a mirror image of the class differences that existed on the cricket field in England. Members of the English high aristocracy, like Lord Hawke, Lord Harris, Douglas Jardine and Lord Tennyson, ensured that gentlemen (amateurs) and players (professionals) did not share the same dressing rooms and entered the cricket field from different gates. In India the princes joined the British establishment to run cricket wherever it was played.

In the influential P. J. Hindu Gymkhana, Palwankar Baloo – a low-caste Hindu but probably the greatest bowler India has ever produced – was not allowed to play for the Hindu team in the communal contests until a press campaign and influence from political leaders like Mahatma Gandhi and Dr B. R. Ambedkar pressurized the Hindus to include low-caste representatives. Even then Baloo and his brother Vithal were not allowed to take lunch and tea with their high-caste colleagues. More than in England, where a social revolution was taking place, in India the spread of cricket was from the top downwards, the top being represented by the British establishment and the Indian princes usually acting in tandem. It was normal to find English selectors and umpires presiding over Indian teams. Sometimes in club matches an independent or 'bolshi' native umpire would be replaced mid-game as a result of pressure from the British bureaucracy.

Before India's independence, three Indian teams toured England in 1932, 1936 and 1946. On these tours the Indian teams were led by Indian princes – the Maharajas of Porbandar (1932) and Vizianagaram (1936) – both of whom were at best club cricketers. In 1946, the English Test cricketer Nawab of Pataudi was appointed captain.

By the 1920s, India's political scene saw the development of anti-imperialist movements under the leadership of the Congress party. Their slogan was 'Swaraj', meaning home rule, and initially the Congress party had the support of Muslim leaders like Jinnah and the Ali brothers. The Congress manifesto was secular and represented the voice of Indians from all communities, especially the two major religious communities: the Hindus and the Muslims. At that time Jinnah was an enthusiastic supporter of Congress's multi-religious anti-British policy. Later, Jinnah left the Congress and joined the Muslim League and took a path increasingly antagonistic to the 'Hindu-dominated' Congress party.

It was inevitable that cricket should reflect the political climate of the times. Cricket matches between the communal teams and their English masters reflected the anti-colonial tenor of the political scene. There was, of course, a competitive edge in the matches between communal teams but these matches paled before the intensity and political fallout of matches between English and communal teams participating in the triangular and quadrangular Championships. By the 1920s, English hockey teams had been overtaken by Indians, who had shown remarkable ability to master the art of hockey and polo. In fact, India won all the Olympic games hockey gold medals from 1928 (Amsterdam) until 1960 (Rome). Cricket was therefore the only sport in India at which the English could demonstrate their superiority.

By the 1930s the communal triangular and quadrangular tournaments had flourished across India but Bombay began achieving centre stage in holding these popular tournaments, where they were played to full houses at the Brabourne Stadium. Inevitably, politics had entered the cricketing domain as the Congress–Muslim League confrontation became more acerbic, causing rioting in many Indian cities.

These opposing ideologies mainly affected Hindu attitudes towards communal cricket. Firstly, the Hindu team had to wrestle with their own internal problems of their caste system. Secondly, the Hindu team was put under extreme pressure by the secular Congress party to boycott the communal tournaments. Consequently, the Bombay Hindu Gymkhana opted out of the communal tournaments between 1928 and 1933. The sponsors and players were opposed to the boycott, claiming that the tournaments helped to douse the fervour of communal rioting that had spread across India due to Hindu–Muslim antagonisms.

Surprisingly, these well-attended grudge matches saw no communal incidents between the throngs of rabid, partisan spectators. The teams also conducted themselves with dignity and with sporting spirit.

The Bombay Pentangular became an annual festival for the cricket-crazy princely states, large and small. Trainloads of supporters would accompany the famous Maharajas and Nawabs from Gwalior, Indore, Patiala, Mysore, Bhopal, Baroda and the smaller states like Porbandar, Kurwai, Vizianagaram, Pataudi, Jamnagar, Dungarpur and Cooch Behar. They would occupy the famous watering holes of Bombay with their retinues of film stars, cricketers and politicians who would do the rounds in a carnival atmosphere. The Cricket Club of India's Brabourne Stadium provided a fitting climax to this special sporting event, as it became the logical culmination of cricketing competition. So great was the interest in the Pentangulars that cricketers invariably recalled these matches as having the intensity of Test matches.

However, it would be an exaggeration to suggest that cricket played a significant role in the foundation of Pakistan that came into being on 14 August 1947. Yet cricket did have an influence – albeit a marginal one – in promoting Mohammad Ali Jinnah's notion of his two-nation theory that became the basis of the movement for Pakistan. This two-nation theory was founded on Jinnah's contention that the Muslims and Hindus of India comprised two separate 'nations', given their separate histories and identities, their differences of ethnicity, culture, language, food, custom and, of course, religion. As a separate and distinct entity, Jinnah claimed that the Muslims of India deserved equal treatment to the Hindus, iron-clad guarantees of their political, cultural and social beliefs. Jinnah's two-nation theory was vehemently contested by the Hindu-dominated Congress party, whose primary aim was self-rule in which all religious communities would participate as Indians and not as Hindus, Muslims, Sikhs and other religions and castes. The Congress pointed to some distinguished Muslims like Maulana Abul Kalam Azad as leading figures in its anti-colonial movement. They also denied Jinnah his claim to represent all Indian Muslims since there were large tracts of Muslims in the Frontier Province under the Red Shirt leader Ghaffar Khan, the Kashmiri Muslim Sheikh Abdullah, the Bengal Muslim Fazlul Haq and the Punjab leader Sardar Shaukat Hayat, who opposed Jinnah's two-nation theory and preferred to seek freedom under 'one united all India' banner.[3]

These competing ideas gained political momentum in the 1930s and 1940s as India's anti-colonial movement began to reach its denouement. The Muslims, frustrated by Congress's denial to grant them guarantees, began veering closer to Jinnah's two-nation concept. At the time, the idea of Pakistan was more a chimera than a geographically defined entity; a bargaining chip for Jinnah, rather than a meaningful option to be pursued at the national level. In those days the two-nation theory drifted towards a vague separate entity of Pakistan that had no clearly defined geographic contours. This was probably deliberate, as defining Pakistan's frontiers would undermine the morale and commitment of Muslims who found themselves outside its territorial limits. Moreover, the two-nation theory was aimed at reviving the glory of Muslim rule, especially under the Mughal Empire, which had been replaced by British rule for the previous 250 years, during which the Muslims languished in a state of supreme decadence and a soporific nostalgia for the glories of the past. Jinnah appeared to revive the spirit of the Indian Muslim with his two-nation theory, often leading to communal skirmishes on the sporting field. For instance, the titanic battles in Calcutta on the football field between rivals Mohan Bagan and Mohammedan Sporting were seen as Hindu–Muslim clashes. The all-Muslim Bhopal Wanderers saw their frequent successes at hockey tournaments across India as being welcomed by the Muslim communities of Madras, Bombay, Lucknow, Delhi and Calcutta. The Sikh-dominated Khalsa college hockey team was similarly a proud representative of their community, especially in the Punjab.

These communal skirmishes on the playing fields of India paled before the gladiatorial contests of the cricket arena. The Quadrangular and Pentangular cricket tournaments played in the port cities of Karachi, Bombay, Madras and Calcutta were brazenly communal and increasingly popular. They were played between Hindus, Muslims, Parsis and the Europeans. Finally, the Rest (comprising Christians, Sikhs, Buddhists, Jews and other religious minorities) joined the contests in 1937 as the fifth team in the Pentangular.

Naturally the communal teams attracted adverse comment from the Congress party leadership as being against the secular tenets of the party, which claimed to embrace all religious denominations. The Congress leadership saw the community-based tournaments as a British attempt to divide and rule in India. More importantly, the Muslim League saw the contests as an example of 'parity' between the Hindu and Muslim communities. Invariably, whenever the Muslims won a tournament, Jinnah would send a congratulatory message to the captain as the Muslims had helped to promote their credentials in Jinnah's two-nation theory. So intense was the public interest in the Pentangular tournaments and so great their propensity to damage the Congress cause that its leaders – Gandhi, Nehru and Patel – intervened with the Hindu team to dissuade them from entering the tournaments. The Hindu team's stalwarts like C. K. Nayudu, Amar Singh and Vijay Merchant, who were keen to continue to participate in the tournaments, claimed that the communal matches lowered community tensions and that no communal incidents had taken place during the matches. They added that the Pentangular provided a huge income for the players and for the organizers. Sensing the Hindu players' reluctance to fall in line, the Congress leadership sought the intervention of the Maharajas of Indore, Baroda and Patiala, who were veering closer to the Congress than the British and were the players' employers, to stop them playing the Pentangular. Mahatma Gandhi wrote to the organizers of the Bombay Pentangular in the following critical terms:

> My sympathies are wholly with those who would like to see these matches stopped … I would like the public of Bombay to revise their sporting code and erase from it communal matches. I can understand matches between colleges and institutions but I have never understood the reasons for having Hindu, Parsi, Muslim and other communal elements. I should have thought such unsportsmanlike divisions would be considered taboos.[4]

The Congress intervention succeeded on two occasions but the Hindu team resumed playing in succeeding years as a result of popular demand, to the chagrin of the Congress party and its supporters and to the delight of the Muslim League. In response to the Congress leaders and the press campaign against the communal tournaments, Vijay Merchant defended the Pentangular in the following terms:

> Communal feeling between Hindus and Muslims is a product of politics not of sport. Cricket and communal series brought them closer together than any other aspect of life.[5]

Other prominent cricketers like C. K. Nayudu, Wazir Ali, Mushtaq Ali and BCCI Chairman A. S. De Mello supported Merchant's contention that the communal Pentangulars should continue.

The other teams in the Pentangular also continued to participate. In particular, the Parsis continued because despite being a small minority they established their credentials as an educated, anglicized and progressive community. The Rest team underlined the fact that several problems did exist with the minority communities.

The results of the Bombay Quadrangular saw the Muslims defeat the fancied Hindus in 1934 and 1935. The Hindu press ascribed their loss to the factions and disunity in the Hindu team. Apart from the habitual caste problem the critics felt that making the Maharaja of Patiala – a Sikh allowed to play for the Hindus – captain of the Hindu team was highly damaging for team unity, especially as stalwarts like C. K. Nayudu and D. B. Deodhar were available. Conversely the less fancied Muslim players were united and showed remarkable team spirit.

In 1936, the Hindus defeated the Muslims in the semi-final and went on to win the trophy against the Europeans, who had the services of the fearsome England fast bowler Harold Larwood, employed as a coach by the Maharaja of Patiala. He played only one match and returned home unable to adjust to the heat, dust and dull pitches of India. The Quadrangular become the Pentangular in 1937, as the Rest team had been admitted to the tournament. At the 11th hour the Hindu team withdrew, ostensibly because they

Figure 1   The 1936 Indian touring team to England. The two stalwarts of the Bombay Pentangular — C. K. Nayudu, captain of the Hindus, and S. Wazir Ali, captain of the Muslims — are seated second and first from the left.

had not received their fair share of tickets, but in fact the raging controversy against the Hindus taking part in the communal championship, abhorred by the Congress, had taken its toll on the players and organizers. The Muslims won easily against the Parsis, who had earlier knocked out the Europeans in the first round. In 1938, the Hindus were back with a bang, led now by the charismatic C. K. Nayudu, but the Muslims again beat the Hindus in the final through a tremendous team effort. The result was reversed in 1939, when the Hindus comfortably beat the Muslims to general acclaim from those elements that supported the holding of the communal Pentangulars.

By 1940, World War II was raging in Europe with wide repercussions across the globe. The Congress party refused to support the British war effort unless Britain made an immediate commitment to Indian independence. The British declined. The Congress leadership, including Gandhi, Nehru, Azad and Patel, were sent to jail for leading their 'Quit India' movement. The Muslims, led by Jinnah, passed the Pakistan resolution in Lahore in 1940 and generally cooperated with the British in opposing the

10

Nazi and Japanese threat. The schism between the Congress and the Muslims raised the political temperature several notches, sparking anti-British riots as well as communal disturbances. In spite of this fraught political atmosphere, the Pentangular was played in 1940 but the Hindu team, under huge pressure from Congress leaders decided to opt out, leaving the field open for the Muslims to defeat the Rest in the final.

By 1941, through public support and pro-Pentangular statements by the Hindu stalwarts C. K. Nayudu and Vijay Merchant, the Hindus were back with a vengeance. They beat the Muslims in the semi-final and went on to defeat the Parsis in the final. Vijay Merchant scored two double centuries in the tournament. In 1942, through immense pressure from the Congress party, now supported by the cooperating princes who banned their players from playing in communal tournaments, the Pentangular was cancelled.

In 1943, despite the increasing Hindu–Muslim riots across India, the Pentangular made a surprising comeback, mainly due to the clamour from Bombay's cricket-mad supporters and the claim by leading cricketers and sponsors that these communal tournaments helped calm rather than exacerbate tensions.

The Muslims beat the Parsis but lost to the Rest in the semi-final. In an epic final the Hindus beat the Rest but only after the Christian Vijay Hazare made 309 not out in a total of 389, still a world record for the highest proportion of runs in a first-class cricket match. The Rest team had arrived and they were feted in the streets of Bombay even though they had lost the final.

The 1944 Hindu–Muslim final was also a classic. By then Congress–Muslim tensions had risen to breaking point and communal riots were taking place all across India. The more rabid Hindu critics of communal tournaments began referring to the Muslim team as 'Pakistan', which increased the needle further. Still there were no incidents on and off the field. In an extraordinary gesture of inter-community camaraderie, C. K. Nayudu, the iconic captain of the Hindu team, found his Indore teammate, the

Muslim Mushtaq Ali, retired injured in the dressing room. Nayudu persuaded Mushtaq to go back and bat for his team, as the match was in the balance. Mushtaq Ali returned to the crease and scored 36 valuable runs, tilting the balance in favour of the Muslims. The final was a classic as K. C. Ibrahim, Merchant's opening partner when playing for Bombay, scored 119 not out to gain victory by one wicket with 20 minutes to spare. Surprisingly, the Europeans had lost in the first round even though they had the services of England players Denis Compton, Joe Hardstaff and Reg Simpson, who were on military duty in India.

The 1945 Pentangular lacked colour as the princes again banned their players from participating, which meant that many stars, like the Nayudu brothers (Hindu), Mushtaq Ali (Muslim), Hazare (Christian) and J. N. Bhaya (Parsi), were not allowed to play. In the final the Hindus beat a rejuvenated Parsi team. After 1945, with the Congress party leading its people towards independence, there were no further Pentangulars.

Altogether the Pentangular was played 11 times between 1934 and 1945. The Muslims won six finals while the Hindus were successful in five, having opted out in two years. At least in the premier cricket tournament in India, the Muslims had underscored Jinnah's claim that the Muslims were a separate nation and deserved parity and equality with the Hindus.

But let us not overstate the influence of cricket on the Indian political scene. Cricket was then an elite sport played mainly by the educated urban middle class. It was only briefly – during the communal tournaments – a mass sport. These communal tournaments were stopped before Independence and the crowds at Brabourne Stadium dwindled to a few thousand for Ranji Trophy matches when, in the past, ten times the number attended the Pentangular matches.

In 1932, 1936 and 1946, India sent teams representing the major communities to play Test matches against England – all three led by rulers of princely states – but they returned defeated without making a political statement against their imperial masters. It was in the popular sport of hockey where India established its identity by winning every Olympic Games in which they participated until 1960. So it was in hockey rather than cricket that Pakistan sought to establish 'parity and equality' with its larger neighbour. Unfortunately, though blessed with superb individual players, Pakistan failed to gel as a team and was eliminated before reaching the finals at the post-war Olympics of London (1948), Helsinki (1952) and Melbourne (1956) to challenge the mighty Indians. The eventual success at the 1960 Rome Olympics, when Pakistan narrowly defeated India, became a huge national morale booster. Overnight, the national heroes were Naseer Bunda, who scored the lone goal, Hamidi, the captain, Anwar Ahmad Khan, Atif and Munir Dar. Sporting pre-eminence was shared between hockey and squash, where a family of Pathans from the village of Nawakili reigned supreme in the world for over two decades.

Meanwhile, on independence, Pakistan was not even given Test match status in cricket. Unofficial tours to Ceylon were arranged and in 1948 West Indies played Test matches against India, peeling off to Pakistan for some 'unofficial' matches. Muslim stalwarts of the Pentangular who had emigrated to Pakistan, like Wazir Ali, Mohammad Nisar, Baqa Jilani, Dilawar Hussain, Dr Jahangir Khan and Nazir Ali, were barely recognized public figures immediately after Independence. By 1951, Pakistan had achieved sufficient success to enter the Test arena and the first official series was played against India, which was lost, but in the Second Test at Lucknow, Pakistan defeated its arch opponents. Three years later, on the first tour of England, Pakistan squared the series through its famous victory at the Oval, thanks to a superb bowling performance by Fazal Mahmud.

Until the 1970s, cricket in India did not have the influence or the popular appeal that it has in South Asia today. Except during the communal Quadrangulars – and especially the Bombay Pentangulars, which were brief seasonal affairs – cricket did not generate mass interest or participation. The Ranji and Duleep Trophy matches, which were non-communal, attracted sparse crowds. Remarkably, the communal tournaments aroused the passionate interest and support of the public. Whole armies of supporters attended these communal matches, invariably in a relaxed and sporting atmosphere. Parsi women were seen to cry copiously after their team's first loss to the Hindus. Initially, the communal teams aimed to defeat the English to make the political point that they were ready for self-rule. The English, on the other hand, wanted to demonstrate their imperial credentials in the only sport in which they could hold their own. As the political climate in India began to heat up, the Bombay Pentangulars became the fulcrum of the mainly Hindu–Muslim rivalry that raged across India. The Congress Party despised the communal tournaments and made stringent efforts to stop them or at least ban the Hindu team from participating. Jinnah's Muslim League wanted the Muslim team to epitomize his claim that Muslims were a 'separate' nation and to seek parity and equality with the Congress in the run-up to independence. By winning the Pentangulars more often than the Hindus, the Muslim team was able to underscore Jinnah's contention. Surprisingly, these politically and religiously fraught matches were played in a sporting atmosphere between spectators and players without an incident taking place in any of the communal tournaments played before packed stadia. Unlike the times when Lord Harris's local English teams would dominate over communal outfits, Indian cricket by the 1930s was strong enough to defeat English teams regularly. British 'supremacy' at cricket had therefore to rely on visiting English teams led by patricians like Lord Hawke, Jardine, Lord Tennyson and Valentine to carry the imperial flag, and to defeat the combined Indian teams that toured England in 1932, 1936 and 1946 captained by assorted Indian princes. England managed to achieve their target by winning all five Test series played against India up to independence in 1947. In India, however, the European (English) team was no match for the communal teams, appearing only once in the finals of the Bombay Pentangular, and that too in the year that the Hindus had opted out.

The Bombay Pentangulars, which carried potential implications for the various religious communities of India and led to heated controversy in the pro-Congress press, were like shooting stars across the Indian political firmament. They left a temporary impact on the scene but not a lasting one. For instance, Hindu–Muslim rioting in Bombay calmed during the Pentangulars, as contended by Indian star players, but resumed again in earnest as brilliantly described by Saadat Hasan Manto, the Urdu short story writer. The Muslim team did engender a certain pride and awakening for the Muslims of India to move closer to Jinnah's concept of Pakistan. But these were fringe influences, as cricket did not, at the time, have the power to affect mass political opinion. The Congress party marched on to independence regardless of the Pentangular 'irritant' of communal teams competing in the tournament. Jinnah would have achieved his dream of Pakistan even if there had been no communal tournaments.

CRICKET ENTERS THE BLOODSTREAM

Some time in the late 1970s, cricket entered Pakistan's national bloodstream. Before that date, it trailed hockey and squash in national importance, and was seen by the masses as a complex, expensive and essentially middle-class sport with scant public appeal. Pakistan in its early years had punched slightly above its weight by winning a Test in its first series with India and squaring its first series with England in 1954. No other major achievements had fallen Pakistan's way and the remarkable achievements of its supreme bowler Fazal Mahmud and the boy wonder Hanif Mohammad's record-breaking feats had received subdued applause without conferring star status on them. In squash, on the other hand, Pakistan had reigned unchallenged in the world for half a century, beginning with the fairy-tale exploits of the 36-year-old, balding, bandy-legged Hashim Khan, who conquered all before him. Hashim Khan's torch was carried later by his fellow Pathans, ending with Jahangir Khan and Jansher Khan. Being top dogs in this sport gave a tremendous boost to national morale for the young nation that in 1947 had started from scratch. Similarly, in hockey, Pakistan dethroned India, the perennial Olympic champions, at the Rome Olympics in 1960, a success that was followed by gold medals in the Asian Games and later Olympics. Hockey was acknowledged as Pakistan's national sport and I recall attending matches played against Germany, Kenya and Holland to packed stadiums in the 1960s and 1970s.

At the time, cricket languished at a low level in the hearts and minds of the Pakistani public. The indifference was partly due to the torpid and soporific contests between arch-rivals Pakistan and India, who played out a succession of boring defensive Test matches invariably ending in draws. Test matches were viewed as a reflection of the political antagonism that had developed between the two neighbours over partition and Kashmir. A Test match was like a battle with neither side prepared to take risks or give ground. Not surprisingly, public interest turned away from cricket. One of the saddest examples of Pakistan's treatment of cricketing heroes involved Syed Wazir Ali, who was the darling of all Muslims in pre-partition India because he vied with great Hindu stalwarts Nayudu and Merchant as India's finest batsmen. Wazir Ali had led the Muslims to famous victories in the Bombay Pentangular. At partition, Wazir Ali emigrated from Jullundur to Pakistan and found himself ignored. He could not even find a small room to house his family and relied on cricketing friends for financial support. He died shortly afterwards – a forgotten hero of pre-partition days.

Then, in the late 1970s, came the sea change for cricket in Pakistan as indeed for the whole of South Asia. It did not happen suddenly, like an earthquake, but over a decade or so beginning in late 1970. The change was noticeable, like entering an air-conditioned room from the searing heat of the street. Suddenly, cricket was being played everywhere, in any open space, with makeshift bats and wickets. Children played in the streets and in village lanes. At night youngsters played under street lamps and with car headlights switched on. They played with tennis balls taped over with electrical tape even inside holy shrines, using gravestones as wickets.

In the orderly rows of middle-class houses in Islamabad, young scions of the family batted in garage spaces against servant boys who had been taught to bowl, with assorted sisters, cousins and cooks doing the fielding. Occasionally even the lady of the house would join in as a fielder. On my afternoon walks past a famous madrassah in Islamabad, I noted that the younger students dressed in skull caps and ankle-length robes preferred playing cricket in their leisure breaks to football and volleyball that their teachers provided for them. My most poignant image of cricket mania was the sight of a group of eunuchs, who lived in their colony near my house in Karachi, playing a cricket match among themselves. In the early 1990s, as Foreign Secretary, I travelled extensively in South Asia where I found the enthusiasm for cricket just as widespread, even in non-Test-playing countries like Nepal, the Maldives and Bhutan.

This cricket tsunami that hit South Asia therefore deserves analysis. What were the factors that shaped this remarkable phenomenon that affected national morale so deeply, sharpened interstate rivalries, while also providing bridges of peace and understanding involving diplomacy, politics and security? Cricket has become a major influence of national life for young and old, rich and poor, Pathan or Sindhi, Punjabi or Baloch. In Pakistan, with the fading memory of its founder Mohammad Ali Jinnah, it is now irreverently stated that cricket is the only unifying force.

Of course there is no single explanation for the timing of this phenomenon. There are several factors that have combined to produce cricket mania. The communication revolution – the easy and inexpensive access to transistor radio and television that took the game from the middle-class drawing rooms to the masses. Most village and roadside tea-stalls had installed television sets to increase custom and to watch a cricket match played out over a whole day, and this was consequently a major influence in introducing the game to the masses. Even the camel-cart driver would listen to cricket commentary on his transistor radio as he slowly wended his way from market to town. There was no other live entertainment, no music hall, no theatre, no concerts and no burlesque, only film songs played over and over again. So cricket became a dreamy pastime for the poor. The arrival of cable TV in the early 1980s and satellite dishes a few years later spread cricket even more rapidly.

A second explanation for the dramatic rise of cricket was the propensity towards idol worship in South Asia. The Hindu religion is deeply imbued with symbols of gods in the shape of idols. Muslims also deeply revere their numerous saints and shrines. The statues of Lord Buddha adorn the temples and museums of South Asia. Cricket, more than any other game, provides an opportunity for the making of stars – idols. It is played over long periods – five days for a Test – and even though like hockey or soccer it is a team game, the opportunity for an individual cricketer to shine over five days rather than 90 minutes is infinitely greater. Hence the great performer assumes the image of a national idol. Television coverage acted as a catalyst to this syndrome and stars like Javed Miandad, Imran Khan, Wasim Akram, Zaheer Abbas, Shahid Afridi and Waqar Younis became household images in Pakistan.

Thirdly, in the 1970s and early 1980s, outstandingly gifted Pakistani cricketers lit up the international stage, not so much as a team but as individuals. They included players like Majid Khan, Mushtaq Mohammad, Salim Malik, Sarfraz Nawaz and Asif Iqbal, all of whom adorned the county cricket scene in England. These charismatic players attracted the interest and pride of the Pakistani public.

Another explanation for the spread of cricket to the common man was the opportunity to make money: the rags-to-riches syndrome. By the 1990s, a lot of money was flowing into cricket worldwide. Central contracts, sponsorship money, huge bonuses, living in five-star hotels, advertising, and, of course, the chance for illicit gains through match-fixing and betting attracted a vast number of new cricketers in the country to try their luck. More than any other team sport in South Asia, cricket provided an opportunity to the underprivileged for spectacular economic advancement.

One final explanation for the cricket craze in South Asia was the success in winning the World Cup. India was first in defeating the invincible West Indies at Lords in 1983. Next, in Melbourne in 1992, it was Pakistan's turn to win the Cup against England, and later in 1996 Sri Lanka defeated Australia in Lahore.

Victories in the World Cup were immense morale boosters for every nation concerned, so that by the turn of the century cricket in South Asia had left every other sport far behind in galvanizing national morale and self-confidence. Cricket, for reasons analysed above, replaced hockey as the national sport and achieved a special role in the national psyche.

I found myself pitched into this highly sensitive and volatile cricket cauldron. Cricket was a supercharged entity, a political prize for the politicians to mould to their advantage. A diplomatic weapon in dealing with foreign countries, a high-profile vehicle that never left national centre stage. I entered this arena in December 2003 and this book recounts my journey across a landscape haunted by demons, wire-traps and pitfalls.

CHAPTER 2

THE CALL

Around 1 December 2003, I received a telephone call from Lieutenant General Tauqir Zia, Chairman of the Pakistan Cricket Board (PCB), at my home in Karachi, informing me that he was resigning from his post as Chairman and that the Patron, President Musharraf, had approved my name as his successor. Would I accept? I asked the General to give me 24 hours to consider. This news came to me as a huge surprise as I had never aspired to the post of Chairman, nor had the media mentioned my name as General Tauqir Zia's possible successor. Tauqir Zia was a cricketing friend who had earlier roped me in to manage the Pakistan team in the 2003 World Cup that had miserably failed to reach the second round. I was now faced with the far more important task of heading the PCB. General Tauqir Zia had been ad hoc Chairman of the PCB for over four years and had been given a torrid time in the national press, especially after Pakistan's failure in the World Cup of 2003.

General Tauqir Zia's nomination as Chairman of the PCB soon after General Pervez Musharraf had seized power in a military coup needs to be viewed in its political perspective. Pakistan has been ruled for nearly half of its 63-year history by military dictators who displaced elected civilian representatives. The first coup was mounted by General Ayub Khan, who after 11 years handed over to General Yahya Khan. There were many successes, especially in the development sector, for Ayub, and Pakistan was seen as a model for economic development. But he significantly failed to liberate Kashmir in the 1965 war with India. Six years later, Pakistan was defeated in its second war with India and was forced to surrender to the Indian Army in Dhaka. Worse still, Pakistan saw its Eastern wing emerge as a separate nation – Bangladesh – compounding the humiliation for the people of Pakistan. After a brief civilian interregnum under Zulfiqar Ali Bhutto (1971–7), yet another coup by General Zia-ul-Haq saw the military take over power, a tenure that lasted another 11 years until Zia was killed in a mysterious plane crash in August 1988. The fourth coup was conducted by General Pervez Musharraf after his disastrous venture to capture the Kargil heights had torpedoed the peace process with India through the Lahore Declaration signed by Prime Ministers Nawaz Sharif and Atal Bihari Vajpayee in 1998.

Atal Bihari Vajpayee's historic visit to Pakistan, when he arrived in Lahore with his entourage in a bus, had raised hopes of improved relations between Pakistan and India. The visit had seen the Indian Prime Minister visit the Minar-e-Pakistan, the monument that symbolized the birth of Pakistan, and ended with the optimistic Lahore Declaration. There were clear indications that both Prime Ministers wanted to move towards a better relationship that could only be achieved through the settlement of the Kashmir dispute. This positive development was based on the personal chemistry between Nawaz Sharif and Vajpayee. They had met on the sidelines during SAARC and Commonwealth summits in which both shared the need to normalize bilateral relations. Clearly, unlike any former or subsequent Indian Prime Minister, Vajpayee was prepared to go the extra mile in seeking a solution to Kashmir. Accordingly, a secret back-channel process was set in motion aimed at reaching a Kashmir solution. Niaz Naik, former Foreign Secretary, represented Pakistan, while Brajesh Mishra, the Indian Prime Minister's principal secretary, represented India. Several rounds of back-channel discussions had been held when Musharraf's fateful incursion into Kargil took place. It immediately derailed the back-channel process as Vajpayee felt that Kargil had been a stab in the back over his effort to normalize relations with Pakistan.

By then Nawaz Sharif had shown himself to be headstrong and erratic as Prime Minister. He had achieved strong backing from the electorate after Benazir Bhutto's earlier dismissal over accusations of corruption. Nawaz Sharif had become Prime Minister based on a 'heavy mandate'. He had demonstrated his power by ordering his goon squad to physically attack the Supreme Court and was intending to achieve the title of Ameer ul Momineen (ruler of the faithful), which had been assumed by famous Caliphs during Islam's glorious conquests. At the other end of these wayward exploits was his decision to improve relations with India, which reflected moderation and good sense, particularly in finding a compromise solution to Kashmir. Kargil demolished these hopes and soon afterwards Musharraf mounted a coup against Nawaz Sharif that saw, yet again, the army achieving the status of the 'patriotic saviour' of Pakistan.

Subsequently, Niaz Naik and important Indian journalists like Kuldip Nayar stated publicly that a solution to the Kashmir dispute had emerged from the back-channel talks. Confirmation of such a formula – called the Chenab Formula – is apparent from the then Foreign Minister Sartaj Aziz's book *Between Dreams and Realities* (OUP, 2009). Kuldip Nayar told me that he had met Vajpayee, who confirmed that a solution of the Kashmir dispute had been agreed in principle when the Kargil attack put paid to the process. The Chenab formula envisaged the handing over to Pakistan of a chunk of Indian territory in Kashmir on the west bank of the Chenab river, which would form the border between Pakistan and Indian Kashmir. Personally, I felt that Vajpayee was the only Indian Prime Minister who could have taken such a daring decision that went against India's long-established position of not yielding 'an inch of Indian (Kashmir) territory to Pakistan'.

Eight years of Musharraf's military rule began reasonably well but gradually degenerated into corrupt political dealings, mismanagement and a lack of direction so that Musharraf's end was ignominious, dragging the armed forces' prestige down with him. After Musharraf's blighted rule, the army under General Ashfaq Kiani has stayed away from the political centrestage, being content to control foreign policy and the budgetary allocation to the defence services under an ineffectual and corrupt political government. The army's lustre has recently faded with the dramatic attack against bin Laden in his five-year hideout which everyone believes was in the knowledge of military intelligence. The end result is that public approval of another military coup to 'save' Pakistan would be difficult to achieve.

During these long years of military rule, it became the norm for military dictators to appoint military personnel to key national institutions like the Pakistan International Airlines (PIA), the Public Services Commission and, of course, the Pakistan Cricket Board. The military leaders felt comfortable with their representatives heading these institutions, even though most of the appointees had neither experience nor expertise to commend them. Moreover, the appointments were a convenient sinecure for retiring generals, admirals and air marshals. These military appointments reflected the general contempt held by the military towards civilians, who were seen as incompetent, corrupt and not sufficiently patriotic, the armed forces having arrogated to themselves the supreme badge of patriotism. Thus, a succession of generals and air marshals found themselves heading the Pakistan Cricket Board even though they had scant knowledge of the complexity and history of cricket. No doubt they were good administrators but had no feel for the game. General Tauqir Zia was an exception to this rule because he was an active cricketer who had a deep understanding of the sport. His problem was that as a serving general and a serving corps commander he barely had time to attend to day-to-day issues that were faced by the PCB. After four years in the saddle, Tauqir Zia faced a growing crescendo of criticism by the media and the public against his role as the PCB Chairman. There were two reasons for this criticism. Firstly, Pakistan had seen a welcome mushrooming of media opinion through the grant of TV licences to private media channels. The print media was also given unprecedented freedom to express their opinions on all issues. Cricket became a target for this newly acquired freedom of the media that began to aim its slings and arrows against Musharraf's military regime, which was generally losing its lustre through half-baked compromise solutions. Politically, criticizing Tauqir Zia was aimed at Musharraf's military regime. Secondly, Pakistan's cricketing performance had been disappointing, typified by its first round exit from the World Cup in South Africa in 2003.

I saw my appointment as a sop to public opinion. As a civilian I would replace a general as head of the PCB. The change might also lead to cricketing performance being improved. I had no doubt that my appointment was part of the political landscape that was developing in Pakistan because Musharraf's regime had begun to lose its shine and was increasingly on the back foot.

There is also a deeper, historical resonance to the ready acceptance by the Pakistani public to successive martial law regimes. I happened to be in Pakistan during each of the four military coups that took place and can testify to the fact that there was a general sigh of relief from the common man whenever the military government took over. The initial reaction was that corrupt politicians had been replaced by patriotic, upright representatives of the armed forces. Initially, the military regimes did not face public resentment at overthrowing the elected representatives of the people. It was only after failures of wars against India and the loss of half of the country that public resentment built up against military power. Ayub failed in the 1965 war, Yahya saw the Pakistan army defeated in 1971 and Musharraf's venture into Kargil was a military and diplomatic disaster. Zia's saving grace was that though he did not liberate Kashmir, he did help in the liberation of Afghanistan from Soviet communists.

24

So why was the advent of military regimes in Pakistan so acceptable to the public? The answer lies in South Asia's history. For 800 years the Muslim invaders from Central Asia, Afghanistan and Iran had invaded and colonized vast tracts of India. The success of Muslim rule was achieved mainly by the military campaigns carried out by the invading Muslim hordes. Several Muslim dynasties, beginning with Mahmud of Ghazni and ending with the magnificent Mughal dynasty, ruled over most of India. This domination of India by the Muslim minority was gained through military prowess – such as the three defining battles of Panipat (1526, 1556 and 1761). Muslim Pakistan saw in its armed forces a reflection and a hope of matching India's numerical superiority. History had provided the Pakistan army with an aura of invincibility that was a factor in the public's acceptability whenever they took over government. Over the years this aura of invincibility began to fade for the reasons given in the previous paragraph. In 60 years of independence, the armed services had lost prestige and respect in the eyes of the public. Musharraf's political demise reflected this disillusionment. My appointment came at a time when Musharraf was halfway down the slide that he wanted to reverse. He was not successful.

The prospect of heading the PCB was daunting. An abrogated Constitution meant that a succession of ad hoc Chairmen had been inducted and removed at the whims of Pakistan's Chief Executives, leading to legitimate criticism that instead of an institutional process, the PCB was run by political nominees who would operate autocratically. It was also apparent that the PCB was faced with diverse pressures from all cricketing quarters that had led to accusations of maladministration, corruption, nepotism and dwindling finances. Cricketing results had been disappointing and the terrorist threat had led to some countries declining to play in Pakistan. Even those countries that did were loath to play in Karachi, where the New Zealand team had aborted their tour after a bomb blast near their hotel in 2002. There were intrigues, with players grouping into separate cabals, and the constant chopping and changing of captains, coaches and managers after every series loss had undermined the stability and continuity of the team. All these negative trends had seen a cacophony of criticism hurled at the PCB and its Chairman. The media clamoured for a change of guard at the PCB with names of former officials like Arif Abbassi, Khalid Mahmud, Zafar Altaf and even cricket-playing generals bandied about as likely successors to General Tauqir Zia. My name was not part of this speculation. I had not been part of the cricketing administration in Pakistan and my experience was limited to two stints as manager of the national team to India (1999) and to the World Cup in South Africa (2003).

An important consideration for me to accept the post of Chairman of the PCB was that the offer had come from President Musharraf. These considerations were both personal and political. Over the years I had established an affable but remote personal relationship with General Pervez Musharraf. This was due almost entirely to the fact that his father had been a colleague in the Pakistan Foreign Office. Musharrafuddin was a Muhajir[1] staff officer from Delhi who, at partition, had opted, like many Muslim civil servants from India, for Pakistan's government service. These civil servants brought much needed bureaucratic expertise that was invaluable for Pakistan's government, which was starting from scratch. Musharrafuddin was assigned to the Foreign Office, where he made his mark as an efficient and capable superintendent. He was subsequently selected for a gazetted (officer grade) post in the new Section Officer scheme, being one of four selected gazetted officers from around 100 qualifiers.

Musharrafuddin was delighted at making the grade and would often drop by my office for a social chat, during which he would proudly inform me of his children's progress. Pervez Musharraf was sent to Forman Christian College, a fine institution, and later joined the Pakistan Army. Musharrafuddin was soon posted out to Turkey as a diplomat and later went to Indonesia.

It was mainly due to his father that I used to seek out Pervez Musharraf for a brief chat, first as a Brigadier and then as a General in the Pakistan Army. I was delighted to see the steep and unusual rise in the cadre of a Muhajir, and rejoiced and was a tad surprised when he was selected as Army Chief. When the Army mounted a coup against Nawaz Sharif's civilian government, I viewed the event with mixed feelings. Politically, as a democrat, a liberal and a firm believer in human rights, I was emotionally opposed to the coup. At the time I was Ambassador in Paris and resigned my post, only to be told my resignation had not been accepted and I should continue 'until further orders'. Moreover, Musharraf's sally into Kargil[2] had been disastrous diplomatically and militarily, seriously damaging Pakistan's international prestige. On the favourable side, I recalled Ayub Khan's decade of governance when Pakistan had made remarkable progress in the field of development and national unity. Ayub was a benign, wise and moderate dictator, and since I knew Pervez Musharraf to be a liberal, sporting, tolerant person, I hoped he could bring order, discipline and direction to Pakistan's policies nationally and externally. Faced with the spectre of religious extremism, I felt only a liberal, courageous and wise leader could overcome the dangers that Pakistan faced. President Pervez Musharraf had idolized Kemal Atatürk and had announced a humane, civilized approach towards weaker elements of society like the minorities. So my objections in principle to military coups were subordinated in favour of promised discipline, progress and reform. Knowing Pervez Musharraf personally made it easier for me to accept the offer.

In the 24 hours during which I weighed up my options, I was encouraged by the fact that Ramiz Raja was Chief Executive of the PCB. I had known Ramiz Raja and had come to respect him as one of the few Test cricketers in Pakistan who was educated, articulate and balanced. Ramiz had received his share of media flak, particularly from Karachi because of his Lahore connections, but it did not alter my perception of him as a rational and competent administrator who was also a former Test captain.

The reason for a Lahore-based cricketer being treated with a degree of animosity by the Karachi lobby (or vice versa, a Karachi cricketer being treated similarly by the Lahore lobby) needs to be set in a wider context of historical regional and provincial tensions.

Rivalries between provinces exist throughout the world. Yorkshire and Lancashire have been traditional rivals reflecting the historical Wars of the Roses. New South Wales and Victoria have a similar rivalry as do the islands of Barbados, Jamaica and Trinidad. Across the border from Pakistan, Delhi and Mumbai are similar adversaries. This rivalry is competitive and mostly healthy. There is the usual hype from the press and public on issues such as selection, and the distribution of loaves and fishes. Pakistan lives with similar rivalries that are perhaps more sinister, and give rise to negative repercussions. This is because of political, administrative and even racial influences.

Let us begin with cricket in pre-1971 Pakistan, before Bangladesh became an independent nation. Until 1971, there was no representation in the national team from East Pakistan despite it having the majority population. There was a club-level cricketer from Dhaka called Niaz Ahmed who was Pakistan's perennial 12th man for quite some time, the Pakistan Cricket Board attempting to give the entirely unconvincing impression that East Pakistan was on the verge of national representation. The fact was that no effort was made by the governments of Pakistan or by the cricket boards to promote cricket in East Pakistan. The result was that although people were full of enthusiasm for the sport, as was evident from huge attendances for the Tests in Dhaka, there was no organized cricket in East Pakistan. Today, Bangladesh is making strides as a junior member of the cricket world and would find some of its players, like its openers, its wicketkeeper and captain all-rounder, walking into the Pakistan national team. Certainly their fielding is more athletic and their fitness and work ethic more apparent. The reason for this neglect of East Pakistan was primarily political. The West Pakistani regarded himself superior, the martial race, with extensive representation in Pakistan's armed services. There was no East Pakistan representation in Pakistan's Olympic contingents and none in its hockey teams. This attitude of superiority was about race, as the smaller, darker East Pakistani was regarded racially inferior and culturally different because they had their own rich language and culture. With the passage of time the East Pakistani was increasingly regarded as having doubtful patriotic credentials.

After 1971, Pakistan was left with an unbalanced administrative structure. Punjab had a population representing 65 per cent of the country with by far the best literacy rate and economic performance. Situated in Pakistan's heartland, Punjab dominated the country politically, economically, educationally and in the control of natural reserves. This inevitably led to the smaller provinces of Sindh, the Frontier[3] and Baluchistan reacting against Punjab's domination. This was especially noticeable in the control of waters from Pakistan's principal rivers, which all flowed through Punjab, and its representation in the armed and civil services based on its advanced education.

Cricket in Pakistan reflected a similar landscape. In the early years there was hardly any challenge to Punjab's domination from the Frontier, Baluchistan or Sindh, except from its Mohajir, Urdu-speaking population that had migrated from India to settle mainly in Karachi and the larger towns of Sindh's interior. This Mohajir population had brought high levels of education with them, a cultural superiority complex as they considered themselves the guardians of Urdu, the national language of Pakistan, and the vanguard of the Pakistan movement under Jinnah's leadership. The Mohajirs brought with them a love and expertise in cricket which presented the only rivalry to Punjab's domination. This Mohajir–Punjab rivalry later became diffused mainly because the Frontier Pathans made sudden and impressive strides in cricket. Secondly Lahore ceased to be the cricketing fulcrum in the Punjab, with other towns like Multan, Faisalabad, Rawalpindi, Sialkot, Gujranwala and Bahawalpur coming to the fore. Karachi, though dominated by the Mohajirs, became a highly cosmopolitan city with large 'settler' populations from the Frontier (including Afghan refugees) and from the interior of Sindh and Punjab. Nowadays the Karachi teams are represented by the offspring of Pathan settlers like Shahid Afridi and Younus Khan, Punjabi 'settlers' like Zaheer Abbas and Asad Shafiq, and members of long-standing Karachi families like Danish Kaneria and Wallis Mathias. These rivalries are played out on a minor scale between the various communities settled in Karachi and on a national scale between Punjab and the rest. The sharpness and negative fallout of the rivalry has been substantially reduced because cricket has reached the smaller towns beyond Lahore and Karachi.

With my appointment, the need to balance the leadership in the PCB between a Punjabi and a Karachi-based Muhajir had been fulfilled. But the basic reasons weighing in favour of my accepting the high-profile post was to improve the cricketing image of Pakistan. I loved the game and wanted to do my bit to change the negative image of Pakistani cricket, and to bring about an air of decency, transparency, merit and financial probity in the Board and in the players.

So after consulting my immediate family, I gave my positive response to General Tauqir Zia, and within a day my appointment was announced, my start date – 16 December 2003 – agreed and my meeting with the Patron scheduled. My son Omar's wise words kept ringing in my ears – that however successful my efforts, my tenure would be seen by the public as a failure except in the unlikely circumstance of Pakistan winning the World Cup in 2007. Another reason for my accepting the challenge was that having lost my mother the year before I was in a state of inert melancholia, attending fleetingly to the publication of her book *Memoirs of a Rebel Princess* and my own account of the 1999 India tour called *Cricket – A Bridge of Peace*.[4] Throwing myself wholeheartedly into the challenge would help me revive my zest for life. The allure of frequent travel, the good life when attending the International Cricket Council (ICC) and the Asian Cricket Council (ACC) meetings and what is enviously referred to as 'foreign jaunts', were definitely not factors in my decision to accept the post. Having served as a career diplomat in the Pakistan Foreign Service, I had travelled across the world for 40 years. As Ambassador and Foreign Secretary, I had dined with kings and presidents. Nor did I cherish the power of being Chairman of the PCB or the publicity that made the post as high profile as any in the country. I regarded the travel, perks and 'high life' as a chore and a necessary responsibility that went against my craving for a simple life.

On my flight to Rawalpindi to call on the President, I reflected on the task ahead. I was a cricket aficionado and had studied the game deeply, but I had no experience of cricket administration in Pakistan beyond my two stints as manager. The first goal that I set myself was to lift the performance of the national team, which had underperformed and seemed to be riven by player intrigue. There had been rapid changes of captain, with Wasim Akram, Rashid Latif, Moin Khan, Waqar Younis and now Inzamam-ul-Haq playing a form of round robin. Coaches and managers had similarly bitten the dust after every series failure. There was a need for continuity, discipline and unity in the team. Part of the problem was the loss of star players after the retirement of Imran Khan, Wasim Akram, Abdul Qadir, Javed Miandad, Saeed Anwar and Waqar Younis – six outstanding cricketers who had seen Pakistan's performance raised to unprecedented highs in the 1980s and 1990s. Now only one player, Inzamam-ul-Haq, merited ranking among the top players of the world, especially after Saqlain Mushtaq's performance seemed on the decline. Pakistan would need to bolster team morale and unity to regain status, and my hope was that rising stars like Shoaib Akhtar, Mohammad Sami, Yousuf Youhana, Shahid Afridi, Younus Khan and Danish Kaneria would knit together to form an effective unit.

Related to this issue was the negative image abroad of the Pakistan team. Match-fixing scandals, boorish, undisciplined behaviour by the players on and off the field, biased umpiring, accusations of ball-tampering and lack of social graces had tarnished the reputation of the Pakistan team. I recalled Ian Chappell's comment that of all cricketing nations, Pakistan was the only team that he and his players found impossible to interact with socially after a day's play. This was probably due to a general inability to converse in English because most of the players were drawn from the 'maidaan' (open space) and not, as in Sri Lanka and India, from English-medium schools and colleges where they received a basic education. Taking cricket to the maidaans was, of course, a welcome development as cricket had been owned by the masses, but the negative side was that many of the players lacked social graces, maturity and balance that comes with education. Many who rose to the top were unable to find the maturity to bridge the gap between relative poverty and sudden riches. I realized that there was no easy solution to this issue because the malaise reflected the lack of education in the whole country, but short-term measures, like English courses in our cricket academies, teaching table manners and lectures on correct behaviour on and off the field, could help remove some of the rough edges, though barely scratching the surface of the problem.

Another task was the need to make the PCB an institution. A comprehensive constitution with every tier of the cricketing responsibility clearly earmarked was vital. The PCB needed to be democratic, representative and transparent, especially in matters of financial probity, and free of nefarious influences that militated against merit.

I recalled some bizarre decisions in which our national leaders had nominated PCB Chairmen from among their friends and colleagues as part of political favours, with scarcely a thought for the incumbent's ability to manage a complex and highly technical game like cricket. These PCB Chairmen included hockey players, business friends, civil servants and army generals. Perhaps the most bizarre of these appointments was the nomination as manager of the Pakistan team to England in 1962 of Brigadier 'Gussy' Hyder – a polo-playing, 'tally ho' type cavalryman who knew absolutely nothing about cricket. In the hallowed pavilion at Lords, he startled MCC members when in a loud voice he joked: 'When do we start the next chukka?' One morning the Brigadier insisted that since the nightwatchman had done his job the day before, he should be replaced by a 'proper batter'. Javed Burki, the captain, argued that it was against the rules, to which the manager replied: 'You are disobeying orders. I will have you court-martialled!' Press ridicule for the doughty brigadier came through thick and fast. Tongue in cheek, English media correspondents asked the most technical cricketing questions to which Brigadier Gussy Hyder would blandly reply in chaste polo terminology. In time our embarrassment gave way to mirth as the Brigadier charged his opponents like Don Quixote!

First-class cricket in Pakistan was also ailing because too many hotchpotch teams were lowering playing standards. Only a few departmental teams had adequate financial resources while regional teams were cash-strapped and poorly organized. Test venues were reasonably well maintained, but other first-class grounds were obviously below standard, mainly due to lack of funding.

As the PIA plane began its descent towards Islamabad airport, I thought also of the decline in grass-roots cricket in Pakistan – the universities, schools and clubs. It was evident that grass-roots cricket had been in the doldrums for the past two decades. The universities that were once the hub of cricket had ceased to play first-class cricket. The heyday of Government College, Lahore, playing Islamia College before daily crowds of 10,000 spectators was over. The last time the Combined Universities team was given first-class status was in the 1990s. The team proved to be so inept that it was soon deprived of its first-class status. The days of university graduate leaders like Hafeez Kardar, Javed Burki, Majid

Khan, Asif Iqbal and Imran Khan were long gone, with Ramiz Raja the lone remaining graduate in Pakistan cricket to assume the captaincy.[5]

Schools cricket, which in the early days had seen the formation of the Pakistan Eaglets, was also in sharp decline. In Sri Lanka schools cricket is the main breeding ground for their Test players. Promising 12- and 13-year-olds are picked up and coached to become rounded Test cricketers. There were no signs of organized schools cricket in Pakistan though it was evident that the Pakistani youth was full of enthusiasm and talent for the game.

Perhaps the decline of club cricket had been the most disappointing at grass-roots level. Club cricket had provided the conveyer belt for players who went on to represent Pakistan. The famous Wazir Ali League in Lahore and the Pataudi League in Rawalpindi had withered on the vine. The same was true of cricket in Karachi. Despite the general enthusiasm for the game, club cricket was in the doldrums, probably because financially club cricket had become difficult to sustain. As I landed in Islamabad, I realized that building up a sound financial base for the PCB was also an essential task that had to be undertaken.

For my first briefing, President Musharraf met me with his customary geniality and, after an exchange of courtesies, underlined that my primary task was to prepare the national team to win the World Cup in 2007. He added that discipline and merit should be strictly enforced and that I could rely on his support over the restructuring of the Board. He had appreciative words for Ramiz Raja and then produced statistics that suggested that some players had not been selected on merit. The Patron had obviously done his homework before meeting me. Significantly, Musharraf emphasized the political importance of winning the next World Cup. Cricket would provide a huge fillip to any government that was in power at the time, as Musharraf intended to be. The general health and development of cricket were subordinated at the very outset to the political benefit of winning the World Cup. I thanked the President for his guidance and added that it would take me a few weeks to assess issues in some depth after which time I would give him my plan of action. He ended the interview by saying: 'Be guided by your conscience and do not be influenced by the media who will be out to criticize you at every step.'

I then proceeded to Lahore for a long briefing with General Tauqir Zia. He was extremely welcoming and we discussed the numerous cricketing issues that he had faced. I recall especially General Tauqir stating that there were some experiments and appointments that he had made which turned out to be failures. General Tauqir graciously offered to pass orders on his last day, correcting these errors so that I would not be burdened with their legacy. I thanked him for this selfless gesture and said that, guided by his advice, I would take the decisions myself in due course and that it would not be right for him to issue such important orders like the cancellation of provincial bodies or the removal of the Treasurer on his last day.

The next few weeks were spent on a roller-coaster ride across the country's main cities, during which seminars, workshops and interviews were held with Test cricketers, administrators, umpires, journalists, district and departmental representatives, selectors, referees and coaches. As a result, within a month I had a fair understanding of the administrative and cricketing issues that were faced by the PCB. I was disappointed to note that most of the criticism addressed to the PCB was personality-based and not issue-oriented. For instance, the Karachi representatives complained bitterly that in team selections, appointment of officials and in development activity, the Lahore-based Headquarters had discriminated virulently against Karachi. Now that a Karachi-based Chairman had been appointed they wanted PCB Headquarters to be moved to Karachi with a fairer dispensation of loaves and fishes. Many other issues were given a personal angle, but at the same time some invaluable suggestions were aired, like Sadiq Mohammad's idea that video cameras should be installed at first-class matches to monitor player performance and behaviour, and umpiring and curator standards.

During this initial period, a spate of critical articles on my appointment appeared in the media. The criticism was based on two counts. Firstly, that by appointing another ad hoc Chairman, the Pakistan team and Board's downward spiral was bound to continue. The only saving grace of my appointment being that I was not a military man but a civilian. This criticism was essentially political, aimed at the President by his opponents for continuing his autocratic hold on Pakistani institutions.

Secondly, criticism was aimed at my lack of cricketing knowledge, as I had not even played first-class cricket. According to these critics, only a former Test player could take Pakistan out of the doldrums. I did not respond to this criticism as it would have been a brazen act of immodesty and in any case it was pointless arguing against shallow and ill-informed criticism. The fact is that the running of cricket in a country demands more than international cricketing experience. It requires experience and ability to organize a huge enterprise that encompasses development, financing, media relations, marketing, human resources, diplomatic interaction, and a comprehensive understanding of the rules and regulations that are part of the International and Asian Cricket Councils. The requirement is therefore of a person who has a basic understanding of cricket as well as experience of supervising a large organization like a bank, airline, ministry or multinational. If my critics had done their homework, they would have recognized that not a single national cricketing board from the West Indies to New Zealand was headed by a Test or even a prominent cricketer. Even the ICC's Chief Executive at the time, Malcolm Speed, cut his sporting teeth on basketball before moving to cricket administration. None of the ICC Presidents of the recent past – Jagmohan Dalmiya, Ehsan Mani, Percy Sonn, Ray Mali, David Morgan and Sharad Pawar – has played cricket at the representative level. I can safely state that Test cricketers today are best suited to becoming selectors, coaches and administrators of cricketing issues and would find themselves ill-equipped to supervise the disparate demands of a huge multinational corporation like a country's cricket board. In the immortal words of C. L. R. James: 'What do they know of cricket who only cricket know?'

As regards my cricketing credentials, my love of cricket was born in me through the influence of my uncle – the Nawab of Pataudi – who played cricket for England and later captained India. Uncle Pat was a regular visitor to Bhopal where hockey was the primary sport, but his reputation and skill imbued in me a love of the game that grew into a passion.

My passion for cricket as a player and as a student of the game has never left me. I could have played first-class cricket but opted out because of my responsibilities as a Foreign Service Officer, which limited my cricketing stints to Headquarters assignments or when I was posted as a diplomat to a Commonwealth country. I became a playing member of the MCC in 1962 and captained an important English club – Wimbledon – during my diplomatic assignments to London, continuing to play serious club cricket in Islamabad until the age of 65. I am one of a few Pakistanis who, as a 14-year-old in 1948, watched Don Bradman from the stands at Lords, Headingley and the Oval.

With due modesty, I felt I had sufficient insight into cricketing issues, just as I also had the necessary administrative experience as head of the Pakistan Foreign Office, which I supervised as Foreign Secretary for four years, and as the UN Secretary General's Special Representative in Rwanda between 1994 and 1996.

CHAPTER 3

INDIA'S PATH-BREAKING TOUR OF PAKISTAN – MARCH/APRIL 2004

When I met the President in December 2003, relations between Pakistan and India were tense after Kargil. Despite this tension, the two cricketing boards had maintained an equable relationship. On assuming charge, I had telephoned Jagmohan Dalmiya, President of the Board of Control for Cricket in India (BCCI), with whom I had struck up warm relations during the Pakistan tour of India in 1999. India's tour of Pakistan was scheduled for March 2004 but given the state of political relations, there were serious doubts that India's first tour of Pakistan after 14 years would go ahead. Dalmiya told me on the telephone that while the BCCI was committed to the tour, it was for his government to decide whether or not the tour would take place as scheduled.

Traditionally, a Pakistan–India cricket series has been seen as a rivalry that goes beyond the cricketing arena. It reflects the political relationship between the two neighbours which, since independence in August 1947, has been tense and confrontational. An added complicating factor has been the relatively recent phenomenon of religious extremism and terrorism that has led to most foreign cricket teams declining to tour Pakistan because of security concerns. When it comes to negotiating an India–Pakistan cricket series, both these factors – the state of bilateral political relations and terrorism – require diplomatic interaction of a highly sensitive nature.

Regrettably, on independence, both dominions were in an atmosphere of hostility to each other. This was not the preferred route of their leaders. Certainly, the founder of Pakistan, Mohammad Ali Jinnah, had conceived a US–Canada type of friendship between India and Pakistan. He intended to keep his family residence in Bombay and seriously considered buying property in Kashmir for his retirement. The immediate cause of this hostility was Britain's shameful and hasty flight from India once partition had been agreed. Viceroy Lord Mountbatten packed his bags, declared victory and vacated the subcontinent with vital issues left unresolved. For instance, there was no arrangement in place for the sharing of rivers. There was neither division of defence equipment nor of finance. In terms of economic resources, India did much better than Pakistan out of partition. It inherited 90 per cent of the subcontinent's industry and the thriving cities of Delhi, Bombay and Calcutta. By contrast, Pakistan's economy, which was based on agriculture and controlled by feudal elites, was left with 17.5 per cent of the British colonial government's financial reserves after partition. Moreover, much of the finances and social capital were concentrated in the hands of the Hindus and Sikhs. Muslims had tended to avoid involvement in colonial schools and Western-style scientific education. The loss of this financial and social capital left a massive gap in knowledge and networks in Pakistan.

The princely states, including Kashmir, were left in limbo, with quirky semi-sovereign princes making quixotic decisions on the fate of millions of their people. Unbelievably, on the day of partition on 14 August 1947, there was no established border between the two neighbouring states so that no one knew where Pakistan began and where India ended. Above all, as the British departed, law and order broke down, especially in the divided provinces of Bengal and Punjab, leading to 2 million deaths. In Punjab alone, ethnic cleansing by Muslims, Sikhs and Hindus led to 14 million people becoming homeless, in what was the largest transmigration known to mankind. These were the issues that saw violence and bloodshed at the time of independence, and invested relations between Pakistan and India with venom and mutual hostility.

After this terrible beginning, the Kashmir dispute exacerbated the already hostile relationship between the two neighbours. Two wars, numerous skirmishes and violent incidents in India and Pakistan have followed in its wake, so that throughout Pakistan's 66-year history relations with India have been tense and hostile. Cricket series have been played against this backdrop and have reflected a rivalry fraught with historic and current tension.

Until 14 August 1947, Pakistan was not on the map of the world. It had no history, no recognizable culture, no identity. On the other hand, India was a known geographical entity with thousands of years of history, identity and culture behind it. Pakistan has since independence sought to fill this void by seeking parity and equality with India. The metaphorical minnow ranged against the mighty and established heavyweight. Sport, and particularly cricket, is an avenue where Pakistan has attempted to achieve this parity by matching India's prowess. Pakistan–India cricket matches reflect this rivalry that encompasses our common history, the recent memory of communal riots, the Kashmir dispute, bloodshed and violence of two wars, the break-up of Pakistan that saw the birth of Bangladesh and the national shame of surrendering 93,000 prisoners of war to India. A cricket series could either exacerbate these relations or act as a balm.

The recent growth of terrorism has seriously damaged cricket in Pakistan, especially because foreign teams have declined to tour Pakistan for security reasons. The onset of the terrorist phenomenon has been influenced by two factors. Firstly, the declaration in Pakistan's constitutions that the newborn state would call itself the Islamic Republic of Pakistan. This title was against the basic principles that Jinnah had articulated in his famous speech of 11 August 1947 in which he clearly advocated a liberal, pluralist, democratic and tolerant foundation for Pakistan:

You are free; you are free to go to your temples, you are free to go to your mosques or to any other place of worship in this State of Pakistan. You may belong to any religion or caste or creed that has nothing to do with the business of the State.[1]

Regrettably Jinnah died after a year of independence and pro-Islamic elements began a successful campaign to convert Pakistan into a more theocratic state. The whole connotation of an Islamic state implies the domination of Islamic theology in the country's society and politics. It has encouraged Islamic extremists in Pakistan to follow the tenets of a doctrine that they consider to be pristine Islam. It is a doctrine that the majority of Pakistanis do not accept, as is apparent in the results of democratic elections whenever they are held. Jinnah's political legacy has been consistently downplayed since his death despite the tremendous respect that he is shown in other realms.

Secondly, the struggle against the Soviet occupation of Afghanistan in 1979 provided a huge boost to the extremist Islamic forces in Pakistan. The anti-Soviet campaign in Afghanistan was fought under the banner of Islam against the forces of 'godless' communist occupation. This war attracted Afghans, Pakistanis and Arabs (including Osama bin Laden) to fight against Soviet domination. It was supported financially and logistically by the West and the Gulf Arabs – a campaign in which the CIA saw the Islamists of Afghanistan and Pakistan as 'our boys'. General Zia, Pakistan's military dictator, himself a staunch Islamist, became an overnight hero in the West. Islamic madrassahs in Pakistan were encouraged and funded to churn out a conveyer belt of students that had been brainwashed to sacrifice their lives for the cause of Islamic 'jihad' against the infidels. At the time, no one gave a thought to the repercussions of producing these Frankenstein's monsters that could spin out of control of their masters. As the jihad gained ground, leading to the Soviet withdrawal in 1989, there followed a disastrous civil war in Afghanistan, which eventually led to the

Taliban – a more extremist group of Islamists – coming to the fore, but even they could not wrest control of the whole of Afghanistan. By then the jihadi forces were rampant in the region.

A 180-degree turn in the government of Pakistan's support for the Taliban occurred after 9/11. This opposition to jihadi forces led to widespread terrorism in Pakistan in which Pakistan's military, civilian and security forces were targeted by terrorists supported by Al-Qaeda and the Afghan Taliban. Nearly every Pakistani city was affected by terrorist blasts and suicide bombers, leading to high security alerts across the country. Foreign nationals left the country in droves, foreign embassies became mini fortresses, and cricket teams increasingly declined to visit a country where foreigners – even cricketers – were at risk. In one of his earlier statements as a politician, Imran Khan publicly stated that no terrorist would dare create a security incident at a cricket match as the people of Pakistan would, en masse, turn against the perpetrators. Alas, a few months later, the Sri Lankan team was subjected to a terrorist attack despite the fact that, by then, Sri Lanka was the only country prepared to tour Pakistan. Obviously, visiting cricket teams are high-profile targets for the terrorists.

In the first week of January 2004, the SAARC[2] Summit produced a revival of bilateral cordiality between the two neighbours, and almost the first step in reviving a better relationship was the announcement by President Musharraf and Prime Minister Vajpayee that the Indian cricket tour of Pakistan would be held on schedule, in March/April 2004.

I had been Chairman for less than a month when the Indian cricket team's visit to Pakistan was announced. It proved to be a momentous event not only in cricketing relations but also in the overall context of public relations and bilateral ties. I immediately contacted Dalmiya, suggesting dates and a schedule of three Test matches and five ODIs. Dalmiya prevaricated. The BCCI wanted to be assured of top security for its team. They declined to play in Karachi and were doubtful about Peshawar. A couple of weeks

42

passed with public excitement building at the prospect of a series between the two rivals.

The Indian tour posed Himalayan challenges for the Pakistan Cricket Board. There were security issues – how were we to ensure foolproof security of the players, officials and the large number of fans that were expected to cross over? ICC officials, umpires and the world media were in the same boat in visiting a volatile country. How would we keep the peace between aggressive, flag-waving fans against the background of hostility? Would Pakistan's right-wing parties match the vitriolic rhetoric of India's Shiv Sena and poison the atmosphere? Would Pakistan's fans riot if an unseemly incident took place on the field? Logistically, the tour presented huge problems for the PCB, such as hotels for players and visitors, their visas and travel and press facilities for the highest-ever invasion of journalists into Pakistan. Transparent sponsorship and television deals had to be in place before the tour began. Pitches and stadia needed to be prepared. It was for the PCB a gigantic task, administratively, security-wise, on the public relations front and in the management of fanatical crowds. As the Urdu saying aptly goes: 'The moment I shaved my head, it began raining hailstones.'

Then, a few weeks after the SAARC summit, the Indian Prime Minister announced that general elections would be held in India at the end of April. This announcement threw a spanner in the works in scheduling India's tour. While the PCB proposed to start the tour in the first week of March and complete it in mid-April, a week before the elections, the BCCI had serious reservations. I could sense that if India were to lose the series the BJP government could suffer reverses in the elections. Moreover, Pakistan–India relations needed to be kept stable before the elections and inflammatory incidents during the tour could jeopardize this stability. The security issue also became doubly important.

Jagmohan Dalmiya proposed that the tour should be split: the three Test matches played in March and the five One Day Internationals (ODIs) in September/October. India felt more confident playing the Tests before the elections and was less sure of success in the ODIs. I rejected this proposal, arguing that the tour would lose focus and that our sponsors would not agree to the split. India insisted, however, on a security check before finalizing the tour. Dalmiya said this was a government requirement. I could have diverted this request to the ICC, which is the final arbiter on security issues, but decided to accept the visit of an Indian security team to all the proposed venues. There were, by then, only two weeks left before the start of the tour, but we put in place comprehensive briefings for the Indian security team through excellent professionals drawn from the Ministry of Interior and our security agencies. Zakir Khan, General Manager of Cricket in the PCB, accompanied the Indian security team and telephoned me from every venue they visited. Zakir told me that in Karachi the briefing had been superbly mounted and he felt sure the Indian security team had been impressed. They loved the new stadium in Multan and wanted a Test to be scheduled there. On the Indian security team's return to Delhi, we waited impatiently for the verdict, having offered to take the Indian cricket team to their ODI at Karachi the night before the match – instead of the regulation two days – and ensuring their exit on the night that the match concluded.

Despite the Indian government and the BCCI having agreed to the tour, I sensed strong reservations re-emerging after the announcement of general elections in India because of the negative fallout on the political spectrum in India if the tour was marred by controversy or if India lost the series. After my rejection of a split tour, Dalmiya counter-proposed that the ODIs should be played first followed by the Tests. I had scheduled the ODIs to follow the Tests for two reasons. Firstly, I considered Test matches to be the real measure of cricketing strength. ODIs, though more popular at the public level, depended more on luck, winning the toss and other factors that decided the fate of matches, compared to sheer cricketing ability. In Pakistan, unlike India, the public is

44

not in general attracted to Test matches and I wanted the Indian tour, taking place after 14 years, to help revive Pakistani spectator interest in Test matches. Secondly, for climatic reasons it would have been sensible to play the five-day Test matches in March, when the weather is fair, than in the searing heat of April. Dalmiya, probably prompted by the BJP government, insisted on a reversal of this scheduling. As a quid pro quo for dropping his proposal for a split tour and the BCCI's agreement to play an ODI in Karachi, I agreed that the five ODIs be played before the Tests. All these decisions were part of high-level cricket diplomacy.

By the end of February all the tour details had been agreed. There would be no split tour but the five ODIs would be played before the Tests. Karachi would host an ODI but not a Test. Peshawar was also agreed as an ODI venue. The security checks had been made and the itinerary finalized. While we waited with baited breath that no terrorist blast would undermine the tour, a final hiccup arrived when the Indian press highlighted that the wives of some of the Indian players, including Tendulkar, Dravid and Kumble, were refusing to allow their husbands to tour Pakistan because of the hostile atmosphere between the two countries. Dalmiya telephoned me to indicate that this was a genuine problem. I replied through a public statement that the Indian team would be given security at par with a head of state and that Pakistan had accepted full responsibility for the safety of the Indian players. The decks were cleared and the tour was finally on – only a few days before the Indian team's scheduled arrival in Lahore on 9 March.

Meanwhile, the PCB was faced with the monumental task of completing the arrangements for the tour within a span of weeks when, normally, it would take months to prepare for a home series of this scale. Moreover, the Indian visit brought special problems of visas for the large number of Indian cricket fans. The first Indian cricket tour in 14 years and the first bilateral series since 1999 was arousing immense enthusiasm both in India and Pakistan, and an additional worry was the accommodation for Indian visitors, who would arrive in hordes from the adjacent regions of Punjab, Delhi and Haryana. Television and sponsorship rights had to be in place, Kargil and other such inflammatory incidents put behind us in the national psyche, and the public mood prepared to provide a sporting and tolerant reaction to the Indian players and spectators. The hailstones were coming down hard on the PCB's newly shaven heads.

TELEVISION AND SPONSORSHIP RIGHTS

The first major issue that I faced relating to the Pakistan–India series was on television rights. General Tauqir Zia's Board had, in 2003, signed a five-year contract with ARY and Ten Sports following an open tender process. The Board had then invited the three top bidders to closed-door negotiations in Dubai that had seen Ten Sports and ARY narrowly outbid their competitors. After the change of leadership in the Board, a virulent media campaign had been launched by the losing party in which they maintained that the decision to award the contract to ARY and Ten Sports was not above board. They called for the annulment of the contract and for fresh tenders to be floated. Meanwhile, this party offered the PCB US$ 15 million for the India series as there was no time left for the bids to be received and processed before the tour began. This media campaign became progressively shrill after a senior representative of the company had called on me in Karachi, urging me to cancel the existing contract and to accept the company's 'generous' offer of televising the Pakistan–India series.

On my return to Lahore, I had the Ten Sports/ARY contract scrutinized by lawyers and marketing experts. They came to the unanimous conclusion that the contract had been negotiated fairly and that it did not have the flaws claimed by the rival competitors. Legal experts warned me that cancellation of the contract would lead to a high-profile court case against the PCB for breach of contract, which would probably succeed as there was no evidence

Figure 2   Cricket icons old and new meet in Lahore, 2004. Fazal Mahmud – a year before his death – with Sachin Tendulkar and Rahul Dravid during the Pakistan–India tour.

of unfair dealing in negotiating the contract. I explained the background of the raging controversy to the Patron and informed him that I had decided to honour the existing contract, signed by General Tauqir Zia, and negotiated with the advice of Ehsan Mani, a highly respected financial expert who later became President of the ICC. On receiving President Musharraf's approval, I made the announcement in a press conference. Immediately afterwards, the aggrieved party trained its guns on me and launched a vituperative media campaign against me, accusing me of nepotism and corruption! I decided not to dignify their malicious campaign with a response. The PCB also calculated that the rival company's 'generous' offer amounted to less than the sum that the PCB had contracted for with Ten Sports/ARY for the Pakistan–India series.

With the Ten Sports/ARY television rights contract settled, it became urgent to address the main sponsorship issue. There was practically no time left to squeeze in the open tendering process that our marketing team – headed by consultant Riaz Mahmood and comprising Ahmad Hosain, a corporate lawyer, and the PCB's able marketing manager, Subhan Ahmed – had set in place. This process required:

- The floating of tenders in the international and local media.
- A cut-off date for expression of interest.
- A period for explanation of the complex issues related to the tendering process.
- A cut-off date for the receipt of the bids.
- The formulation of a reserve price for each of the 11 streams that were being tendered.
- The public opening of each tender by our solicitors duly recorded in a register, followed an hour later by the announcement of the bids in front of all competing parties present at PCB Headquarters.

This totally transparent process saw each bidder announce their own bid in front of all gathered competitors. We decided that, in order to ensure maximum transparency and financial probity, there would be no closed-door negotiations with the top two or three bidders. Instead, the highest bidder would be awarded the contract, provided the party met the reserve price. In seven of the 11 streams on offer, the bids cleared the reserve price and the top offer was accepted. In the four streams that did not meet the reserve price, a re-tendering process was ordered within 24 hours. Meanwhile, the reserve price was slightly lowered. The next day, the bids for all four remaining streams crossed the reserve price and the contracts were awarded to the highest bidders.

By making the tendering manifestly transparent and awarding contracts to the highest bidders instead of taking the top two or three bidders into closed-door negotiations, the PCB lost out marginally on a higher return, but the price of total transparency in the PCB's dealings was worth the financial sacrifice. In fact, the best compliment that we received for the PCB's marketing effort was the comment by a losing bidder, who said: 'We are disappointed to lose the title sponsorship bid, but the tendering process was the fairest and most transparent of all such tenders that we have participated in.'

The marketing of sponsorship rights led to an unexpectedly high return of US$ 21.7 million, a record by far for any sponsorship contracted by the PCB. The credit for the remarkable achievement goes to the late Riaz Mahmood and his marketing team, who ensured that the bidding by tenders was completed in the shortest possible period and that the bidding process was flawlessly transparent. This process, which was repeated in all subsequent tenders, helped to project the image of fair play and integrity in the Board.

GROUNDS, PITCHES AND STADIA

There were barely two weeks left before the start of the Indian tour and the grounds, pitches and stadium facilities needed to be brought up to scratch to meet ICC standards. Ramiz Raja, the Chief Executive, had wisely decided to invite Andy Atkinson, the famous English curator, to help prepare our pitches. Atkinson duly set about his task in earnest. A heavyweight, he could be seen driving the roller and squatting down on his knees to scrape the pitches himself in the scorching heat. We knew that the pitches in Karachi, Peshawar and Rawalpindi were reasonably bouncy and favourable to our fast bowlers, but the Lahore, Multan and Faisalabad pitches were 'low and slow' and needed to be quickened so that our fast bowlers could challenge the battery of India's superb batsmen.

I decided to make a quick tour of the venues and found the stadiums in Lahore, Karachi and Faisalabad reasonably well equipped. Multan was a magnificent new stadium but had not been equipped with seats in more than half the stands. Because of the shortage of time, I decided, with the help of the excellent PCB official Naveed Cheema, to short-circuit the long process of advertised tenders, and called established seat-making firms for quotations on the telephone and awarded the contract to the lowest bidder. Our adversarial reporters highlighted these lapses of 'financial probity', but it was clear that the work had to be completed and there was no time for tendering in the normal manner.

In Rawalpindi, to my horror, I found the stadium to be in an appalling condition. The dressing rooms and umpires' rooms were almost derelict, there was no hot water and I found the grass in the outfield knee-high! I had to telephone the Governor of Punjab to seek his assistance, and the splendidly efficient General Khalid Maqbool arrived the next day in a helicopter to survey the dismal scene. He sought the assistance of the Rawalpindi corps commander, who immediately set his units to work. They completed their job of preparing the outfield, building new washrooms and sprucing up the main stands in record time. Finally, my visit to Peshawar found the stadium in reasonable shape, but there was only one men's toilet and none at all for women spectators! Again, contracts to construct men's and women's toilets were short-circuited and the Peshawar stadium had a much cleaner and spruced-up appearance by the time the Indian team played their One Day International.

TICKETS AND VIP FREELOADERS

A last hurdle to overcome before the start of the series was the issue of tickets. In the past, the distribution and control of tickets in Pakistan's stadiums had been chaotic. Forged tickets, leaking-in of friends by policemen on duty and corrupt practices in the sale of tickets had contributed to the PCB's poor reputation in organizing international matches. Most of my cricketing friends preferred to watch the matches on TV at home, even when they had the option of buying the best tickets. They argued that invariably they found relatives of VIPs sitting in their seats, with no official prepared to make them budge from their unauthorized occupancy. The most famous chaotic scene took place at the Gaddafi Stadium, Lahore, which was hosting the World Cup Final in 1996 between Sri Lanka and Australia. At the presentation ceremony, Prime Minister Benazir Bhutto was surrounded and jostled by about 50 VIPs on the dais. Neither the TV presenter nor the PM could be heard in the milling, jostling crowd. This shameful scene was witnessed by millions of cricket-watchers across the world and provided the shoddiest image of Pakistan's civilian government. Earlier, at the start of play, the large number of foreign VIP invitees to this special event had found their seats occupied by grubby-looking acolytes of the Chief Minister of Punjab, who had, that morning, ordered the takeover of the entire VIP stands so that his party members and their relatives occupied the seats reserved for ICC invitees. Among the invitees was my cousin, the Nawab of Pataudi, and his wife Sharmila Tagore, who took one look at the scene and, like most others, drove straight back to their hotel.

I was determined to avoid such ignominious scenes that damaged Pakistan's image as a disciplined and organized country. I was especially determined to root out, as much as possible, the VIP culture of freeloaders being given preference over genuine cricket-lovers who buy their tickets. I could see the sceptical look in the eyes of my colleagues when I discussed my anti-VIP-freeloading campaign with them, but I was bent on doing my utmost. I had one advantage that I owed nothing to any VIP, whether they were a federal minister or a provincial Chief Minister, a member of parliament or a general. I told them politely that we were not issuing complimentary cards or tickets and that all categories of tickets were available in the market at reasonable prices for cricket-lovers and their relatives. I could sense shockwaves registering with the personal secretaries of the VIPs, who would casually 'demand' complimentary tickets for their bosses and their families, and when denied would turn nasty and abusive with my junior colleagues at their boss having been 'insulted'. On the other hand, I must record that several VIPs engaged wholeheartedly in the process. I saw, at Lahore, four federal ministers with their families watching the match from the stands with tickets that they had bought. The same was true of three senior generals and a chief of police.

My task of preventing freeloading was made easier by President Musharraf's personal example. After I had explained my anti-VIP-culture policy, he publicly announced that he would pay for his ticket for every match that he attended. Staff and family members of the President's entourage would also pay for their tickets. I widely publicized this Presidential statement and then circulated it to the offices of the Prime Minister, the Governors and Chief Ministers, who felt obliged to follow suit. This led to the PCB's ready response to irate VIPs demanding complimentary tickets by stating: 'The President has paid for tickets for his staff and family, so why can't you do the same?' One could almost hear the gnashing of teeth at the other end of the line.

Limiting the freeloading VIPs was only part of the ticketing issue. Forgery and massive leaking in of interlopers into the stadium by the police and security staff were highly damaging to the PCB because genuine ticket-holders often found themselves

Figure 3   Chacha Cricket and Indian fans in Lahore.

unable to occupy their marked seats. To reverse this trend, we decided to engage a computer-based company that would print non-forgeable bar-coded tickets. Also, the tickets could be bought on the Internet by international cricket fans. This was another first for the PCB in that the PCB would be selling tickets on the Internet against foreign exchange. Again, there was no time to advertise and we knew that only one company, Suhail & Co., was capable of mounting this effort. So I decided that in order to check the sale of each ticket with bar codes and offer tickets on the Internet, the ticket contract be signed with Suhail & Co. Of course, there was more criticism of nepotism but my conscience was clear. I had never met Suhail before but he was the only man who could deliver a completely computerized ticketing process. Suhail is a computer genius who has suffered at the hands of corrupt governments, but I found him to be a man of integrity who kept his word.

With cricket fever in both India and Pakistan building up to unprecedented heights, I had to make a decision on whether Indian fans should be placed in separate enclosures from the Pakistani public, or allowed to mix. Separate enclosures were the safer option, but I had sensed a welcoming attitude to Indian visitors and decided that there should be no separate stands.

I then embarked on a public campaign to urge our spectators to appreciate good cricket and sportsmanship from both sides, and to welcome the Indian team and their supporters with our traditional hospitality. I addressed the national team in similar terms, asking them to play hard but fair, and to act like true sportsmen on and off the field. The image of the country was in their hands as millions would be watching the series at home and abroad, and I wanted our cricketers to lead the way in showing Pakistan as a moderate, disciplined and welcoming nation. I told them that an acrimonious incident on the field would have a multiplier effect on the watching public. Inzamam cooperated fully in aiming to achieve this task.

While we sorted out the problems leading up to the start of the series, both teams were preparing themselves for the contest. The general view was that the decisive battle would take place between India's master batsmen – Tendulkar, Dravid, Ganguly, Sehwag and Laxman – and our fast bowlers – Shoaib Akhtar, Mohammad Sami, Umar Gul and Shabbir Ahmed. On the spinning front, Indian spinners Anil Kumble and Harbhajan Singh had an edge over Danish Kaneria, but Pakistani pitches were not expected to help spinners. John Wright had been a successful coach for the Indian team, while the ubiquitous Javed Miandad was a high-profile demonstrative coach for Pakistan.

It is sometimes questioned why Pakistan has such a fearsome fast-bowling armoury, producing a battery of fast bowlers ranging from Mohammad Nisar to Khan Mohammad, Fazal Mahmud, Imran Khan, Wasim Akram, Waqar Younis, Mohammad Sami and Shoaib Akhtar, as opposed to the wily and guileful spinners from India such as Mankad, Gupte, Bedi, Prasanna, Chandrashekhar, Venkataraghavan and Kumble. There are many exceptions to this generalization, like the Pakistani Abdul Qadir and India's Kapil Dev, but every knowledgeable cricketer recognizes that India's cutting edge in its attack lies in its superb spinners while Pakistan has relied on pace.

In my view, there are three reasons for this difference. Firstly, the physique of the Pakistani – particularly those from the northern belt of Punjab and Khyber Pakhtunkhwa – is more robust so that their fast bowlers can propel the ball at high velocity.

Secondly, the pitches in Pakistan are generally of higher bounce and fast bowlers are able to obtain greater purchase for seam and fast bowling. Karachi, Rawalpindi, Sialkot, Peshawar and several other first-class grounds have provided happy bowling grounds for faster bowlers while the pitches in Lahore and Faisalabad have been low and slow, prompting Dennis Lillee to vow that he would never again visit Pakistan because of its graveyard pitches. The reason for these faster pitches is that Pakistan's soil is conducive to harder and faster wickets and it is sometimes exported to countries like UAE and Malaysia to provide relatively fast tracks. I played most of my club cricket in the Islamabad/Rawalpindi region and generally found wickets with the kind of bounce and carry that I often encountered in England. In contrast, most Indian pitches tend to be low and slow, discouraging the faster bowlers so that Indian teams tended to rely on the slower bowlers. This is now changing because expert Indian curators are preparing faster wickets. In any case, in the port cities of Mumbai, Chennai and Kolkata, the humidity provides lateral movement that encourages seam and swing bowlers.

Thirdly, and most interestingly, the question arises as to whether the psyche and character of the two countries leads to this distinction. Recalling the very first sentence of this book, does what is bred in the marrow collectively come out in a nation's cricket? On the one hand the Pakistani is extrovert, aggressive and carefree; on the other hand the Indian is introverted, guileful and cast in the Gandhian mould of non-violence. Of course there is no single generalizing answer to the question, but cricket certainly reflects the national character of a people.

During the hectic preparations for the series, I had telephoned my friend Nusli Wadia, Jinnah's grandson, inviting him to one of the matches. Nusli told me that his mother was in Mumbai for a visit from New York, where she lived, and suggested that I join him in trying to persuade her to come too. Quaid-e-Azam Mohammad Ali Jinnah, the founder of Pakistan, and my grandfather, the Nawab of Bhopal, had become close friends during the Pakistan movement – a friendship that had been maintained by succeeding generations. I therefore spoke to Mrs Dina Wadia on the telephone. Though uncertain at the beginning, she agreed to visit Lahore for the ODIs on condition that the visit would be strictly private and that the family would visit Pakistan not as the government's, but as my personal guests. I then spoke to the President, who was glad to confirm the arrangement for the Wadia family's first visit to Pakistan since Quaid-e-Azam Mohammad Ali Jinnah's funeral in 1948.

Figure 4   Dina Wadia – Mohammed Ali Jinnah's daughter – and her son watch the ODI in Lahore, seated with President Musharraf. It was the only occasion since Jinnah's death in 1948 that his daughter and grandson visited Pakistan.

In a separate message from Dalmiya, I was informed that Priyanka Gandhi, her husband and her brother Rahul wanted to witness the ODI in Karachi. I immediately sent an invitation to them, so that two high-profile visitors had already confirmed their visits to Pakistan for the series. I had also invited my Cambridge friend Natwar Singh, who was later India's Foreign Minister, but because of the election campaign he could not accept.

By the time I left Karachi to attend my first meeting of the ICC in Christchurch, New Zealand – a journey that took 72 hours there and back – the Indian team had arrived in Lahore, tense and apprehensive at the prospect of playing before hostile crowds and an 'enemy' environment. The first ODI was scheduled to be played at Karachi, which was seen as the centre of terrorism in Pakistan. The Indian media kept reminding everyone that unruly crowds had disrupted the previous six matches in Karachi. Most foreign teams avoided playing in Karachi, which had led to resentment from the Karachi public. This was exploited politically by the MQM,[3] Karachi's main political party. They now had a Karachi-based

Chairman and looked to him to end the cricketing drought in Pakistan's largest city.

Before I left for Christchurch, we had moved mountains to prepare the physical arrangements for the tour. Hotels and airlines had been booked thanks to the indefatigable logistics man Asad Mustafa, the huge media invasion from India had been catered for by our enterprising media manager Sami Burney, stadiums and ground conditions improved, security arrangements finalized, and the computer-based bar-coded ticketing set in place. Of course, given the extreme shortage of time, corners had been cut and 'due process' replaced by the pressure-cooker, but given the high-profile importance of the Indian team's first visit to Pakistan in 14 years, these measures had to be taken.

I viewed the tour at two equally important levels. Firstly, the cricketing encounter between two arch-rivals was obviously going to be intense. There was a need to avoid acrimony and incidents while maintaining a sportsman's spirit in the matches.

Secondly, I saw the series as an opportunity to redress Pakistan's distorted image abroad, particularly in India. Slanted propaganda had projected Pakistan in a highly negative light. The trigger images were of terrorist bomb blasts, paramilitary elements armed to their teeth ruling the country, home-bound burqa-clad women denied basic human rights, bearded fundamentalists spewing hatred against foreigners and in particular Indians, of unruly cricket crowds and seating arrangements that had seen mayhem in the VIP stands because of freeloaders and VIPs who muscled their way into the enclosures.

In the build-up to the series, I had exhorted the Pakistani crowds to show sportsmanship and a welcoming spirit to the Indian team and their supporters. I had especially challenged the Karachi public to demonstrate their discipline and a sporting spirit in order to remove the blot against Karachi. With the active support of President Musharraf and Prime Minister Shaukat Aziz, I had tried to bring order into the VIP boxes and enclosures.

THE ONE-DAY SERIES – 13–24 MARCH 2004

I returned to Karachi from Christchurch the night before the first ODI. My driver told me that there had been some chaos at the ticket counters, which had been sorted out by PCB officials and the police. As scheduled, the Indian team had arrived from Lahore 36 hours before the match, enabling them to practice at the National Stadium. Rahul and Priyanka Gandhi had also arrived. As I drove with bated breath to the National Stadium, I was pleased to see that there were no traffic bottlenecks and long lines of spectators were queuing to pass the security checks into the stadium. They carried flags, seemed relaxed and in a festive mood.

I went briefly to the Pakistan dressing room to greet the team and to remind the captain that a huge responsibility rested on him and his team. I also shook hands with Indian captain Sourav Ganguly with whom I had struck up a warm relationship during Pakistan's 1999 tour of India.

The National Stadium soon filled up to its capacity of 55,000. I could sense that the Karachi crowd was friendly and responsive, cheering the stars of both teams during practice. The Indian supporters were not yet visible in large numbers and were mainly those who could afford air journeys from India and abroad. They could be seen seated and relaxed with Pakistani supporters, their large Indian flags evoking not a whiff of hostility. Just as the captains went out to the toss on a sunny day, Priyanka Gandhi, her husband and her brother Rahul arrived in the Chairman's box, escorted by a bevy of Indian and Pakistani security personnel. I had met Priyanka and Rahul with their mother at Prime Minister Rajiv Gandhi's funeral. Both children, then in their early teens, had seemed remarkably poised and dignified in their moment of supreme grief.

Now a young, married woman with a striking presence, Priyanka was gracious and friendly. All three Indian VIPs settled into the front row of the Chairman's box as the match began, with Pakistan winning the toss and putting India in to bat. Inzamam probably banked on early moisture helping his fast bowlers to gain quick wickets.

Sehwag and Tendulkar – Pakistan's nemeses of the World Cup in 2003 – opened for India against the fearsome speed of Shoaib Akhtar and Mohammad Sami – both regularly bowling at over 90mph. The battle was commenced with India's superb batsmen against Pakistan's fast bowlers. As at Centurion in 2003, Sehwag and Tendulkar started at a gallop, slapping Pakistan's fearsome duo to all corners of the field. They reached 60 at eight runs an over and had given India a magnificent start. The crowd was neither hostile nor silent. They cheered every boundary by the Indian openers, and soon Priyanka and Rahul left the VIP box and, to the consternation of the security staff, waded into the public stands, where they were warmly greeted by Pakistani spectators. Tendulkar was out at 69, but Rana Naveed began with a succession of no-balls and wides in a 13-ball over that seemed to demoralize him and the rest of the team. India continued its onslaught with Sehwag, Ganguly, Dravid and Kaif scoring freely, closing on a massive 349 for 7. The defining moment of the innings was when Dravid reached 99. The crowd erupted by clapping him on to his century – an unbelievable sight in 'hostile' Karachi. The encouragement seemed so overwhelming for Dravid that he was bowled on 99!

Pakistan began their seemingly impossible task by losing both openers before reaching 35. Then Yousuf and Inzamam began a consolidating partnership of 135 runs when Yousuf got out to Sehwag. Inzamam, now in full flow, played one of the finest innings of his illustrious career. Hitting all round the wicket, Inzamam reached his century by pulverizing the Indian bowling with Younus Khan giving him valuable support. At 275 for three in the 42nd over, a miraculous victory was on the cards and I could see Priyanka and Rahul's earlier ebullience giving way to nail-biting concern. Inzamam and Younus were out by the 45th over, but the free-hitting Razzaq and Moin Khan could complete the job if they stayed at the wicket. Razzaq and Shoaib Malik were soon gone and in the last over, superbly bowled by Ashish Nehra, nine runs were needed for victory. The Pakistani batsmen managed only four, and the magnificent match was lost by four runs. It had been the highest-scoring ODI ever[3] and an exhilarating spectacle for the spectators. Perhaps Pakistan's indiscipline in the shape of 29 no-balls and wides against nine from India made the difference.

The Karachi crowd had been superb – sporting, disciplined and welcoming. Even in losing there was no hint of acrimony and everyone trotted home happy to have witnessed such a magnificent game of cricket. The Karachi match had removed all the demons that had inhabited Karachi's reputation as a cricket centre. The Indian team publicly appreciated the welcome that Karachi's citizens had given them on and off the field, and their manager announced that they would, next time, willingly play a Test in Karachi, something that came to fruition during India's next visit to Pakistan in 2006. The first match had been a huge success with pulsating cricket and magnificent crowd behaviour to which both teams had responded. It set the tone for the remainder of the tour.

The teams then moved to the capital, where the second ODI was scheduled at the Rawalpindi stadium. By now, a large number of Indian fans had crossed the overland border at Wagah and made their way to Rawalpindi. Many of the Sikhs stopped over at their holy shrines on the way from Lahore to Rawalpindi. At the stadium, with a capacity of 17,000, I could sense an electric and enthusiastic atmosphere. The players were relaxed and it was evident that rather than hostility the Indian fans were being royally welcomed by the Pakistani public. The Karachi match had ensured that the tour got off to a superb start.

This time Pakistan elected to bat on winning the toss and Yasir Hameed, opening with the flamboyant Shahid Afridi, gave Pakistan a rollicking start, with an opening partnership of 138.

Both openers made 80s and the remaining batsmen chipped in with useful scores that led to Pakistan scoring 329 for six.

India's openers again began with a 50 partnership, with Tendulkar in masterly form. At 244 for three, with Tendulkar well past his century, the balance had tilted in India's favour and another exciting finish, going to the wire, was on the cards. Then Tendulkar, Dravid, Yuvraj and Kaif were out between the 39th and 45th overs. Balaji and Zaheer then swung hard, bringing the crowd to its feet in excitement, but both perished in the 49th over and Pakistan were home by 12 runs with eight balls remaining. The Rawalpindi match was again played before a marvellously supportive crowd and in a highly competitive but sporting atmosphere.

With the series even after two exciting matches, the whole country was consumed by cricket fever. There was no tension, only amity between the fans. For their next match, the Indian cricketers proceeded to Peshawar by road, where they were seen visiting the famous Kissa Khwani bazaar and open-air restaurants with hardly a security guard in sight. Sadly, such has been the deterioration in the security situation since 2004 that it would be inconceivable to hold a match in Peshawar today. The city has been ravaged by multiple terrorist attacks. The hotel where the Indian team stayed was destroyed by a bomb in June 2009. In the same year, the Kissa Khwani bazaar was the site of another bomb blast.

At Peshawar, with the stadium filled well beyond capacity and in a joyful mood, Inzamam won his third consecutive toss and elected to field – a normal ploy in all day matches because the morning dew livens up the wicket for a couple of hours and when it evaporates, batting is made easier in the afternoons.

This time, India lost early wickets – Sehwag, Tendulkar, Laxman – to the lanky Shabbir, and despite a valiant 65 by Yuvraj, the Indian batting subsided to a modest 244. Pakistan began equally uncertainly and were 65 for four with both local heroes – Afridi and Younus – dismissed cheaply. The third Pathan in the team – Yasir Hameed – held the innings together with a fine 98, but at

173 for six, with both Inzamam and Hameed back in the pavilion, another nerve-tingling finish was in sight. However, Razzaq and Moin held firm, playing aggressively and leading Pakistan to a victory in the 48th over with an unbroken partnership of 74 runs. The match could have tilted towards India if either of the experienced stalwarts had been out earlier.

The two final ODIs to be played in Lahore were to be the icing on the cake in this superbly contested series, with Pakistan favourites after their two victories in Rawalpindi and Peshawar. Lahore was agog with anticipation and famously welcomed around 20,000 Indian fans – a figure well beyond the 8,000 visas agreed by the government – who had somehow reached Pakistan not only from across the border, but from Oman, UAE, Singapore, Canada, Saudi Arabia and even Japan. On the morning of the Lahore ODI, two private jets owned by India's leading business houses landed in Lahore. They carried India's top businessmen, film stars and pop icons. Somehow we found space for them and the visitors thoroughly enjoyed their stay in Lahore. The newspapers and TV channels carried stories of restaurant owners, rickshaw drivers and shopkeepers refusing to take custom from Indian fans and showering them with the warmest of welcomes. This welcome from the Pakistani public in all the cities where the Indian team played was totally spontaneous. One senior Indian official told me that he was returning home worried that when Pakistan visited India for the return series, the Indian public would not be able to match the warmth and hospitality that the Pakistani public had shown to Indian fans.

My favourite story relates to the visit of a Sikh family from across the border. Two young fans had brought their elderly mother with them, as she wanted to visit her former home that she had left in 1947 in Wazirabad – a township 15 miles outside Lahore. While the sons went to the Lahore stadium, they arranged for a taxi to take their mother to visit her former birthplace and home before she emigrated to India.

Hesitantly, the old lady knocked at the door of her old home and when the housewife opened the door, the old mother explained with diffidence and many apologies that she only wanted to see her old birthplace from the outside. She would now return to Lahore having satisfied her wish and did not want to impose herself on the housewife's family. Having heard the old lady's story, the housewife insisted that the mother share a cup of tea with her and look over her old home. Touched by the welcome, the old woman entered the house and was shown around the building. The housewife then excused herself as she made tea in the kitchen while her young family made small talk with the visitor. After a while, the housewife produced a sumptuous meal for the old mother, with traditional cakes, sweet dishes and, of course, tea. The old lady was overwhelmed by this welcome and thanked her hostess profusely. Before taking leave, the hostess asked the mother to wait a few more minutes and returned with six beautiful *joras* (dresses), which she asked the old lady to accept as a present for coming all the way from India to visit her birthplace. The old mother burst into tears at this gesture and the women hugged each other before making their way out to the waiting taxi.

There, outside the house, a large number of neighbours had gathered as word had quickly gone round about the old Indian lady's visit. The neighbours then presented the old lady with 64 *joras* that they had gathered as a mark of their affection for the family that had been obliged to leave home and hearth at the time of partition. The old mother wept and wept and asked how she could take back 70 *joras* to Lahore. 'We shall send them to you in another taxi. Tell us where you are staying,' said the women neighbours. Completely overwhelmed by her welcome, the old lady got into the taxi and returned to Lahore with tears streaming down her cheeks throughout the 40-minute ride. When she arrived at her guest house, the taxi-driver refused to accept the fare.

Pakistanis, and Lahoris in particular, had opened their doors and hearts to their Indian guests. The Indian visitors returned home with many stereotypes shattered.

By the time the Lahore ODIs began, my friend Nusli Wadia, accompanied by his mother, Dina, his wife Maureen and his two sons Ness and Jay, had arrived in his private jet. Security arrangements, cars and a suite in the state guest house were quickly arranged by the Punjab governor, General Khalid Maqbool, who was extremely helpful in the low-key welcome of Quaid-e-Azam's family's visit to Lahore. The news of this visit added a new dimension to the public relations factor. At the stadium, large crowds gathered outside the entrance to catch a glimpse of the founder's daughter and, every time she was visible, she received warm applause from the people. I could see that Dina – who bears a striking resemblance to her father – was moved by the welcome of the people at the stadium.

As the fourth ODI started, the Chairman's box had an electric atmosphere. Apart from the Wadia household, the graceful and elegant Maharani of Jaipur – a family friend – had arrived at my invitation. My dear friend Raj Singh Dungarpur was also present, and soon President Musharraf joined the group and engaged in a

Figure 5   Relaxed Indian fans enjoy the welcome of Pakistani crowds at the Lahore ODI, 2004.

warm discussion with Dina, Nusli and the family. The bonhomie in the box was unbelievable, with hardly anyone noticing that Inzamam had won the fourth toss of the series and decided to bat. Two wickets fell early but Inzamam was in imperious form. With the help of Yasir Hameed and Younus Khan, he took the score to 264 for four in the 38th over, scoring his second century of the series. The crowd was full of good cheer, with Pakistani and Indian fans exchanging humorous banter and running around with their flags joined together in a show of joyous festivity. The Pakistani crowd expected an acceleration by the lower order, so that with a score of around 350 the match and the series would be won for Pakistan.

It was not to be. The Indians fielded like tigers, with Mohammad Kaif taking two incredible catches in the deep. Pakistan's lower order subsided for the addition of only 30 more runs after Inzamam and Razzaq were out and the total of 293 fell far short of the expected target. India then batted sensibly and with the Pakistani bowlers handicapped by a dew-laden outfield, Dravid, Kaif and Yuvraj comfortably took them to victory in 45 overs. The fourth ODI was the first game of the series that did not go to the wire but the crowd went home happy, with the teams locked at 2–2. The decider was to be played two days later.

In the decider, incredibly, Inzamam again won the toss and this time elected to field. After an early loss, Laxman scored a superb century and helped India to exactly the same total – 293 – as Pakistan had made in their first innings of the fourth ODI. India had made the runs easily but now Pakistan's suspect batting faltered, leaving them at 96 for six in the 23rd over. Moin and Shoaib Malik then shared a valiant partnership of 108, but could not maintain the momentum. The turning point of the match was Tendulkar's catch at deep mid-off when Inzamam, in full cry on 38, struck Kartik for what seemed a six, but Sachin, running at full speed, plucked the ball with one hand before it could land over the ropes!

India won the match and the ODI series, which most observers felt was in Pakistan's grasp after going 2–1 up at Peshawar. Lahore's sporting crowd was stunned but not hostile and filtered away silently. Next day, the expected criticism in the media and the press roundly denounced all cricket stakeholders in Pakistan. Inzamam for his inept leadership, despite being selected man of the series, the selectors for playing profligate fast bowlers, coach Miandad for his balcony histrionics, the PCB for mismanagement and denying Test players complimentary tickets. The more serious commentators noted that India's batsmen had successfully overcome Pakistan's fast-bowling barrage. In fact, its less fearsome medium pacers, Nehra, Balaji, Zaheer Khan and Pathan, had more successfully undermined Pakistan's brittle batting, with the exception of the imperious Inzamam and the consistent Yasir Hameed. Secondly, under their excellent coach John Wright, India was a more efficient team. There were few extras, their fielding was alert and they played to their strengths. In contrast, Pakistan appeared to lack strategy and dynamism. Their fielding and running between wickets was shabby, and a large number of no-balls and wides gave away precious runs. This made the difference between two well-matched sides. There was a cavernous gap in discipline, fitness and professionalism between the two teams.

THE TEST SERIES – 28 MARCH–16 APRIL 2004

Traditionally, Pakistani crowds, unlike the Indians, are not supportive of Test matches. We had hoped, however, that we could reverse this trend when playing against our arch-rivals after a gap of 14 years. We therefore proceeded to the 'city of saints', Multan, for the First Test in the expectation that we could win the Test series to compensate for our ODI series loss.

Controversy erupted before play had even begun with the pitch shaved bare, clearly a batting paradise. It was generally felt by the media that Inzamam, supported by his vice-captain Yousuf

Youhana, had asked the curator to take off all the grass from the pitch – a move that was seen as highly defensive as the bald pitch would draw the sting from our fast bowlers, neutralizing our main advantage. The dead pitch would enable our suspect batting to build a score against India's less fearsome but accurate bowlers, who had troubled our batsmen in the ODI series. Miandad was unhappy with the shaven pitch and so was the PCB management, as the pitch was certain to favour India's batting.

Dravid, who had taken over as captain from the injured Ganguly, won India's first toss of the series and batted. Virender Sehwag went immediately on a rampage – smacking Pakistan's bowlers to all corners of the field. The sparse crowd at Asia's most beautiful stadium watched in silence while Sehwag and Tendulkar murdered the Pakistani bowling, increasing the criticism of taking off the grass. On the second day, India declared their innings at 675 for five, with Sehwag hitting a magnificent triple century and Tendulkar scoring 194 not out.

Pakistan then went in to save the follow-on but were bowled out for 407, Yasir Hameed making a valiant 91. Following on, they batted until the close of the fourth day's play, but could not save the match, which Pakistan lost by an innings and 52 runs, Yousuf Youhana scoring a despairing century in a total of 216. The resounding defeat was a heavy blow to Pakistan's morale, our fast bowlers having made no impact on the Indian batting. The shaven pitch had backfired on Pakistan.

For the Second Test at Lahore, the crowd was split almost 50–50, with buoyant Indian supporters mixing freely with Pakistani fans. India won the toss and after a sedate opening, Umar Gul, in a memorable spell, turned the tables on India. In the space of ten overs, he captured four top Indian wickets with rearing seamers delivered from a high action. Though limping towards the end of his spell, Gul broke the back of India's batting as they were all out for 287. Pakistan went in and consolidated carefully with Inzamam, as always, the rock of Pakistan's batting. Next day, the young Karachi left-hander Asim Kamal gritted his way through the remainder of the innings, giving the home side a decisive advantage. Pakistan made 489, leaving India with a mountain to climb.

With their tails between their legs, India could muster only 241 in the second innings, even though their first innings destroyer Umar Gul was off the field with an injured back. Pakistan then carefully made the 40 runs required, levelling the series at 1–1 and looking to win the Third Test in Rawalpindi.

By this time, the friendly Pakistani crowds had selected their favourite in the Indian team. He was not one of the high-profile stars in the Indian team, nor one of the Muslims playing for India – Pathan, Zaheer or Kaif – but the unknown South Indian newcomer, Balaji, who somehow endeared himself to the crowds by his smiling demeanour and gritty performance with bat and ball. Every time he fielded the ball, shouts of 'Balaji, Balaji' went up from the crowd, and he was given a rousing welcome every time he bowled or batted, to the obvious amusement of his teammates. Balaji was a quiet, modest and cheerful soul and it is amazing how crowds can discern the character of a player.

The Third Test at Rawalpindi was a huge anti-climax for Pakistan. Put into bat, our batting sank without trace for 224. Then Dravid made an imperious 270 for India in a total of 600. In the second innings, Pakistan batted gutlessly for 241, giving up the chase, as in Multan, long before the painful end. It was not the heavy defeat – by an innings and 131 runs – but the manner in which the team played that made me angry. There was no gritty, over-my-dead-body resistance, no attempt to play for a draw. I doubt if any of our players would have known that Atherton had batted 13 hours in Johannesburg to draw a Test. Or even heard of Watson and Bailey, let alone our own Hanif Mohammad, who batted 16 hours to save a Test in the West Indies. Our cricketers knew little of cricket history and drew no inspiration from it. With the exception of Asim Kamal (60 not out), the second innings was played in a cavalier manner – with glorious but risky shots played all around the wicket. Yousuf Youhana and Shoaib Akhtar were the worst culprits, playing festival shots as they holed out, accepting the inevitable without the semblance of a fight. The team had shown no character and no fighting spirit, as much a reflection on the players as on the coach.

At the cricketing level, the loss of both series was extremely disappointing. A torrent of criticism was directed at the players, the coach and the board, with Test players and cricket commentators highlighting Pakistan's cricketing failure at every level. The President was annoyed as he telephoned to ask why, with victory in the ODIs in our grasp and going in 1–1 in the Test series, Pakistan had meekly succumbed. I had no answer for the Patron.

However, in the public relations domain the Indian tour had been an unbelievable success. It left a benchmark at the political level that

Figure 6 Priyanka and Rahul Gandhi leave the VIP box and wade into the public stand to watch the Karachi ODI, 2004.They were given an enthusiastic reception by the crowd. Rajiv Shukla, current Vice-President of the BCCI and cabinet minister (right), joins them in the open.

69

raised people-to-people goodwill levels that neither government could disre-gard. The spirit between the Pakistani and Indian fans reflected a desire for peace regardless of the daunting issues, like Kashmir, that had divided the two nations for nearly 60 years. The presence of the Quaid-e-Azam's family in Lahore, Priyanka and Rahul Gandhi in Karachi, and a bevy of Indian VIPs heading 20,000 Indian cricket supporters, added a special flavour to the series that the public and media began to call the Friendship series.

Accolades for the success of the series poured in from all quarters. Laurens International, the world's leading sports concern, nominated the India and Pakistan cricket teams as joint winners for their annual team sports prize. The UN recognized the impact of the series in peacebuilding by announcing a special tribute to both teams as ambassadors of peace. For Pakistan these international tributes were of special significance as they projected the moderate, peaceful and hospitable image of the country that had been tarnished by exaggerated accounts of internal events.

Almost nine years have passed, but people from both sides of the border regard the 2004 tour as the standout, path-breaking series between the two countries. Using a memorable phrase, the Indian High Commissioner, Shiv Shankar Menon, told me while taking leave in Lahore: 'Shaharyar Saheb 20,000 Indian cricket fans visited Pakistan. You have sent back 20,000 Pakistan Ambassadors to India. Thank you for your hospitality.' The PCB had passed its sternest test. It had demonstrated that Indian players and fans would not only be secure but welcomed in Pakistan. Everything had worked – visas, transport, accommodation, attending to the journalist invasion, sponsorship – and though we lost the series, the cricket had been absorbing and played out before sporting crowds that showed no rancour or boorish behaviour. Both teams had dignified captains who behaved superbly. Above all, from every point of view, the PCB had demonstrated that it could deliver.

Looking back, I regard India's tour of Pakistan in 2004 as the most important and defining event of my three-year tenure as

Chairman. It happened to be the very first tour of my chairmanship and threw me into the deep end from the moment that I took over. The tour encompassed politics, diplomacy, logistic arrangements, public relations, overcoming interstate tensions, handling the largest invasion of Indian fans and media, watertight security, marketing the series efficiently, and urging the Pakistani public to treat the contest as a sporting contest and not as a battle between two antagonistic neighbours. All this had to be achieved within the space of seven weeks between the sudden announcement of the tour and the Indian team's arrival. The tour was to be India's first visit to Pakistan after a gap of 14 years, raising huge expectations – and fears. The tour tested our mettle to the hilt and deserves detailed analysis to highlight the vital issues that the PCB faces.

Six years later, terrorists attacked the Sri Lankan cricket team, with no security cordon in sight. The Pakistan cricket team has been accused of drug-taking, spot-fixing, indiscipline and breaking into factions. Cricket results have been appalling. We have slumped from being second and third in the international table to being near the bottom. The management of the team has been lax and was found incompetent. A revolving door of captains and coaches has again plagued the cricketing establishment. Why the sharp decline? The answers to these questions are discussed in Chapters 8 and 9 of this book.

CHAPTER 4

WOOLMER ENTERS THE FRAY

After the India series, Chief Executive Ramiz Raja and I did a bit of soul searching. We needed a fresh start and a coach that could inspire and lead from the front. Javed Miandad had been a highly demonstrative coach who had worked hard in improving technique, gleaned from his experience as a master batsman. He was undoubtedly a great batsman who relied on instinct and natural genius, but he was not an analyst. Miandad had failed to instil a fighting spirit in the team and often complained of lack of cooperation from the senior players. This was not new for me, as during the 1999 tour of India, when I was manager and Miandad the team coach, I had noted similar tensions between Javed and senior players.[1] For these senior players, Miandad remained primarily a former captain rather than a coach.

Ramiz and I felt that by employing a prominent professional coach, we could help the team turn the corner. Miandad still had about a year left on his contract, but we thought that the approach of the World Cup demanded an immediate change. Three coaches were in our sights – Greg Chappell, Bob Woolmer and Barry Richards. All three were attending an ICC coaching clinic in Pakistan and we held discussions on cricketing techniques with all three. I had thought about the impact of inducting a foreign coach and had the experience of seeing the players' reaction to Richard Pybus, a South African who had coached the Pakistan team while I was manager for the 2003 World Cup. The only issue

Figure 7   Bob Woolmer takes over as national coach, July 2004.

between Pybus and the players was that he was not an established Test cricketer. Otherwise I noted no difficulty with regard to race, communication in English or social standing. In the end, Ramiz opted for Woolmer and I gave him the green signal to negotiate a contract with him. Soon, Woolmer had agreed terms. I then called on President Musharraf and gave him the reasons for the PCB taking this vital step. I told him that the PCB would be severely criticized for replacing a Pakistan icon by a foreign coach, but the President, after giving me a full hearing, asked me to go ahead.

The appointment of a foreign coach was not in itself such a major issue. Most other cricketing nations had foreign coaches. In South Asia, India, Sri Lanka and Bangladesh had all decided on a foreign coach. In fact, Pakistan had twice appointed the South African Richard Pybus in place of a Pakistani. What made Woolmer's appointment much more controversial was that he was replacing a national hero, Javed Miandad.

It was therefore a question of emotional patriotic support for a national icon whose coaching method was based on experience and intuition against the technical prowess of a coach who had achieved excellence by graduating to the highest echelons of professional coaching. The Pakistani public was divided on this emotive issue. The more sober elements welcomed Woolmer's appointment, especially as Miandad had not been particularly successful. At least, they felt, an expert of Woolmer's known calibre should be tried and judged on his results. The other half's response was nationalistic and emotional. How could a foreigner replace a cricketing great and a national icon? It was as though a foreign expert were to be appointed as the Governor of the state bank to overcome an economic crisis, or a foreign police chief to head the police force when law and order had broken down. Nationalistic attitudes would not accept such an appointment.

Before negotiating a contract with Woolmer, I had wrestled with the controversy of employing a foreign coach instead of a Pakistani. There were arguments in favour and against on both sides of the fence. A foreign coach was considered to have a communication problem of language and of not being familiar with the 'culture' of the Pakistani team. On the other hand, a foreign coach would be better qualified technically in the art of coaching in a game that was becoming increasingly complex and specialized. Various grades of coaching qualifications were prevailing in all cricketing countries, ranging between Grade I up to Master Coach. In Pakistan, at the time, we had only three Grade III coaches and one Master Coach (the late Wasim Raja) who lived abroad. A top-qualified coach had to be a proven master of his profession.

Conversely, indigenous coaches had no language or cultural gaps to fill. They tended to be former Test stars, such as Intekhab Alam, Waqar Younis and Javed Miandad, and even though they were not highly qualified technically in the art of coaching, their familiarity with local players and the national scene was regarded as an advantage. However, indigenous coaches were prone to be influenced by player divisions and intrigues. Some, like Miandad, had been playing colleagues of Waqar Younis, Wasim Akram and Inzamam, and carried with them their likes and dislikes in coaching the team.

In selecting Bob Woolmer, I felt the language barrier had been overstated because nearly all of our players had played league or county cricket in England. They had sufficient knowledge of English to understand directions from an English-speaking coach. The cultural gap was more significant but bridging the gap depended on the sensitivity of the foreign coach. Greg Chappell had been a failure in India, but Bob Woolmer, Dav Whatmore and John Wright had quickly adjusted to their new cultural milieu. All things considered, I felt no hesitation in employing a highly qualified and famous coach, Bob Woolmer, to take on the mantle. After all, the last time our hockey team had won a World Championship was under a Dutch coach!

I had developed a happy relationship with Miandad when he was national coach during the Pakistan team's tour of India in 1999. Therefore, the task of informing him that he was sacked was difficult to handle. Naturally, Miandad was disappointed and upset but did not remonstrate with me at the time. I offered to make him head of the National Academy and to honour his contract in full by paying all his dues. Miandad left, disconsolate, adding that he would think about the offer. His supreme ego had been hurt and he subsequently addressed a barrage of criticism against me, the PCB and the appointment of Woolmer.

The news of Woolmer's appointment was generally well received, especially by the more serious cricket followers in Pakistan. The PCB's regular snipers and the Miandad lobby went into an overdrive of criticism, but the die had been cast and only future performance would show if we had taken the right course.

I met Woolmer for the first time as national coach during the ICC annual meeting at Lords. Ramiz and I invited him to dinner at a hotel near Lords, and I was impressed by his down-to-earth attitude and his cricketing vision that he had developed as a highly innovative and professional coach. Woolmer expressed his concern

75

about being able to communicate with the players, as he understood they were not fluent in English, adding: 'I intend to learn Urdu, but it may take time to become proficient in the language.' Ramiz and I reassured Woolmer that most of the players had regularly played league and county cricket in England and had sufficient knowledge of 'cricketing English' to follow his instructions. We did not anticipate a communication gap because of language.

During the dinner Ramiz and I briefed Woolmer on Pakistan cricket. We told him that with the exception of Omar Kureishi and very few others, the press was looking to sensationalize the most trivial issues. As Woolmer was going to be part of Pakistan's cricket establishment, he could expect gratuitous criticism based neither on reality nor reason. We advised him to disregard such salacious comments.

Woolmer wanted his own team of physical and fitness trainers to which I readily agreed. Woolmer brought two South Africans with him: the experienced Murray Stevenson (fitness trainer) and young Darryn Lifson, who had high recommendations as a physiotherapist from knowledgeable South African cricket administrators.

During dinner we witnessed Woolmer's expert player-management capability. After the Rawalpindi Test defeat, Shoaib Akhtar had walked out of the national camp because he felt slighted by the medical inquiry following his 'breakdown' in the Rawalpindi Test. The media and public had speculated that Shoaib's injury had been faked or exaggerated in front of his home crowd, where he had failed to deliver. Woolmer telephoned Shoaib, who was in England at the time, and spoke to him with sensitivity and understanding. He said: 'I regard you as a vital member of the Pakistan team. Now that I am taking over as national coach, I want you to put all your problems behind you. I can assure you of my full support and commitment. You can rely on getting a fair deal from me. We are turning over a new page for Pakistan cricket. I'm sitting here with the PCB Chairman and the Chief Executive and have their support as I talk to you. Now promise me that you will join the camp.' Shoaib Akhtar responded immediately and positively to Woolmer's persuasive call. One call from Woolmer had resolved a grating issue within minutes!

Woolmer and his team arrived in Pakistan on 1 July 2004. The criticism by the PCB's habitual opponents and the Miandad lobby referred to the 'huge' expenditure on Woolmer and Pakistan's lack of success with a former foreign coach, Richard Pybus. This criticism was pernicious and baseless. Woolmer's remuneration was almost exactly the same as Miandad's. Miandad was given Rs. 8 million per year. Woolmer was contracted for £80,000, which was equivalent to Rs. 8.1 million. They had the same privileges of travel and daily allowance when on tour with the team. Woolmer had additional perks of paid visits to his home in South Africa, but the anticipated expenditure on five-star accommodation was nullified by Woolmer and his team, deciding to occupy simple, no-expense accommodation at the National Academy. The Academy accommodation was fairly basic, but Woolmer said he wanted to be near or at his place of work where he could interact with the team – whether national, 'A' or under-19 – and get to know the boys personally. A year later, when India replaced John Wright with Greg Chappell, he received a salary three times the one that Woolmer had been contracted for. South African Graham Ford was offered US$ 300,000, which was more than twice Woolmer's salary. Recently, India are reported to have engaged Duncan Fletcher for a fee of £800,000 per annum. Yet Woolmer was recognized internationally as the world's outstanding coach. In talking to Woolmer regularly, I felt that his decision to coach the 'talented but difficult' Pakistani team was a challenge for him and he accepted the assignment at well below his market rate.

Most of the Test-playing countries at the time had opted for foreign coaches too – Sri Lanka (Whatmore/Moody), India (Wright/Chappell), Bangladesh (Whatmore), England (Fletcher), West Indies (Bennett King), Zimbabwe (Simmons). Only New

Zealand (Bracewell), South Africa (Mickey Arthur) and Australia (Buchanan) had their own nationals as coaches. Mickey Arthur was for a period employed as Australia's coach and Duncan Fletcher (Zimbabwe) is the national coach of India. England are coached by Andy Flower, also of Zimbabwe.

Except for Greg Chappell, none of the coaches had been international Test stars. Some had played a few Tests – Whatmore, Woolmer, Wright, Bracewell, Simmons – while the most successful coaches, Buchanan and Fletcher, had barely played first-class cricket. As regards recruiting famous national players as coaches, some of the all-time greats like Vivian Richards, Sir Garfield Sobers, Clive Lloyd, Javed Miandad and Kapil Dev had not been successful national coaches. This was due to the fact that coaching cricket has now become a science, a discipline that requires a coach to be part technician, part medico, part psychologist, part teacher and wholly computer literate. To become a successful coach, it is necessary to pass through the academy of coaching, going from Grade I to Master Coach, like taking a university degree. Being a great cricketer does not automatically qualify a person to perform the role of a national coach. He needs to acquire basic technological skills.

Immediately on arrival, Bob Woolmer was thrown into the deep end, taking over the national camp for the forthcoming Asia Cup. The players had been selected and I could see from my office window that Woolmer was wholeheartedly engaged in supervising the new fielding drills, the batting and bowling practices in a completely different and innovative manner. Woolmer told me that players mostly saw fielding as a chore and he had devised a system that would be competitive and retain their interest. Haroon Rashid, the team manager, assisted him, while Murray Stevenson and Darryn Lifson went about their duties of trainer and physio in a highly professional manner. The batting practices in the nets were organized to simulate cricket in the middle, with two batsmen per net facing three or four bowlers performing as though playing in a Test match. An umpire signalled no-balls and wides while the two batsmen called for runs and alternated the strike. Fielding was given special importance as was curbing of no-balls and wides.

After a couple of days, Woolmer told me that in all his coaching days he had not supervised such a talented bunch of fast bowlers. He was aware of our opening-batsman problems, but felt that the middle order was in the safe hands of Inzamam, Yousuf and hopefully, Younus Khan, when he curbed his natural aggression. The all-rounders were also excellent and he felt enthused by the team after his initial encounter with the boys. Bob Woolmer was, however, highly critical of the team's fitness levels. I recall him saying that fitness levels in the squad were no higher than 30 per cent and he was even more critical of the medical support staff attached to the team. The medics were not qualified in sports medicine and the National Academy lacked equipment that was essential to raise fitness levels. Bob said that it would take him six months to build up fitness levels to near the 100 per cent that was required of a national team.

I immediately ordered the equipment required and upgraded the Academy's swimming pool so that the team could perform its aquatic routine and relax after a coaching session. Murray Stevenson and Darryn Lifson also set up a computerized database for the players. A thorough medical examination saw three players of the national squad with serious dental problems that needed to be addressed immediately. One player had a blood infection that had led to constant debilitation and another had astigmatism that required contact lenses. The camp was now humming with activity and the boys were, for the first time, being introduced to individual computerized data sheets showing their cricketing flaws, their medical data and their fitness levels that could now be measured on the computer.

Woolmer said that he had numerous ideas on training schemes, facilities and equipment for the Academy, but that he would wait until after the Asia Cup to discuss them with Ramiz and me. He was upbeat about moulding the team into a successful unit. The players had also warmed to Woolmer's innovative coaching methods, his sensitive concern for players, whom he encouraged to see him at any time, and his tactical vision to optimize the team's potential. Bob told me that he had struck up a good relationship with captain Inzamam, insisting that their joint leadership in their differing roles was essential for the team's success. Woolmer considered Inzamam an outstanding batsman and though the player was laid-back, overweight and not fluent in English, Woolmer felt he had an excellent cricketing brain and had the full support of his team. Bob made it clear to Inzamam that as coach he would prepare and strategize for the team at practice and before every game, but once the skipper went out to the toss, all decisions would be made by the captain. Woolmer would be in the dressing room but would not interfere in the decision-making process once the match was under way. This was in sharp contrast to the role that Javed Miandad had assumed as coach, waving and gesticulating from the Pakistan balcony to the batsmen and fielders and sometimes even changing the batting order to the annoyance of the captain.

The team was now ready to proceed to Sri Lanka for the Asia Cup under its new coach. The media was agog with anticipation at the new coach's performance.

At the Asia Cup we defeated India in a league match – the acid test for the Pakistani public. We then lost to Sri Lanka and were eliminated from the finals by India's better point count. August saw the triangular Videocon Trophy in Holland, with India and Australia the other participants. Here we again defeated India but narrowly lost to the Australians in the final. We then proceeded to Lords to play Australia in a one-off match to 'compensate' us for Australia's unwillingness to tour Pakistan. Again we lost narrowly by ten runs when we appeared to be coasting to victory. Every time we had played against the mighty Australians we had stumbled at the last hurdle due to nerves, and lack of crisis management by our batsmen. Later in the autumn at the Champions Trophy in England, we again defeated India at Edgbaston for the third time under Woolmer's tutelage, but lost to a weak West Indies team in the semi-final by deciding to bat first on a lively Rose Bowl wicket that eased out later in the day. This was a tactical error that deprived Pakistan of a place in the final.

On return to Pakistan, Bob, Ramiz and I held long discussions on the organization of the National Academy. It was generally recognized by every visitor that Pakistan's National Academy was the world's finest in terms of construction and facilities, for which credit must go to my predecessor, General Tauqir Zia. The issue now was the coaching structure and aims of the National Academy.

Bob Woolmer offered to head the academy, but Ramiz and I declined his offer because Bob would be away with the National Team for long periods and the Academy required a chief coach and administrator to be on the spot on a permanent basis. Woolmer also recommended that cricket players should be encouraged to play other games like tennis, squash, table tennis, badminton and even hockey, as it would develop stamina and hand-eye coordination that would be helpful in improving cricket performance.

Woolmer kept underlining the lack of fitness of our cricketers. In the few first-class games he had seen, he found fitness and therefore fielding levels deplorable. He made it clear that however promising a young bowler or batsman may be, he would find no place in his squad if he was not personally committed to full fitness. I recall particularly an 'A' team camp at which the selectors were looking for a wicketkeeper. Karachi had sent a highly recommended young keeper, Amin-ur-Rehman, who had performed well at first-class level. Karachi had traditionally provided the national team with top wicketkeepers, including Wasim Bari, Moin Khan and Rashid Latif. From my office window I watched Amin-ur-Rehman keeping brilliantly in the trial matches but his name was missing from the final squad. Intrigued, I asked Woolmer for his opinion of the young Karachi keeper. Woolmer replied: 'He has the best pair of hands I have seen among Pakistani keepers but his fitness level is appalling. I told him, "Go back to Karachi and get fit. You will then walk into the national squad. Your future is entirely in your hands. I can't make you fit, only you can.'" This was Woolmer's refrain to all his players. A coach can guide and point the way, but it is for the player himself to heed the advice and take corrective action. The coach cannot do it for him.

Defeating India three consecutive times since Woolmer had taken over, even though we had not gone on to win any silverware, was viewed as a success for Pakistan. Under Woolmer there was a new buzz and fighting spirit in the team. Woolmer was disappointed that we did not beat the Australians when we had them under pressure. He kept saying: 'We must develop the winning habit. We need mental strength and a belief in ourselves. Success will follow.'

Bob Woolmer's method was not that of a severe disciplinarian. He used a soft touch with the players, of persuasion and pointing out their deficiencies personally through computer images of their play. Woolmer would frequently talk to players, one on one, showing them their faults on the computer and telling them that it was for the coach to show the way and for the player himself to take corrective action. His coaching techniques were innovative and carefully crafted from his successful experience, and his attempt to make practice interesting and competitive rather than a chore galvanized the team. Woolmer had no problem with communicating with his players as they had more than sufficient knowledge of English cricketing terminology, so any deficiency in fluent English was easily overcome. In fact, more than any Pakistani coach, Woolmer was able to come down to the level of the players and teach them from that perspective rather than from the perspective of a past player. It is difficult for a supremely gifted sportsman, like Miandad or Vivian Richards, to understand why their pupils could not play like them.

Woolmer's own relatively humble background – he was far from the English public school type – helped to bridge this potential social gap. He had made his way up the cricketing ladder from a Kent ground staff hound to an England Test player. He later joined the Kerry Packer tours. The respect that he gained from the Pakistani players was mainly due to his fairness, total availability and an absence of any racial condescension in his attitude. Unlike Richard Pybus, he also had the advantage of being a Test player with two centuries against Australia.

Woolmer based his coaching method on what he referred to as the six Ss – skill, speed, strength, stamina, suppleness and spirit – that required both physical and mental capabilities. Woolmer was a deep student of cricketing technique and voraciously read books written by great exponents of the game like Don Bradman and C. B. Fry. He advocated players reading and absorbing techniques passed down by great players. His own experience as a successful Test player and coach was used to formulate coaching techniques that related to grip, stance, weight of bats and wrist action for spin and swing bowling. Woolmer gave Jonty Rhodes's commitment to technique, speed, strength and suppleness as a prime example of hard endeavour. Rhodes became the finest fielder of his generation, but even that status was not enough for a Test place until Rhodes's batting improved, as it did under Bob's coaching.

Bob's interaction with the players had led to a growing respect for his coaching methods, especially with the junior and middle-ranking players. His gentle, personalized approach was appreciated, as also the computerized data that he collected on each player. For instance, Shoaib Malik had been under a cloud over his bowling action due to a bent elbow at the time of delivery. With the help of the physio Darryn Lifson, Bob diagnosed that Shoaib Malik's bent elbow was due to a faulty operation on his arm, which had led to one of his tendons being shortened, preventing a straightening of his arm at the elbow. Bob sent Shoaib's reports to one of the top sports medical specialists in South Africa, who advised an operation that would straighten his arm. Shoaib was greatly enthused at the prospect and wanted to undergo surgery immediately to get the cloud over his bowling action lifted. This space was difficult to find as Shoaib Malik was a vital player in the national team, but an opportunity was found and Shoaib returned from South Africa after the operation with arm straightened, and has since bowled without any difficulty in satisfying umpires about the legitimacy of his action. Remedial action with Shabbir was more difficult and Bob Woolmer put in hours of work to rectify the apparent jerk in his action. Shabbir was sent to Australia, returning with partial improvement, but he was prone to fall back into a doubtful action when bowling under stress. Bob Woolmer generally favoured tall fast bowlers like Shoaib, Shabbir and Umar Gul, who hit the deck hard from a high action, as opposed to shorter 'skid' bowlers like Mohammad Sami and Yasir Arafat, even though they bowled at a high pace.

Bob's relations with senior players were sometimes less than smooth. Soon after taking over, he told me that they tended to treat the physio as a personal masseur, calling him up for body massages at odd hours. Bob explained to the players that Darryn Lifson was a highly qualified physio who would attend to injuries in a professional manner during reasonable hours. He was not a personal masseur as previous Pakistani medical attendants had been. Initially, there was resentment from the players, but in due course they came to appreciate Lifson's professional qualities. Bob Woolmer's relationship with the captain, Inzamam-ul-Haq, was also central to the success of the team. Inzamam was a towering figure as Pakistan's leading batsman and most senior player who was held in awe by his fellow players. Inzamam was a brooding, introspective man who was not, by nature, an inspiring captain, even though he had a deep understanding of cricket and tactics. Bob made a special effort to establish a close, cooperative relationship with Inzamam, which was, in the main, successful. Sometimes, Inzamam would go into a silent and childish huff with Woolmer over trivial issues and it would take a major effort by Woolmer and by myself to put the relationship back on an even keel again. Sometimes, these stand-offs were due to Woolmer not paying sufficient attention to Inzi's batting practice. In another case,

Inzi took umbrage (during the Bangalore Test) when Inzi, while batting, sought Woolmer's advice on the timing of the declaration. Woolmer did not respond to Inzamam, believing that it was for the captain and not the coach to decide on the declaration. I remember berating Bob for overemphasizing the principle that after the toss it was for the captain to decide on cricketing issues. I said that sometimes, out in the middle, it is difficult to make the calculations for a crucial declaration and Inzi was within his rights to seek guidance from the coach that was not forthcoming. Bob accepted my reasoning and apologized to Inzamam.

Though generally cooperative, the Woolmer–Inzamam relationship had its discordant moments over control of the team.

THE CAPTAINCY

When I took over as Chairman, Inzamam-ul-Haq was already nominated Pakistan's captain and was leading the team in New Zealand. He was the obvious choice as the senior-most player and the only player in the team of international repute. The issue of captaincy rested squarely with the Chairman, and I wholeheartedly supported Inzamam's captaincy, especially as it ensured continuity and consistency in the leadership that had sadly been lacking in the recent past. There were regular criticisms of Inzamam's captaincy from the media for his defensive laid-back approach as also for his lack of articulation, especially in English. In the early days, Yousuf Youhana was his deputy but was by no stretch a rival. A year or so later, Younus Khan was made vice-captain, replacing Yousuf. I had got to know all three players during my two stints as manager. I had a deep respect for Inzamam for his dignity and composure. He was a sensitive, brooding soul whose cricket stature and knowledge were unquestionable, as of course were his cricketing credentials. I had also gained the highest regard for Younus Khan for his commitment, enthusiasm and growing cricketing credentials. Inzamam and Younus were, however, opposites in character and in their leadership qualities. Inzamam was uncharismatic, defensive and laidback, while Younus was ebullient, demonstrative and active in his leadership. Clearly, Inzamam sensed a rival and his innate insecurity led to a distance between the two. Inzamam rarely consulted Younus on the field and on the few occasions that Younus acted as captain, the contrast in leadership was obvious. When Pakistan performed badly – as against Australia and India – a cry went up from the media to replace Inzamam with Younus, which heightened Inzamam's insecurity. He also tended, therefore, to be oversensitive to what he sometimes considered as lack of support from Woolmer in matters of tactics and team selection.

Here, despite his obvious credentials, Inzamam's insecurity needs to be explained. Hitherto, captains, coaches and managers had bitten the dust after almost every series loss. They were sacrificed to hungry media wolves by Chairmen who sought public approval by their peremptory measures. Secondly, there was no institutional process for the appointment of a captain as the Chairman had the power to make changes without accountability. Much depended, therefore, on the Chairman's whim. Thirdly, players relied on a degree of backing from political elements for their support. Inzamam, coming from a lower-middle-class Multan family, had none. Hence his insecurity heightened.

For the sake of continuity and stability I set out to confirm Inzamam's leadership by appointing him over long periods and not on a series-to-series basis. With the approach of the World Cup, I was convinced that Inzamam was the obvious, though not perfect, choice as captain. His father met me once and told me that he had informed his son that I was his strongest supporter! To maintain equilibrium between Inzamam and Younus, I told Younus that every captain has the right to mould his team according to his priorities and style. Younus needed to bide his time in order to make his mark on the team and on the occasions when he substituted for Inzamam, he had to be careful not to draw too great a contrast with his own style of leadership in contrast with Inzamam's, as it would give rise to unnecessary factionalism. Younus understood my message. His time would come.

Throughout my tenure, until the World Cup, Inzamam was confirmed as captain, but his insecurity saw him gather a coterie of senior players who tended to undermine Younus's leadership claims. I remained convinced, despite reservations on Inzamam's excessive religiosity, that continuity in leadership was essential for the team.

Inzamam sought total control of his team in terms of loyalty, which he achieved through his seniority and as a towering religious figurehead. The senior players Razzaq, Yousuf and Afridi gave him this support, while Shoaib Akhtar and Younus Khan were not part of this inner cabal.

Overall, until the tour of England in 2006, Woolmer had achieved an equable and positive relationship with Inzamam. The senior players were sometimes uncooperative but Woolmer's gentle and sensitive handling of the team had gained him general respect. Sometimes, a player dropped from the squad would behave rudely with Woolmer. When informed, I would be ready to come down heavily on the player but Woolmer would invariably ask me to desist. He would say: 'No Chairman. This is my job. You pay me for this responsibility and I shall carry it out.' He would visit the offending player in his room, reason with him gently and urge him to try harder in the future so that he could return to the team. Usually the unpleasantness was forgotten and the player's commitment to the team revived.

One of Bob Woolmer's regrets while coaching in Pakistan was that he was unable to watch first-class cricket in order to assess talent that could be groomed for the national team. This was due to the heavy schedule of our national team that required Bob's constant presence. Occasionally he snatched a day or an afternoon in Lahore or Rawalpindi to watch a first-class match, but a regular survey of first-class cricket was beyond reach.

Partly to make up for this inability, I tasked Bob after the Australian tour to proceed directly to Zimbabwe and Namibia, where our 'A' team was playing these countries. Our 'A' team included opening batsmen who had scored heavily in the domestic season. Given the failure of several opening batsmen at the national level, I hoped that Bob would be able to find a nugget or two on the Africa tour who could be tried at Test level. We also had a clutch of aspiring fast bowlers who could be considered as understudies to Shoaib, Sami and Shabbir. Returning from the Africa tour, Bob gave me a disheartening report of the two heavy-scoring openers. He said one was overweight and unfit; the other had a poor technique and was not a team player. Neither had scored heavily on the tour and both were therefore discarded. The 'A' team leg-spinners were impressive, but with Kaneria and Mushtaq around there was no vacancy. The fast bowlers were good without being outstanding, but most disappointingly the standard of fitness was extremely poor. Overall, the second line of hopefuls was not impressive, at least on the 'A' tour of Africa.

CHAPTER 5

URGENT ISSUES FACING THE PAKISTAN CRICKET BOARD

After the 2004 India tour and four months into the assignment, I had a fair idea of the main issues faced by the Board. I analysed the flaws and shortcomings of cricket in Pakistan to mirror those that have damaged Pakistan at the national level. They could be summarized as: A) lack of institution building; B) the government's inability to follow through with long-term improvement of structural issues; C) Reviving grass roots; D) corruption, graft and political pressures. These issues are discussed in this chapter under the four headings mentioned above.

A. LACK OF INSTITUTION BUILDING

In Pakistan, over the years, there has not only been a dearth of institution building, but also existing institutions have been gradually undermined by successive governments, both civilian and military. For instance, the civil services like the administrative, taxation and police have been damaged by the exercise of political pressure. The judiciary has been attacked physically and through political pressures exercised by the executive and a pliant parliament. The expenditure on the armed services and the ISI is accountable to no one. The Pakistan Cricket Board has suffered similarly by not having a permanent constitution and by a lack of accountability.

Drawing Up a New Constitution

The Pakistan Cricket Board had previously been governed by five constitutions that had all been annulled by various governments, often acting on whimsy. In the early days, PCB constitutions would hardly have qualified as comprehensive legal documents. For instance, the Fida Hussain constitution during President Ayub's tenure was a one-page note on cricket that was converted into a constitution. Later, Justice Cornelius provided a legal document that served as the PCB's first real constitution. Subsequent documents missed out on a number of issues, but the main reason for flouting the constitution was because successive chief executives wanted to place his or her own nominee in this high-profile post. Five previous constitutions were, therefore, torn up and thrown out of the window, following changes of government.

I was uncomfortable with my appointment as an ad hoc Chairman and wanted the PCB to be governed by a constitution that would give it an institutional frame. Before leaving the board, General Tauqir Zia had set in motion a process to revise the previous constitution that had been partially abrogated. I inherited this draft and on review felt that it needed to be expanded, as it repeated several gaps and anomalies that had led to previous constitutions becoming ineffective. Moreover, I felt that a new constitution should not be born from the PCB's womb but should be the product of independent, respected, legal and creative minds. After consulting our excellent legal adviser Asghar Haider, I decided on an independent constitution committee that would draft a new constitution. This panel was headed by Justice (retd) Karamat Bhandari, who had previously been involved in cricketing issues and was a highly respected retired judge of the Punjab High Court. Makhdoom Ali Khan, a distinguished lawyer from Karachi, and Senator Zahid Hamid, a Member of Parliament and also a lawyer, were nominated to the constitution committee.

The task for Justice Bhandari's committee was to draft a new constitution for the PCB and to convey it as early as possible to the Patron. The PCB gave Justice Bhandari copies of all previous constitutions, including the draft that General Tauqir Zia was examining when he resigned. We also collected constitutions of the cricket boards of other nine Test-playing countries and handed them over to Justice Bhandari. I sat with Justice Bhandari and discussed the discrepancies, omissions and contradictions that had led to previous constitutions becoming ineffective. The mandate was for the committee to complete its task in six months; that is, by the end of the year.

Justice Bhandari and his panel soon set about their task in earnest. However, shortly afterwards, Makhdoom Ali Khan was appointed Attorney General of Pakistan and a week or so later Senator Zahid Hamid was nominated Minister of State for Defence.[1] The elevation to these high government posts meant that two out of three members became extremely preoccupied with their official duties and difficult to consult, leading to a delay in deliberations. It was virtually impossible to find all three personalities free and in one place, with the result that the Chairman was reduced to sending written notes to his colleagues. For legitimate reasons, therefore, work on the new constitution slowed down, with Justice Bhandari given authority by his colleagues to consult various stakeholders on their behalf. Justice Bhandari drew up a questionnaire and circulated it to senior Test players, former administrators and to district association office-bearers for their comments. He then toured Karachi, Islamabad and Peshawar to consult with district associations. This process took much longer than had been anticipated, mainly because of the heavy preoccupation of the two panel members and because the Chairman was carrying the full burden of travel and consultations.

Meanwhile, there was impatience in the media and among some members of the Senate Sports Committee at the delay in announcing the new constitution. The clear implication of this criticism was that the Chairman of the PCB was deliberately delaying the process in order to maintain his autocratic hold on the PCB. The truth was that the delay was due to the elevation of two panel members to important government posts and that it was not the PCB but the constitution committee that was responsible for drafting the new constitution.

Eventually, in February 2005, Justice Bhandari informed me that he had almost completed his draft and wanted a final discussion with the PCB. I agreed and scheduled an ad hoc committee meeting at which the learned Justice presented his draft and explained the rationale for his recommendations. Ad hoc committee members stated their reservations, preferring an elected rather than a nominated Chairman, a corporate culture in the Board, and the need to keep the Executive Committee small and cohesive. In early March 2005, Justice Bhandari was ready to present his revised draft. It had taken three months longer than I had anticipated but the reason for the delay was understandable. Certainly there was no ulterior motive to prolong the ad hoc status of the PCB.

Meanwhile, Senator Enver Baig and some political opponents of the government on the Senate Committee for Sports were baying for my blood, as the promised draft had not been produced. I told the committee that the draft was ready, but it was my duty to present it first to the Patron and only then to any parliamentary committee. I was ready, however, to explain the main differences between the Bhandari draft and the previous constitution that had been partially abrogated. Senator Baig did not listen and walked out of the committee meeting to create a grand-standing furore. The media was only too glad to feed on the rumpus for several days.

Nevertheless, I formally presented the draft constitution to the presidency on 6 June 2005. I explained to General (retd) Hamid Javaid, the President's Chief of Staff, the reasons for the delay and suggested that the draft be vetted by the Law and Sports ministries and by anyone that the Patron wished to consult. I expected that the new constitution would be ready for promulgation a couple of months later. I left the Presidency relieved that, though delayed, the draft of the new constitution had been delivered to the Patron. There was no response from the Presidency for weeks. Then after several months had passed, I began to badger the Chief of Staff and others for the Patron's response. Nothing emerged. I even asked ad hoc committee member Dr Nasim Ashraf, who was close to the Presidency, to assist in eking out a reaction, but the draft constitution remained buried under the Presidency's files. Either more important issues were given precedence or the Patron did not want a change in the ad hoc basis of the PCB. Since then my successors, Dr Nasim Ashraf and Ijaz Butt, have pressed for a constitution but there is no permanent solution as yet.

The impression that I gained from this long delay in approving the draft constitution and subsequent shillyshallying by the succeeding governments is that the Chief Executive – for example, the Patron – does not want a democratic constitution that withdraws his patronage to nominate a Chairman of the PCB, nor to see his nominees' powers reduced by the new constitution's checks and balances. The Chief Executive therefore prefers to exercise political power through his nominated Chairman.

Recently the ICC has ordained that the constitution of national organizations must allow for election of their respective heads through a democratic process. This edict affects Pakistan, Sri Lanka and perhaps Zimbabwe. The reason for Pakistan having so far nominated its chairman by the President or its Chief Executive is not difficult to understand. As with most other institutions, Pakistan started from scratch and there was no proper structure to the PCB. With the passage of time, it was realized that cricket in Pakistan required an upright and motivated head of cricket and indeed of most other sports to be nominated, as sport had assumed a national dimension in building morale. It was therefore considered important that the President select a Chairman to oversee the activities of the Board. This was true of cricket as well as hockey and squash, and therefore found itself reflected in the

Board's numerous constitutions. Inevitably, this led to Presidents and Chief Executives nominating their political associates, especially when Nawaz Sharif, Benazir Bhutto and Asif Zardari headed political governments in Pakistan. During the long rule of military dictators, army generals tended to be nominated as Chairmen of the PCB.

Recently, with cricket assuming greater importance in building national morale, the need to have a reliable chairman of the cricket board became all the more important. It was felt that an elected chairman would be open to corrupt practices and such a process could lead to the election of an individual who was crooked, inexperienced and politically covetous. Elections could throw up an unscrupulous charlatan or gangster who would be attracted by power and the pot of gold that lay within the Board's compass. Sri Lanka has passed through such a phase, prompting the government to replace its Chairman with a government nominee. Ideally, the PCB Chairman should be elected by its general body but the democratic process has its obvious drawbacks. Clearly, the Pakistan Cricket Board needs to reach a compromise between the appointment of a purely elected Chairman and his approval, though not nomination, by the President or Chief Executive.

Ideally, the Chairman of the PCB should possess the following four qualities. Firstly, he should be a person of unimpeachable integrity. Secondly, he should have experience of managing a large organization like the PCB. Thirdly, he should have a deep understanding and knowledge of cricket, of its intricacies and tradition. Fourthly, he should be impervious to the inevitable political pressures on him from politicians, the media and the cricketing lobby.

Restructuring and Reorganizing the PCB

When I took charge, it was apparent that the PCB was poorly structured in its management and organization. Clearly, some officials were incompetent, while others were square pegs in round holes. There were some outstandingly able officials like Subhan Ahmed[2] (who would adorn any organization and who shouldered the main burden of the PCB's administrative activity). Most appointments seemed to have been made on a personal basis without having gone through 'due process' in their selection. There was no system of financial or administrative accountability in the Board. In order to set matters right, I asked Pakistan's premier university and business School, the Lahore University of Management Sciences (LUMS), to carry out a structural and organizational study of the PCB and to make its recommendations in three months. The Vice Chancellor himself was enthused at the task and a professional team of organizational and financial experts quickly engaged. They went about their task through interviews and data processing.

After three months, the LUMS experts had completed their survey and gave me their report, whose recommendations I summarize below.

The report found the PCB's financial wing to be exceptionally weak. They recommended the appointment of a qualified chartered accountant as its head and doing away with the post of Honorary Treasurer. Moreover, LUMS proposed the appointment of an internal auditor who would monitor all financial transactions and report independently to the Chairman. The LUMS report focused on the need for a separate HR department headed by a qualified senior manager. The absence of a security officer was also a source of concern for the LUMS experts, as there was no check on visitors roaming about the corridors. Valuable equipment and documents had been stolen from the premises. The issue of monitoring betting and match-fixing had also to be addressed. The LUMS report therefore proposed the appointment of a security officer.

The LUMS report drew up a new organogram for the PCB, which was not drastic but proposed a rational distribution of work and responsibilities. For example, the report recommended a separate marketing department in place of the current ad hoc appointments that had been made with the imminence of the India tour in mind. The report further recommended that a senior manager should separately head international and domestic cricket. Also, that grass-roots and womens' cricket should be overseen by separate district representatives in the regions in order to monitor and promote cricket activities at the grass-roots level.

The report recommended a revised constitution that should reflect modern realities. It underlined the need for a paid Chief Executive and a vibrant general body with local associations being given a pivotal role.

I accepted the LUMS report recommendations and placed it on the PCB website. Some of the recommendations were immediately implemented, while others that required selection though a transparent process were actioned over a period of time.

Basically, I wanted to change the culture in the PCB from being a dictatorial one-man show to an institution with a corporate structure. This meant that senior professional managers of each department would have responsibility to take decisions through a process of managerial devolution as, say, in PIA or a large conglomerate or a government ministry. Educated Test cricketers would head cricket-oriented departments like the selection committee, the National Coaching Academy and the umpiring and curators committees, while professionals and experts would head marketing, finance, audit, public relations and administrative divisions. The Chief Executive would ensure cohesion and direction, while the Chairman would play an overseeing role coordinating the various elements of the PCB.

One of the LUMS report recommendations that I was personally eager to pursue was the appointment of PCB representatives in the nine regions. Traditionally, the activities relating to cricket in the country had been centralized from Headquarters in Lahore and partly from Karachi. There was no PCB representation in the provinces and local cricket organized by the district and regional associations. These local associations were seldom efficient and were mostly ineffective and corrupt. Most of these local associations served as personal fiefdoms selecting favourite players, dispensing largesse or engaging in ego trips of cricketing warlords for political gain. Frankly, I found most such local associations rotten to the core, barely serving the needs of grass-roots development, the upkeep of grounds, coaching youngsters and so on. I found it odd, almost bizarre, that the PCB with its vast responsibilities for cricket and cricketers had no one at the ground level to oversee and monitor cricketing developments at the base.

The appointment of these Regional Development Officers (RDOs) was not welcomed by the local organizations. They felt it was an intrusion into their domain, but after explaining to them that the RDO was appointed to help and not to interfere in the district organization's activities and that it was to serve as a bridge between the local organizations and PCB Headquarters, they tended to relent. Of course, these appointments, involving the RDOs' salaries, allowances and minor perks, appeared to place an additional financial burden on the PCB, but in reality the LUMS report, after its streamlining of staff and personnel of inefficient dead wood, would result in net savings for the Board.

It was evident that in the 60 years of the Board's existence, no one had attempted to develop the PCB as an institution. There was no constitution, no system and no accountability. Instead, it was regarded as a convenient handmaiden of the political ruler of the time.

Ramiz Raja

When I took over as Chairman, Ramiz Raja was occupying the post of Chief Executive Officer (CEO). General Tauqir Zia had presided over his own team of senior officers on the Board, though a few of them had preceded his four-year tenure as Chairman. The press expected me to make wholesale changes to the Board, anticipating a clean sweep of the CEO and senior officers, which would provide it with fodder for juicy stories. I had no such thing in mind as I intended to take my time – several months – before assessing the calibre of each officer. Continuity and experience were also important factors in retaining the staff I had inherited. I had known Ramiz Raja earlier and had formed a healthy respect for his qualities and personality. Ramiz Raja had been under criticism from various lobbies, particularly Karachi. Some of the criticism referring to his holding two jobs – his TV broadcasting contract and being CEO of the PCB (albeit honorary) – appeared to be justified on the principle of conflict of interest. Though I had no intention of replacing Ramiz Raja, I was inundated with personal requests by former CEOs and assorted aspirants for the appointment of Chief Executive, some of them pleading with me through friends. When they realized that their requests were not being accepted, they turned their guns on me through personal attacks on television and in newspaper articles. The only immediate changes I made were to relieve the marketing manager of his post because his reputation and method of work did not suit my work discipline. The second change was that Wasim Bari was made Chairman of selectors in place of Aamer Sohail, mainly because there had been a plethora of changes in the captaincy and players during his tenure and I wanted to start with a clean slate.

I was in no hurry to replace Ramiz Raja who was an ideal Chief Executive. The Patron also held him in high regard. I spoke to Ramiz about the issue of principle and offered him a substantial salary as CEO if he were to withdraw from his television contract. Ramiz told me that his emoluments from his television contract were substantial and no salary, even if considerably elevated, could compensate for his earnings from television. Moreover, his television expertise was his chosen career, which he could not jeopardize for a salaried post that was temporary. He thanked me for my confidence in him and accepted that he could not on principle hold on to both assignments. I appreciated his honest reply. In due course, he would step down and continue with his television assignment. He added that he would look around for a suitable replacement. In Kolkata, for the Jubilee match, Ramiz and I agreed at breakfast that the change had soon to be effected. I had explained the issue to the Patron, who agreed with a heavy heart that on the principle of conflict of interest, Ramiz had to be replaced.

The Board needed an educated and balanced Test cricketer to be selected as CEO. My first choice was Majid Khan, but his son Bazid was on the fringe of the national team and I did not want Bazid to be accused of receiving favouritism if his father became CEO. I then proposed the name of Zafar Altaf who was a PhD, a senior government servant, and had been selected in the Pakistan team that toured India in 1962. The Patron, however, declined his nomination for some unexplained reason. The choice was extremely limited and eventually, after advice from cricketing friends, I selected former Test player Salim Altaf and had his nomination approved by the ad hoc committee. With hindsight I have to admit that Salim Altaf's selection was an error of judgement. I should not have insisted on Ramiz's resignation on grounds of principle and should have continued my search for a replacement. It did not surprise me that both my successors Dr Nasim Ashraf and later Ijaz Butt eventually decided to dispense with Salim Altaf's services.

At the time of Ramiz Raja's resignation as Chief Executive, it was necessary to reconstitute the ad hoc committee. I wanted a mix between senior Test players and executives who had a deep knowledge of cricket. From the Test stalwarts I selected Imtiaz Ahmed and Salim Altaf, the new Chief Executive. Among the executives, I requested Moin Afzal – an MCC member and financial expert – and Ali Raza, Chairman of the National Bank of Pakistan. As the ad hoc committee required the approval of the Patron, I was in regular consultation with the President's house regarding the proposed nominees. There was general approval on my selection of the ad hoc committee but the Presidency kept insisting on having Dr Nasim Ashraf appointed to the committee. I had never met Dr Nasim Ashraf but learnt that he had for many years been a doctor working in the USA. He had played serious cricket in Pakistan before emigrating to the USA and was now heading the newly formed Human Development Corporation aiming to raise funds from the USA for investment in Pakistan's development projects. Dr Nasim Ashraf had the status of Minister of State. I was initially reluctant to include Dr Nasim Ashraf in the committee because I did not relish the thought of a Minister of State being part of the PCB's set-up. However, when the Military Secretary to the President conveyed the President's express wish, I accepted his nomination.

Throughout our meetings, I found Dr Nasim Ashraf to be balanced, knowledgeable on cricket issues and generally supportive of the PCB's plans and objectives. An added advantage of his presence on the ad hoc committee was that he as Minister of State had regular interaction in Islamabad with the President and his coterie. At the back of my mind was the thought that the good doctor was familiarizing himself with cricketing issues and would, one day, wish to be Chairman.

The State of First-Class Cricket in Pakistan

There was a general consensus among players, administrators and commentators that Pakistan's first-class cricket programme was unsatisfactory. Too many matches were played with too many players participating, lowering the quality of cricket. No real challenges were posed to the cricketers in the extended first-class schedule and a hotchpotch of regional teams and departmental outfits was detrimental to the standard of cricket. We calculated that Pakistan had more cricketers participating in its first-class schedule than any other country in the world.

In the past, the departmental teams like PIA and the major banks had been instrumental in developing cricket in Pakistan as they had the financial resources to employ players, and to provide them with jobs and facilities like coaching, grounds and support staff. Over the years, many of these departments had scaled down their financial support to their sports activities. The result was that some departments had opted out of organized cricket altogether, while others reduced their commitment by not giving their players regular posts but employing them as seasonal mercenaries. Most of our Test cricketers came from the stables of these departments, playing also for regional teams for little money. Pakistan's first-class programme was therefore split between departments and regional teams – frequently changing its format from year to year because there was no constitution or institutional order in place.

Except for Pakistan, every cricketing country based its first-class programme on regional competition. Australia has six state teams, England 18 counties, the West Indies six islands; India has a mix of states and cities in their Ranji Trophy, while South Africa, New Zealand and Sri Lanka also have regional teams playing in their first-class competition. Only Pakistan has (well-endowed) departments and (poorly financed) regions.

When I took over as Chairman, I held several seminars and workshops across the country in which the organization of first-class cricket was the most important issue on the agenda. There was a clear divide between participants. At one extreme was Imran Khan's view that Pakistan's first-class programme should comprise only six or seven regional teams playing each other home and away. Imran felt that departmental teams were an anachronism and should be excluded from first-class cricket. He was adamantly against Karachi and Lahore fielding two teams each. Imran quoted Australia as his model, stating that Sheffield Shield interstate matches had the challenge, competitiveness and tension of a Test match. Interstate cricket ensured that only the best players were selected. These matches were a real test of mettle and cricketing ability and prepared players for cricket at the national level.

At the other extreme were Test players, administrators and commentators who insisted that departmental teams should continue to play first-class cricket and that Pakistan should have two first-class competitions – one for regional teams and the other for departments. These commentators insisted that most first-class cricketers were employed by affluent departments and Imran's suggestion of six or seven regional teams would affect the livelihood of first-class players, especially as the regions did not have the financial resources to support their players, coaches and back-up staff. Moreover, following the Australian model was not appropriate as Pakistan had a population of 180 million compared with 20 million in Australia. Restricting the competition to six regional teams would mean denying a large number of deserving players exposure to first-class cricket. Admittedly, most of these former Test players and administrators had been employed by the departments and were therefore loyal to them. There was clearly an element of nostalgia in the pro-department lobby.

Having heard the arguments on both sides, I handed over the problem to a special committee charged with making recommendations on first-class cricket, headed by CEO Ramiz Raja. My personal opinion was closest to the Imran Khan view that Pakistan's first-class cricket should be regional, with some reservations. I felt that the regional competition need not comprise six or seven but ten to 12 teams playing each other. I also felt that the departments should be gradually phased out as, even though they had made a huge contribution to Pakistan cricket in its early days, departmental commitment to cricket was diminishing. As the Chairman of Pakistan's leading bank stated at one of our seminars, the large conglomerates were focusing increasingly on their basic mandates, banks on financial issues, PIA on running an airline efficiently, Customs on their specific mandate. Sponsoring sports teams and cultural troupes was being phased out and given low priority. The departments had played their role for the promotion of cricket in the early days after independence. It was now time to move on. These were pragmatic but ominous words against departmental cricket. The basic question was how would the regions take over the financing of first-class cricket, especially providing a livelihood for first-class players? Clearly, the financial issue had to be addressed before plunging headlong into making drastic changes in Pakistan's first-class structure.

The season before I took over, the PCB had created nine regions that would play first-class cricket competing for the Quaid-e-Azam Trophy. These nine regions comprised:

- Karachi
- Hyderabad
- Multan
- Lahore
- Faisalabad
- Sialkot
- Rawalpindi
- Peshawar
- Baluchistan

Karachi and Lahore fielded two teams each. This division of regional cricket in the country was based on the following rationale:

Firstly, unlike most other countries where regions, counties, states and provinces were evenly balanced, Pakistan's administrative division was highly disproportionate. The largest province, Punjab, represented over 60 per cent of Pakistan's population and was by far the most advanced in promoting cricket. In Sindh, only Karachi had real nurseries for cricket, while the rest of Sindh, though enthusiastic, was a long way behind in facilities and talent. The Frontier (now Khyber Pakhtunkhwa) had only recently emerged as a cricket nursery, its earlier sporting talent having been drawn to hockey, squash and football. Baluchistan, with a population of 4 million, had no tradition for cricket, but as Pakistan's largest landmass needed to be included as a region. Thus the dispensation of nine regions – five from Punjab, two from Sindh and one each from the Frontier and Baluchistan – that I inherited appeared to be based on rational grounds.

The second reason for the regional devolution was that over the past three decades talent was emerging from smaller towns all over the country. In the first three decades of Pakistan cricket, nearly all the Test players came from Karachi or Lahore.

Currently, the Pakistan team comprises players from smaller towns like Multan, Mardan, Sialkot, Mianwali, Peshawar, Faisalabad and Jhelum. It was imperative therefore that the opportunity to play first-class cricket should be available to budding players across the country and should not be restricted to the mega-cities. Thus the nine cricketing regions allowed for their talented cricketers to demonstrate their prowess through regional teams competing in the Quaid-e-Azam trophy. Nine regions and 11 teams was more than Imran's limit but covered the entire country in a more rational dispensation.

Before the 2005 season I decided on a fine-tuning amendment to the Quaid-e-Azam trophy. We decided to divide the regional participants into two groups – the Gold and Silver groups – based on the previous year's results. Both divisions would retain first-class status. Competition would be for prize money and prestige. Two teams from the Gold group would be relegated to the Silver group and two from the Silver group promoted to the Gold. There would be no relegation for the two bottom teams in the Silver group. In this way we would ensure that competitive interest would be retained throughout the season as the Gold team leaders would vie for the enhanced prize money, while the teams at the lower end would fight to remain in the Gold league and avoid relegation to the Silver group. According to the principle enunciated earlier, there would be no relegation from the Silver league. This format was based on the successful system in the English county championship that led to sustaining competitive interest throughout the season. Otherwise, a large single league led to early laggards losing interest and approaching matches without incentive and as routine.

Another fine-tuning exercise that the PCB introduced to the Quaid-e-Azam Trophy was to increase the cricketing regions from nine to 11. It was evident that one region for the entire Frontier province (Peshawar) was no longer enough. The Frontier's

Figure 8   The Peshawar regional women's team that participated in the first national women's championship in 2005. Fourth from left (seated) is Imtiaz Ahmed, cricketing icon, who was appointed adviser on women's cricket. Peshawar is one of the most conservative regions in Pakistan.

performance at all levels had recently been outstanding. Peshawar won the Quaid-e-Azam Trophy in 2005. They provided several players to the national, 'A' and under-19 teams, and at the schools level they reached the finals of the schools championship. There was tremendous enthusiasm for the game in NWFP and many of their top players had migrated to other regions to find a permanent spot. For instance, Younus Khan and Shahid Afridi have played for Karachi-based teams. The Pathans, with their robust physique and superb hand-to-eye coordination, have recently taken to cricket and performed superbly. The result is that, apart from Younus Khan and Shahid Afridi, the national team have recently included Yasir Hameed, Umar Gul, Arshad Khan, Fazle Akbar, Wajahatullah Wasti and Riaz Afridi. Several others are knocking at the door. Even at the women's level, players are emerging from the Frontier, and a strapping, athletic young woman, Asmavia Iqbal of Abbotabad, opens the bowling for the national women's team.

105

The second change related to the demand by so far unrepresented regions of Pakistan, Azad Kashmir and the northern areas, to be included. Both these areas had a different constitutional status from the remaining provinces of Pakistan and though their cricketing infrastructure was sparse and underdeveloped, there was, as in the case of Baluchistan, great enthusiasm among the people of the region to join the mainstream of cricket in Pakistan. In any case, following the PCB's principle of including the whole of Pakistan in its cricketing regions, it was evident that Azad Kashmir and the northern areas, despite their limited resources, needed to be included in Pakistan's cricketing set-up. In fact, there had been much progress and development of cricket in Azad Kashmir thanks to the enthusiasm of a committed administrator, Shahid Rafi, who built two beautiful stadiums in Mirpur and Muzaffarabad, the capital. Unfortunately, the terrible earthquake in October 2005 damaged the Muzaffarabad stadium at a time when it was nearing completion. It also damaged the five-star hotel that overlooked the stadium. On completion of both projects, Muzaffarabad would have the credentials to host international matches. Mirpur stadium was not affected by the earthquake but no five-star hotel is nearby, although several three-star hotels have been built, and during my visit to Azad Kashmir, I urged Mirpur hotel owners to raise their hotels' status by constructing facilities such as gyms and swimming pools that visiting cricketing teams always look for.

Another reason why I was personally in favour of Azad Kashmir being included as one of the regions is that I wanted to attract the large number of British Kashmiris who are now emerging in fair numbers into the first-class scene in English county cricket. Amongst these players are Adil Rashid (Yorkshire and England), Bilal Shafayat (Nottingham and England 'A'), Sajid Mahmood (Lancashire and England) and several Azad Kashmiris who play for Midland counties. From my diplomatic experience in the UK, I know that over 60 per cent of the Pakistani population there is from Azad Kashmir. They are enthusiastic cricketers and a large number of these school and club cricketers are pushing their counties for a first-class place. These British Azad Kashmiris could play for their 'home' side in Azad Kashmir after summer in England and add immense value and quality to Pakistan cricket. I notice that the first step in this direction has been taken by Bilal Shafayat playing for one of the Pakistani teams in the Quaid-e-Azam Trophy.

Central Contracts

The signing of central contracts with players had become increasingly prevalent in the cricketing world. England and Australia already had their players signed up on central contracts, and other countries, notably India, were in the process of following suit. Before I took over as Chairman, the PCB had decided to engage its players on central contracts and the Pakistan team to New Zealand (2003) had carried unsigned central contracts with them in their pockets. Hitherto players had been paid match fees for Tests and ODIs based on seniority. On return from New Zealand, Inzamam told me that the players had not signed the contracts because they felt that financial and other conditions needed to be reviewed, especially as the players were liable to have their freedom of signing commercial deals circumscribed by the contracts.

I had several meetings with Inzamam and senior players before a fresh central contract scheme was finalized. Inzamam and his colleagues initially insisted on equating their contracts with the vast sums being paid to Indian players. However, I explained to them that Pakistan was in no position to match Indian rates because of the BCCI's huge financial reserves and commercial clout. I also stated that the contracts would be flexible in permitting players to sign commercial deals provided they did not offend the PCB's own contractual commitments with commercial concerns. For instance, a player could sign a contract with a watch or soap company but not with a drinks company or a bank, because PCB had signed long-term contracts with Pepsi Cola and ABN AMRO Bank.

By June 2004, an agreed formula had been negotiated and central contracts signed. I was impressed by Inzamam's mature approach to the grading of players in various categories (A, B and C). He felt that seniority should be given due weight and that performance should not be the sole criterion in grading players as, over time, there was an ebb and flow in every player's performance. He reasoned that the overall points system should not lead to resentment, with young players leapfrogging over established members of the team. He stated that in Pakistan's culture, seniority was important, while in other cultures like England and Australia players would accept performance as a major criterion.

B. THE GOVERNMENT'S INABILITY TO FOLLOW THROUGH WITH LONG-TERM IMPROVEMENT OF STRUCTURAL ISSUES

Grounds and Stadia

The PCB faced a monumental problem of not having sufficient grounds and stadia at all levels of cricket, ranging from the international to the grass roots. My predecessor had made a huge effort to construct grounds and stadia to provide facilities for first-class cricket, especially in the deprived towns of interior Sindh and Baluchistan. There was an urgent need to continue this process.

Starting at the top, Pakistan had ICC-approved Test-playing centres at Karachi, Lahore, Rawalpindi, Faisalabad and Peshawar. To these centres, General Tauqir Zia's administration had added a magnificent stadium in Multan and a brand new stadium in Quetta. Of these seven Test-playing venues, only three – Karachi, Lahore and Quetta – were owned and controlled by the PCB. The remaining four were owned by local government organizations, which presented serious problems of maintenance for the PCB. Local administrations gained financial returns from these stadia by receiving rent from the shops around the perimeter. They were also inclined to lease out these grounds for non-cricketing functions such as political rallies, fairs, large wedding receptions and so on that damaged the playing area. Maintenance of these four stadiums was invariably unsatisfactory and frequently, as international series approached, the PCB had to step in to ensure that the ICC's standards for international matches were met.

Apart from these seven Test and ODI centres, Pakistan had in the past hosted international matches at Hyderabad, Sheikhupura, Gujranwala, Sialkot, Sukkur and Bahawalpur. These grounds could no longer be used for international matches because ICC regulations now require a four- or five-star hotel to accommodate visiting teams, umpires, referees and other international officials. There was a great deal of chagrin in these former centres at the PCB not scheduling international matches at these venues, but our hands were tied by the ICC's strict conditionalities.

In the three stadiums at Karachi, Lahore and Quetta, the PCB employs maintenance staff to keep the ground and stadiums in tip-top order. In the four remaining international centres, maintenance of grounds as well as player facilities in the dressing room area was an uphill task. Maintenance at these four stadiums is at best sporadic, often leading to mini-crises before a Test or ODI. I took up the slack vigorously after becoming Chairman and lobbied with the Patron and with provincial Chief Ministers for the cricketing control of the four centres. Everyone agreed, but there was no movement on the ground. So after sensing local reluctance to hand over revenue-bearing assets, I modified the income-sharing formula so that local bodies would retain ownership of all revenue from the commercial facilities while the PCB would be given cricket control of the ground and facilities. This would mean no political rallies or agricultural 'melas' (fairs) on the ground, but rent from shops and such would continue to be collected by the local administration.

I explained to government authorities that the PCB planned heavy investment in these stadiums by upgrading dressing rooms, spectator facilities and hospitality boxes, and constructing regional academies with gyms and practice grounds, electronic scoreboards and floodlighting that would enhance their international status, but I would not undertake the investment unless cricket control of the ground was passed to the PCB. All my efforts, like my predecessor's, were in vain. Dr Nasim Ashraf, who succeeded me, also returned to the charge but without result. This apathy and indifference by government has been a huge negative factor in developing our Test centres in the four venues, made all the more critical as Pakistan was scheduled to host the Asia Cup in 2008, the Champions Trophy in the same year and the World Cup in 2011. So acute is the problem of maintenance that after the last ODI at Peshawar, the ICC formally conveyed to the PCB that the ground conditions and facilities in Peshawar were below acceptable standards and that the ICC would no longer accept Peshawar as an international venue unless corrective measures were taken. Nothing has happened and I noticed that recently a mass funeral was held at the ground, which ended in mayhem! Alas, today, Peshawar is the centre of terrorist activity in the region and it may have to say goodbye to international cricket for quite some time.

Coming down a rung, to the state of first-class venues, each region had one or two major cities that hosted Pakistan's extensive first-class schedule. Lahore and Karachi had several such grounds while other cities had at least one ground for first-class cricket, maintained by the local associations, which were often cash-strapped. General Tauqir Zia had built new stadiums in the interior of Sindh, at Mirpurkhas, Sukkur, Thatta and Khairpur. In the Frontier Province, Kohat had a brand new stadium, as did Abbotabad, while in Baluchistan as well as the main Bugti Stadium, new grounds were constructed near Quetta. The problem with these new stadiums was their maintenance, as the local associations had neither the finance nor the staff to maintain the grounds. The PCB had, therefore, to pay for maintenance staff for the upkeep of these grounds and prevent their decline. To raise finances, the local associations were obliged to rent out these grounds for non-cricketing functions, which led to their deterioration.

I was also determined to extend first-class cricket into the smaller towns to provide spectators with the opportunity to watch first-class matches and to help the less fashionable district associations with extra financing. Thus Bahawalpur and Okara were given first-class fixtures in the Multan region, Kohat and Abbottabad in the Peshawar region, Sargodha in the Faisalabad region, Gujranwala in the Sialkot region and Thatta, Sukkur and Mirpurkhas in the Hyderabad region.

At the grass-roots level the dearth of grounds was apparent everywhere. Cricket matches were played in *maidaans* (open spaces) with teams overlapping into each other's territory. Schools and clubs were facing a squeeze in this regard and thus the huge enthusiasm for cricket had no outlet. In my travels into the interior, I had seen many sports fields lying derelict and fallow. These unused grounds belonged to government organizations like the railways or local sports departments that could not afford their upkeep due to lack of interest or financing.

In an effort to utilize these fallow grounds, I proposed to the Patron that a commission for the procurement of playing fields should be appointed with the Pakistan Olympic Association, the Sports Ministry, the PCB and local government bodies playing a lead role. The PCB would lend its full support in eking out these grounds for club, junior and women's cricket and other sports. As always, despite initial enthusiasm, no action was taken on the proposal.

Could the government have done more for Pakistan cricket? The answer to this question is most emphatically in the affirmative. Given that cricket enjoys a special place in building up national morale the government needs to sustain a serious and focussed support to the build-up of cricket in Pakistan through its main institution – the PCB. This has not been forthcoming. For instance, only three Test grounds are under PCB's control. The remaining Test venues remain under the control of local government bodies. Even with exiting Test stadia there are legal and territorial issues that could easily be sorted out by government backing. Government has failed to persuade wealthy semi-government bodies like the PIA to provide low-cost sponsorship for cash-starved regional cricket. Also, at the grass-roots level there has been no government initiative to convert fallow grounds and open spaces into playing fields for cricket and all other sports.

Sponsorship of Domestic Cricket

The first step towards financing domestic cricket came from ABN/AMRO's[3] generous offer of sponsoring first-class cricket in Pakistan. ABN/AMRO is a progressive bank which at the time was working under two dynamic cricket-loving executives – Naved Khan and Salman Butt (not the cricketer) – who put together a package that injected Rs. 92 million into first-class cricket in Pakistan. This was a huge boost for Pakistan's domestic cricket and was the first time that any organization had exclusively sponsored Pakistan's domestic first-class cricket.

Boosted by ABN/AMRO's support, the PCB was able to pay players salaries when they played for regional teams. We hired coaches, improved first-class cricket pitches and provided decent accommodation for players, umpires and support staff that attended first-class cricket in the country. I recall former Test players like Imtiaz Ahmed and Zulfiqar Ahmed recounting how they were obliged to take long overnight train journeys in cramped railway bogeys, stay in sleazy rat-infested hotels and appear the following morning to represent their teams in a first-class fixture. Though conditions had slightly improved from those days, regional cricket was played on a shoestring budget. ABN/AMRO's sponsorship saw players paid Rs. 30,000 salary per month, provided with air travel and lodging in decent hotels. Travel and daily allowances were reasonable and the feeling among players that only the departments paid salaries and that there was no financial incentive to play for the regions was gradually being eroded. Most first-class players were now able to receive financial reward by playing for both departmental and regional teams.

Television coverage of domestic cricket would help attract companies from the private sector to sponsor regional teams.

My fervent hope was that the departmental teams participating in the first-class Patron's Trophy would agree to sponsor one of the regional teams and merge their considerable facilities (grounds, coaches, senior and junior players and academies) into the regional set-up. Through these mergers the departments would be able to continue participating in first-class cricket and our domestic cricketers would have the benefit of regular employment and significant funding. Exposure to television would provide an additional boost to the first-class programme. In conceiving this scheme, I was mindful of the need for the new draft constitution to reflect the vital importance of the regions in our domestic set-up as also for the regional sponsors to be enabled to play their role in financing domestic cricket.

I presented this plan to the Patron, who graciously agreed to prod the semi-government organizations such as Sui Gas, PIA and others to sponsor regional teams. Private companies like Adamjee, the Eastern Federal Union and Deewan Motors had already indicated to me that they would sponsor a regional cricket team. Instructions were given to the Chief-of-Staff but there was no indication of implementation. A few months later, I again made the request, but despite promises there was no action.

Security

From the late 1990s the issue of security has cast a deep shadow across Pakistan's political spectrum. This issue directly affected Pakistan's cricket with increasing instances of violence, suicide bombings and religious intolerance. In order to induce foreign teams to play in Pakistan, trouble spots like Quetta, Peshawar and Karachi had to be avoided. Gradually, even the 'settled' cities like

Lahore were engulfed in the spectre of insecurity, particularly after the impact of 9/11.

The security issue increasingly impacted Pakistan cricket. Several governments declined to send their sports teams to Pakistan. We were deprived of hosting the Champions Trophy and 2011 World Cup matches. Pakistan could not play home series and was obliged to play host in third countries like UAE, Malaysia, Sri Lanka and England. The Pakistan public at home saw no international matches, leading to financial loss and diminishing public interest. Improving the security climate was out of the PCB's control and the only option left was to manage the problem as best as possible. Most ICC countries were sympathetic towards Pakistan's dilemma and the ICC has formed a task force, headed by Giles Clarke, head of the ECB, to examine how best to assist Pakistan in breaking out of this isolation.

I believe the security problem will remain on the horizon for a long time ahead – perhaps decades – so that Pakistan needs to adopt remedial measures to overcome the cricketing and financial loss due to the prevailing political insecurity in the region. One step would be to construct five-star hotels on or adjacent to the Test stadiums in the country. As a diplomat I had noted that many countries that hosted international conferences, like Zimbabwe, Kuwait or Saudi Arabia, built five-star hotels adjacent to their international conference centres. This meant that a security cordon could be thrown around the hotels and conference centres where the VIPs would be staying and meeting. The delegates could then even walk across from hotel to conference centre reassured of security across the whole area. Potential security problems are aggravated when delegates or players are required to travel by car or coach to their hotels, even if they are just a short ride away.

On a medium- and long-term basis the government and the PCB need to construct such facilities for visiting teams. Usually there is ample space in Test venues to accommodate a five-star hotel, to obviate any need for unsafe travel between hotel and Test ground, as was the case with the Sri Lankan team in Lahore in 2009.

C. REVIVING GRASS ROOTS

Long before I had assumed charge as Chairman it was apparent to any discerning observer of cricket that the grass roots of Pakistan cricket had declined sharply over the past two decades. University cricket was no longer a force, club cricket – the real nursery for budding cricketers – was decaying and school cricket was being undermined by government's educational policies and lack of facilities. The drying up of these vital nurseries was an issue that deserved immediate attention and reversal.

University Cricket

The universities of Pakistan had provided Pakistan with its initial core strength that led to its early recognition as a Test-playing country. Abdul Hafeez Kardar was a product of Government College, Lahore, from where he graduated to Oxford and Warwickshire.

Javed Burki and Imran Khan followed his lead. Majid Khan captained Cambridge and like his father, Jahangir Khan, was held in the highest esteem at Fenner's. Government and Islamia Colleges of Lahore produced most of the famous cricketers that made up the early Pakistan team, with stalwarts like Fazal Mahmud, Imtiaz Ahmed, Shujauddin Butt and Maqsood Ahmed all part of the 1954 Test team that achieved its famous victory at the Oval. In the early years of Pakistan cricket, Government College and Islamia College engaged in titanic annual battles that attracted around 10,000 spectators per day. Karachi University was not far behind and the annual fixture between Lahore and Karachi Universities was given first-class status, like Oxford and Cambridge. These were the early nurseries for Pakistan cricket. The large-scale interest and crowds ensured that there was pressure to perform and the result was a stream of players whose temperament for a larger stage was already put to the test. University cricket thus provided a vibrant base of educated and talented cricketers that formed the nucleus of the earlier Pakistan teams.

University cricket then began to taper off. Until Misbah-ul-Haq was appointed Test captain in October 2010, Imran Khan (1982–7, 1988–92) and Ramiz Raja (1995–6, 1996–7) were the last of the university graduates to captain Pakistan.

When I took over, there was an urgent need to revive this vital artery of Pakistan cricket, especially as the infusion of educated cricketers would add an important dimension to social and behavioural patterns in our team. I therefore decided to write to 52 Vice-Chancellors proposing a cricketing renaissance in their respective university. The response was lukewarm even though I proposed a revival of a Combined University team in the first-class structure.

Schools Cricket

Schools cricket was also in the doldrums despite the huge enthusiasm for the game at junior level. This was due as much to the lack of structure and organization as government's educational policies that gave priority to pure education rather than sporting and cultural activity that is such a vital part of educating children.

An example of this policy was evident when I paid an unannounced visit to a government boys' school in Islamabad, where my sons had received their early education in the 1960s and 1970s. My boys had played cricket at school and I had frequently played club cricket at their well-maintained school ground. Thirty years later, in January 2004, I visited the school again, and was warmly received by the headmaster, who took me around the school. I noticed that one of the school grounds had disappeared under a new classroom block, while the only available sports ground was in poor shape as it was used for football and hockey as well as cricket. There was no structured cricket practice and the headmaster informed me that since the school ran two schedules, the first from 8 am to 2 pm and the second from 2 pm to 8 pm, there was no time for the schoolboys to play sports. Compulsory sports periods have been scrapped. In my tours of the districts the same problem of lack of facilities meant that most schools denied their students basic cricket-playing facilities. Only the well-established private schools and cadet colleges had proper facilities with grounds, elementary coaching, equipment and practice facilities, and even here, the sports fields are being replaced by classroom blocks.

The prospect of breathing life into schools cricket was not as daunting as with the universities. With the help of stalwarts from Peshawar, Karachi and Lahore who had dedicated their lives to promoting junior cricket, such as Javed Zaman, PCB's honorary advisor on schools cricket, a national schools competition was conceived for which I lassoed a sponsor. After contests at the local level, regional schools winners would play each other, with the two top schools reaching the final. In 2005, over 450 schools participated in the schools championship and the final was played between a Karachi school located in its Pathan sector and an Urdu-medium school in Lahore. The final was a splendid occasion where the PCB invited the parents of the players. Governor Khalid Maqbool gave away the prizes, which included a well-equipped kit bag for each team. The following year was an even greater success as over 700 schools participated, with a Peshawar school taking the trophy against a school from Layyah, a non-cricketing district from central Punjab. In this way, the PCB attempted to revive school cricket. I had hoped that the finals would be shown on television but that event would have to await the launch of a national television sports channel.

In Sri Lanka, schools cricket draws huge crowds. Rashid Latif, Pakistan's former captain, told me that on one of Pakistan's tours to Sri Lanka, Pakistan was playing a tense Test match at Colombo. The match had drawn good crowds on all four days, but on the final day, when the match was evenly balanced, there were hardly any spectators. Rashid Latif enquired about the reason for the low turnout and was informed that the spectators had gone to witness a local school derby that would normally attract crowds of around 10,000. There is no similar tradition in Pakistan, but I wanted to encourage government and private schools to engage in competition with a certain pride attached to winning the national school's title. A fixture between Aitcheson College Lahore and Karachi Grammar School should reflect a traditional rivalry like the annual Eton versus Harrow match in England that is played at Lords.

To engender this enthusiasm and spirit among the juniors, it is vital that government organizations at the local level should coordinate schemes with the PCB to promote schools cricket. The PCB cannot achieve this task on its own. Government and semi-government (Railways, Customs, PIA etc.) have large budgets to dispense on local sports. They have control of local grounds and can afford to provide equipment and maintenance to these grounds. I noted that local government sports bodies and the PCB acted on parallel lines with hardly any coordination between them. I sensed that government officials jealously guarded their parishes and were loath to admit the PCB into their domain. I mentioned the need for effective coordination to promote cricket at the local level to prominent figures on the political scene, who readily agreed to my ideas but implementation was not followed up.

Club Cricket

Traditionally, club cricket has been the nursery and conveyer belt for our national team. Given the decline of university cricket, the role of club cricket has become even more important. Talented young players from schools and from the 'maidaan' are usually snapped up by local clubs and provided opportunities to perform. Regrettably, club cricket was also in decline during the past decade. The reason for this decline was not so much structural or organizational as financial because the cost of maintaining grounds, pitches and players by the clubs had become prohibitive over the years. Most clubs were financed by local enthusiasts, but the high costs of supporting club activities led to a steady evaporation of financial support.

The revival of club cricket was, therefore, a serious challenge for the Board. One solution was to provide the districts and regions with greater financing so that the financial back-up of club cricket would be revived. The downside of this process was that district association office-bearers would aim to retain control by registering bogus or fake clubs that would then vote for them at the time of elections. Financing was liable to be diverted to funding-favoured or bogus clubs rather than the promotion of healthy club cricket. Extra financing of district associations was therefore fraught with problems.

Clubs often formed into cartels, monopolizing selection to district and junior levels. These favoured clubs prevented the smaller clubs from putting forward their players for district selection. This monopolistic process is described in a later chapter dealing with corruption in Pakistan cricket.

With the worldwide decline in university and schools cricket, whether in England, Australia or Pakistan, club cricket becomes the most important grass-roots nursery. Most university students, while attracted to the idea of representing Pakistan, realize that their chances of making it to the highest level is minuscule. In that event choosing a 'traditional' profession – doctor, engineer, accountant, lawyer – is by far the safer option. First-class cricketers do not earn enough for university graduates to consider cricket as a career option. Moreover, the few recent graduates who have attempted to follow the cricketing path have found that navigating the maze of nepotism and corruption that has bedevilled the game is extremely difficult. This is described in greater detail in Chapters 8 and 9. Club cricket requires funding and a viable structure.

Women's Cricket

In discussing grass-roots cricket, it is necessary to refer to women's cricket. Over the decades, the main activity in women's cricket had been spearheaded by two Karachi sisters, who were keen cricketers and who organized women's cricket mainly in the Karachi region. These sisters came from an industrial family background and were able to sponsor women's cricket through family financing. They had net practice facilities on their premises and were able to provide board and lodging when needed to outstation women cricketers. The sisters played women's cricket in England and were able to network with English officials and organizers.

In due course these Karachi-based sisters sponsored a women's organization that claimed national representation. Some up-country women cricketers – mainly from the Punjab – were included in the 'national' team, but their main activity remained rooted in Karachi. Through their links with the International Women's Cricket Association [IWCA], which was an independent organization, the sisters had their organization recognized by the IWCA as Pakistan's national representatives and began participating in international fixtures. At the time, as in most cricketing countries, national women's associations were not affiliated to men's cricket nor was the IWCA affiliated to the ICC.

Sometime in the 1990s, a women's group from the Punjab also began to claim national representation, contesting the Karachi-based group's credentials. This group was based in Lahore and at one stage arrived at an international tournament in Kolkata with a document from the Sports Ministry supporting their credentials. The IWCA, which had earlier recognized the Karachi-based representation, was placed in a dilemma but decided not to accept the Lahore group's claims. All this time, the PCB had kept its distance from the wrangling between the Karachi and Lahore women's groups.

The battle between these two groups subsequently intensified, each claiming national representation, and was eventually taken to the High Court of Punjab. The Court sought a report from a committee of experts appointed by the PCB. In due course the committee gave its report to the High Court in which it stated that neither Karachi nor Lahore groups could justifiably claim national representation. The report criticized the organizational capabilities of the two groups, finding that no real structural or organizational women's cricket had been put in place.

Meanwhile, movement at the international level had taken place. The ICC decided to place the IWCA under its aegis and recommended that all national cricket boards should similarly bring their national women's organizations under their respective Boards' umbrellas.

When I took over the chairmanship of the PCB, I was intent on promoting women's cricket. Given the twin support of the High Court that urged the PCB to take over and organize women's cricket and the ICC decision for national Boards to assimilate national women's organizations, I began a search for a dedicated and high-profile woman who would head Pakistan's women's cricket. Clearly neither the Lahore nor the Karachi associations could fulfil this role, and we needed to make a fresh start.

The serious promotion of women's cricket by the PCB raised some fears in my mind related to women taking centre stage in a popular sport in a Muslim country. The religious right-wing elements were campaigning to keep women behind veils and hijabs and regarded women participating in sports as anti-Islamic. The Indian mullahs had already objected to Sania Mirza wearing shorts while playing tennis. In contrast, I was intent on promoting women's cricket because I wanted women to play their full part in a liberal, democratic and moderate Pakistan. I therefore anticipated a clash between the more extremist mullahs and the PCB. None came. I did receive one letter from the representative of the Lahore Jamaat-e-Islami, in chaste Urdu, who politely stated that while his party recognized women's cricket as beneficial for the players' health, he hoped that their dress would reflect Islamic traditions and that they would not be allowed to play in front of men! I replied welcoming the writer's appreciation for better health in women cricketers and confirming that women cricketers were appropriately dressed. I referred to one of the national players, our wicketkeeper-batsman from Toba Tek Singh, who played in a hijab. I made no comment on men watching women's matches. I received no further complaints over women's cricket.

In promoting women's cricket, the example set by the late Benazir Bhutto was immensely beneficial. She represented the modern Pakistani woman in the best possible light and her party, that formed the majority in Parliament, would not suffer any slights against women taking centrestage in Pakistan.

After a long search, I appointed Mira Phailbus, who had dedicated her life to women's education, having been a highly successful principal of Lahore's Kinnaird College for over 25 years. She had been recognized for her dedication by being awarded the Sitara-e-Pakistan. Mira Phailbus was not herself a cricketer but a well-known administrator of educational institutions. Phailbus launched herself enthusiastically into organizing women's cricket in Pakistan. She was aided by the excellent player and administrator Shamsa Hashmi, who was probably the best woman cricketer in Pakistan even though she was over 35. An all-rounder, her performance on the field for the Lahore region was outstanding. Shamsa was also a qualified umpire and coach. She was doing her PhD in Sports psychology from Punjab University and became a dedicated administrator supporting Mira Phailbus. All nine regions were activated and a programme to promote women's cricket at government school- and college-level taken in hand. I nominated Test icon Imtiaz Ahmed to assist women's cricket and he formed an excellent team with Mira Phailbus and Shamsa Hashmi to place women's cricket formally on the map in Pakistan.

In 2004, the Pakistan Women's Cricket Association (PWCA) held its first national championship, which has since been organized efficiently every year. Karachi were first-time winners and Lahore had their revenge the following year. Predictably, the Karachi and

Lahore groups that had previously claimed representation refused to cooperate, with Karachi refusing to allow our best batsman and international record-holder Kiran Baloch from participating at the national level. There was such an enthusiastic response from women cricketers all over Pakistan that the PWCA went ahead with organizing the first women's national team. It was a pleasure to note that though the bulk of the national team came from the two large metropolises of Karachi and Lahore, several players from districts such as Abbotabad, Toba Tek Singh, Multan and Hyderabad were selected for the national team. Thus Pakistan, with zero experience, began playing international women's matches. An Asia women's cup was organized in which India with 17 years' experience and Sri Lanka with eight years' experience participated in Karachi. Predictably, Pakistan was defeated in all its matches, easily by India but narrowly by Sri Lanka. India won the first Asia Cup by defeating Sri Lanka. Later, Pakistan went to South Africa and though it defeated a provincial team in a side match, it lost to the South African national team.

The crucial test for the women's team came in the World Cup eliminator against Hong Kong, which included players from New Zealand and other cricketing countries with experience of provincial cricket. Pakistan won all its matches against Hong Kong and qualified to play the eight members' eliminating round in October 2007. Amazingly, the Pakistan women's team came second to South Africa and have qualified for the Women's World Cup, defeating long-established teams like Scotland, Ireland and Holland in the qualifying round. The credit for this stage in women's cricket goes to the players and to the coaches and trainers acting under the dynamic leadership of Mira Phailbus, Shamsa Hashmi and Imtiaz Ahmed. I am sure that the enthusiasm that has been generated will be continued under the enthusiastic leadership of Bushra Aitzaz, who deserves full support from the government and PCB.

D. CORRUPTION, GRAFT AND POLITICAL PRESSURES

The Selection Process

On assuming the Chairmanship, I appointed former Pakistan wicketkeeper and captain Wasim Bari as Chief Selector, to be assisted by former Test cricketers Iqbal Qasim (the former left-arm spinner who was highly respected as an administrator) and three other Test players – Azmat Rana, Ehteshamuddin and Abdul Raquib. There was also a junior selectors' panel headed by Iqbal Qasim, who provided a link between senior and junior selectors. I made it clear to the selectors that I would not influence or interfere in their selection process and that I expected them to resist the pressures of politicians, media and cricketing icons in arriving at fair assessments based entirely on merit. I asked them especially to pay heed to domestic performance and to prepare a back-up squad for our national team. In every country, there have been differences and tensions between selectors, captain and coach. My instructions to the selectors were that they needed to formally sit down with the captain and coach and receive their input. The final decision was for the selectors to take. When on tour, once the squad was finalized, it was for the tour selection committee – normally captain, coach and vice-captain – to decide who made the final 11.

My problem with the selection process was not at the national level (i.e. national squads, 'A' teams and junior squads), but with the need for emerging talent at the district and domestic first-class level to be recognized on merit and given due weight. As the PCB was investing so heavily in regional domestic cricket, how was it possible to ensure that talent from local clubs or schools was represented on merit in the district teams? Who monitored the performances of the district championships? Or did the selectors rely exclusively on scoresheets? How could the PCB ensure that political pressures would not affect selection because local selectors were heavily influenced by coteries of cricketing and political pressure groups?

In order to prevent local bias and corruption asserting itself, Ramiz Raja had devised a system in which all regional first-class teams were selected by the PCB's national selectors. Thus, for each region, about 200 players from the districts were called up for two days of trials in the nets under the supervision of two national selectors who were parachuted into each regional centre. There was vehement criticism from the district associations to this over-centralized selection process. They asked how two national selectors who had no familiarity with local cricket and who did not even recognize the players could select a team on the evidence of two-day nets attended by 200 or more players. They claimed that it was for local selectors to decide on team selection.

I felt there was merit in this argument, especially as I was in favour of decentralization in every domain. Therefore, I struck a balance by asking each region to nominate upright and fair-minded selectors for approval by the PCB. Once approved, they and not the national selectors would propose their regional squads that would be finally approved by the PCB. In order to check local bias and malpractice, I appointed regional development officers (RDOs) to each region, as recommended in the LUMS reorganization report, to supervise all forms of cricket. An important element of their mandate was to ensure that local cricketing bodies acted fairly in their selection process.

At the national level, most of the teams normally selected themselves. One or two marginal places were subject to criticism. For example, should Kaneria be selected for the one-day squad when Afridi would competently assume the role of a leg spinner? Which of the six openers that Pakistan had regularly alternated should be selected for a series? Bari was generally conservative in his policy as was the captain, so that selections were relatively smooth, with few surprises or out-of-the-box selections. Occasionally there were differences between chief selector and captain, as when Bari wanted to play young Kamran Akmal and Inzamam insisted on retaining an out-of-form Moin Khan. Bari sought my help and I discussed the issue with Inzamam. He agreed that Moin's form had been poor, but as captain he wanted a senior, experienced player near him in the middle for consultation. He said the senior players – Yousuf, Razzaq and Shoaib – generally fielded on the boundary and he could not interact with them easily. Moin was always at hand and Inzamam found his mature counsel to be invaluable. I accepted Inzamam's reasoning on cricketing grounds rather than personal grounds but felt it was more important to give Kamran a chance. Against the general impression that Inzamam always had his way, Kamran was selected and soon established himself in the team.

Illegal Actions

Even before I had taken over as Chairman, I was struck by the number of our top bowlers being questioned for illegal actions. Shabbir Ahmed, Shoaib Akhtar and Shoaib Malik were the more prominent examples, but some of our bowlers, both fast and slow, who represented the 'A' and under-19 teams were reported by international umpires and referees for doubtful actions. When I assumed the Chairmanship, I was appalled at the number of 'chuckers' that were playing first-class, club and schools cricket. Chucking seemed to have reached epidemic proportions in Pakistan and no one seemed to take on the responsibility of corrective action, certainly not the umpires who obviously looked the other way and left it to others to take remedial measures.

Soon after I took over, our under-17 team won an international tournament in Dhaka. Pakistan's hero was our off-spinning all-rounder who almost single-handedly won us the final. He was feted and garlanded in his small hometown and was regarded as a certain national player of the future. The only problem was that his action had been reported and when I asked Bob Woolmer to have a look at the young prospect, Bob told me: 'Chairman, he is full of talent but unfortunately he is a chucker.' The PCB tried its best to correct his action. He was sent to Australia but to no avail. The poor boy has since faded from the cricketing scene. Another example was when I went to watch a local schools match. Khizer Hayat, our head of umpiring, accompanied me in a well-organized match with professional umpires, scorers, screens and so on. Then a bowler was introduced who, even from the boundary, seemed to be a huge chucker. After a few balls, I asked Khizer Hayat if he felt there was some doubt about the bowler's action. Khizer agreed that the bowler was patently chucking. 'Then why are the umpires not intervening?' I asked. Khizer had no reply but he ran out to the middle to have a word with the umpires, and soon the fielding captain was obliged to take the offending bowler off.

In first-class and club matches there was usually at least one bowler per team who had a doubtful action. My last example is of my visit to Faisalabad, where while visiting a prominent club at practice, I was informed by enthusiastic officials that they were coaching an 11-year-old bowler who could 'turn the ball a mile'. The boy was duly brought to the nets and bowled his sharply turning off-spinners, except that he 'bowled' them with a pronounced throwing action. I turned to the eager officials and told them that although they had discovered a gem, the boy's action was completely illegal. It was unfair on their part not to correct the boy's action while he was still young and impressionable. None of the experienced club officials seemed to have a clue about illegal actions, seemingly believing that anything goes!

Disturbed at this trend, I addressed a gathering of accredited umpires and told them emphatically that stopping and reversing this scourge was their top priority. They did not have to be confrontational by openly no-balling a chucker, but all doubtful actions had to be reported to the match referee, the managers and of course the PCB. I followed up by writing to all the district associations, to the umpires and officials, raising the issue prominently at my press briefings. I was particularly insistent that junior cricketers with a problem should have their actions corrected early, with the offending bowler being confidentially reported to his school coach or sports master.

In the 2006 season, 29 first-class bowlers were reported for doubtful actions. This is a huge number, indicating that an average of two bowlers per first-class team have potentially illegal actions. Corrective measures have been taken, and with the realization that the PCB will not allow bowlers with doubtful action to operate, improvement is likely to take place over time. But years of neglect have led to this scourge contaminating Pakistan cricket.

In my view the large number of 'chuckers' in Pakistan cricket is due to lack of coaching facilities at the junior level. In most countries a boy would have his doubtful action corrected by a school coach or sports master. Unfortunately, most of our cricketers are not coached and learn their cricket in the *maidaan* or street. Here they often play with taped tennis balls on which purchase for spin or speed can better be obtained by a throwing action. These bowlers then graduate to higher levels of cricket, often unchallenged by umpires, and become set in their actions. Of course, Pakistan is not the only country that has 'chucking' problems. Who can forget Meckiff, Rorke and Slater of Australia, Griffin of South Africa, and Griffith and Clark of the West Indies? At least, today, through modern technology, doubtful actions can be checked by high-speed photographs, and the ICC has prescribed regulations limiting the flexion at a bowler's elbow to 15 degrees.

CHAPTER 6

CLIMBING UP THE INTERNATIONAL LADDER UNDER WOOLMER

Before embarking on highly challenging tours of India and Australia during the winter of 2004–5, Pakistan played a one-day triangular series against Zimbabwe and Sri Lanka in which the teams played two matches each followed by a final. Sri Lanka arrived earlier to play two Tests. This series was followed by a one-off Jubilee Match between India and Pakistan at Kolkata to celebrate the BCCI's 75th Anniversary.

Pakistan's relations with Sri Lanka and Zimbabwe had been excellent at both political and cricketing levels. Pakistan had supported the Sri Lankan government throughout its civil war and the two countries had cooperated closely on the diplomatic front at conferences such as SAARC. On the cricketing front, Sri Lanka (then Ceylon) had been the first country to engage with Pakistan in 1949 when Pakistan toured and later it received Sri Lanka for bilateral cricket series. At ICC and ACC meetings I made it a point to support Sri Lanka on several awkward issues.

Pakistan–Zimbabwe relations at the political level were also cordial. Soon after achieving independence, Zimbabwe's air force was trained by a Pakistani air force contingent, which had led to an especially warm bilateral relationship. Pakistan had exchanged cricketing visits with Zimbabwe at both national and 'A' team levels. The icing on the cricketing cake was Zimbabwe's hosting, during a Commonwealth Summit, of a festival cricket match between Commonwealth leaders and an international team in which Prime Minister Nawaz Sharif hit five sixes in his two-over innings. Prime Ministers John Major and Bob Hawke were paired for their two-over stint during which the Australian Prime Minister constantly stole the strike, leaving John Major with only three balls to face much to his chagrin. Clive Lloyd and Graeme Hick also took part in the festival match. That day, Nawaz Sharif was the toast of the Commonwealth Prime Ministers. Sri Lanka and Zimbabwe agreed without hesitation to tour Pakistan at a time when most other teams declined to do so for security reasons. Pakistan was therefore grateful to these countries for engaging in a trilateral series.

In the ODI triangular league, we swept all before us, comfortably winning all four matches. The team stumbled again in the final, in which Sri Lanka defeated Pakistan easily to win the trophy.

PLATINUM JUBILEE, KOLKATA

We now left for Kolkata to play the high-profile Jubilee match against India, celebrating 75 years of BCCI stewardship of Indian cricket. Despite the festive background, there was a high comptetitive interest in the game as with all Pakistan–India matches, especially as Pakistan had defeated India in three consecutive matches played since Bob Woolmer took over as coach.

A vast, 90,000-strong crowd was present at Eden Gardens when Shoaib Akhtar opened the bowling to Sehwag and Tendulkar, who had been Pakistan's nemeses over the years. Sehwag, Laxman and Ganguly played steady knocks and Yuvraj seemed to take the game away from Pakistan with a quick-fire 78, leading to a respectable total of 292.

Pakistan was soon in trouble with Younus Khan, being tried as an opener, falling early, but Salman Butt and Shoaib Malik steadied the innings. Inzamam then joined Salman Butt and played an imperious, commanding innings of 75, adding 98 with Salman Butt (108 not out) to guide Pakistan home to a magnificent victory in the 49th over. Salman Butt had played the innings of his life in winning the platinum Jubilee Match for Pakistan. It was a huge boost to the team as they achieved their fourth consecutive victory under Woolmer against arch-rivals India. Bob Woolmer returned highly encouraged by the spirit and unity in the team, with Inzamam acting as a rock of Pakistan's batting, and allaying doubts about his leadership qualities.

AUSTRALIA, DECEMBER 2004–JANUARY 2005

Pakistan was thus primed for the daunting tours of Australia and India away from home in the coming months. Pakistan's political relationship with Australia had been friendly. There was much appreciation in the Pakistani public of Australia's stupendous sporting achievements. Its hockey team was top of the ladder, Geoff Hunt had been a superb squash player and Australia's swimmers, tennis players and golfers had set the world alight. Australia's cricketing icons like Don Bradman, Keith Miller, the Chappell and Waugh brothers, Dennis Lillee and Shane Warne were household names and were held in awe by Pakistanis. Cricketing relations between the two countries had seen a little bit of angst mainly because of much-publicized incidents like the Miandad–Lillee ruckus and, of course, Shane Warne and Mark Waugh's accusation of match-fixing against Salim Malik. The impression that Australian umpires had denied Pakistan victory in crucial Tests, at a time when Pakistan fielded a particularly strong team with Imran Khan, Waqar Younis and Wasim Akram at the height of their powers, had dismayed Pakistanis. Especially galling for the Pakistani public was Australia's constant refusal to tour Pakistan, which led to one of its tours being scheduled offshore. Australia regarded Pakistan as dangerous but unpredictable opponents capable of producing flashes of match-winning performances.

For the tour of Australia, Pakistan selected Salman Butt and Imran Farhat as their preferred openers. Two young fast bowlers, Mohammad Khalil and Mohammad Asif, who had performed well in the domestic season, were also included. Bob Woolmer insisted that Pakistan should proceed ten days ahead of schedule to Western Australia, where the First Test was to be played at Perth, and which was famous for its fast, bouncy wickets that were in sharp contrast to the low and slow tracks of Pakistan.

Woolmer's apprehensions about adjusting to the fast Australian wickets were justified as Pakistan performed poorly against state and scratch sides in the practice matches. Inzamam was not fully fit, with back trouble, and a succession of low scores by our leading batsmen appeared to lower confidence and morale.

So far Woolmer's stewardship had been a success. Though Pakistan had not won a trophy, four successive wins against India and robust performances against Australia had seen Pakistan improve its discipline and performance. The Test series against Australia was, however, disastrous. Pakistan was whitewashed comprehensively, like a head teacher putting an upstart schoolboy in his place. The Triangular series, shared with the West Indies, was not much better, Pakistan losing all but one of its matches against Australia and scraping through to the finals because the West Indies were worse. We lost these matches, albeit narrowly, to return home with our tails between our legs.

Pakistan's abject performance in the Test series led to criticism of Pakistan's leadership. Inzamam especially came under fire for not being able to lead from the front and for his fitness. Woolmer's coaching techniques were also questioned by his various critics. Shoaib Akhtar had performed poorly after Perth, where he did not bowl in Australia's second innings. He was also criticized for breaking curfews and leading a high life while the team plunged into the doldrums. I met the Patron after the tour and he expressed his displeasure at the team's discipline, and insisted that a more authoritarian disciplinarian replace the manager, Haroon Rashid.

Though we were soundly defeated in Australia in both Tests and ODIs, I could not help feeling that decisions by Australian umpires standing in ODIs had often gone against Pakistan. I am the first to recognize that accepting human error is part and parcel of cricket and that the bad decisions usually even out in the longer term. Moreover, as the losing side, it would not be appropriate for the PCB to return to the charge of appointing neutral umpires in all international matches, including ODIs. Bob Woolmer returned from Australia seething with indignation at the umpiring. Typical of Woolmer's meticulous preparation, he told me that he had collected a video database of 29 marginal decisions during Pakistan's tour of Australia, of which 25 had gone in favour of Australia and only four in favour of Pakistan. Bob showed me the video in Lahore, which confirmed my own impression. Consequently, in a telephone conversation with ICC Chief Executive Malcolm Speed, I raised my concerns regarding Australian umpires, relating it to my proposal for neutral umpires. I was also aware of the impression by other visiting teams to Australia that Australian umpires, though highly qualified, tended to lean towards the home team at critical points in the game. Malcolm Speed appeared to scoff at my complaint but agreed to have a look at Bob Woolmer's video. Surprisingly, several weeks later, an ICC official admitted to me that the Woolmer video confirmed that 25 of the marginal decisions had gone against Pakistan. He immediately qualified his remark by adding that the umpiring decisions were not regarded as biased! Why these marginal decisions (and other similar ones) went against Pakistan is examined in subsequent chapters.

PAKISTAN'S TOUR OF INDIA, MARCH/APRIL 2005

After the disappointing tour of Australia, Pakistan had to face the formidable challenge of a return visit to India. There was enormous media hype on both sides, and the cricket-mad public looked for a repeat of the exciting series and the public goodwill that had been witnessed during India's visit to Pakistan the year before. I had, with Inzamam's consent and after consulting my colleagues in the ad hoc committee, decided that Younus Khan should replace Yousuf Youhana as vice-captain purely on cricketing and leadership grounds, with an eye to a smooth transition to captaincy when the 35-year-old Inzamam decided to call it a day. I called in Yousuf Youhana and explained to him that Pakistan needed him to focus exclusively on his batting away from the burden of office. Yousuf took the decision manfully and calmly, indicating his full commitment to the team's success.

Before the tour began a few problems of a political and diplomatic nature had arisen in scheduling the Tests and ODIs. The BCCI had proposed Ahmedabad for a Test, which I thought was asking for gratuitous trouble, as Ahmedabad had earlier been the centre of Hindu–Muslim riots that had drawn the attention of the world to the abuse of human rights. The Chief Minister of the region during the riots, Narendra Modi, was still in office and it was common knowledge that tension between the communities existed beneath the surface and a spark at the stadium could ignite an ugly bonfire. After all, it was the stadium at Ahmedabad where Imran's team had taken the field wearing helmets. At an ICC meeting, I spoke to Jagmohan Dalmiya – suggesting an alternative venue to Ahmedabad. I reminded Dalmiya that in 1999 he had himself moved Pakistan's First Test from Mumbai to Chennai after threats from the Shiv Sena. Dalmiya prevaricated, stating that rescheduling Ahmedabad was a political decision that only the government could take. He understood my reasoning but in order to help him obtain government concurrence, he asked me to write to him stating my reasons. On reaching Lahore, I responded to Dalmiya's suggestion and wrote to him requesting an alternative to Ahmedabad. Regrettably, the Indian government chose to publicly refer to my letter as an unwarranted interference in India's internal affairs when Dalmiya himself had asked me to write the letter! Some of the Indian media called it a tit-for-tat Pakistan response to India's objections to playing in Karachi. The reality was that I wanted to avoid a venue that could spark a religious incident. President Musharraf backed my reservation to Ahmedabad and the issue began to create gratuitous tension. However, with the help of my Cambridge friend, Foreign Minister Natwar Singh, and political troubleshooter Rajiv Shukla, the matter was resolved diplomatically with Pakistan agreeing to play an ODI in Ahmedabad.

Another problem related to the Pakistan team playing its first warm-up game at Dharamsala, located in the beautiful mountain state of Himachal Pradesh. Dharamsala has been the home of the Dalai Lama since his dramatic escape from Lhasa and I felt that the team's visit to Dharamsala could cause unnecessary embarrassment to Pakistan–China relations. These apprehensions were confirmed when the Indian press put out the news that the Dalai Lama wanted to visit the ground to 'bless' the two teams. I immediately telephoned Dalmiya to point out the adverse political implications for Pakistan of the Dalai Lama's presence and told him that I wanted to avoid political incidents, and unless the BCCI took appropriate steps, I would order my team not to meet the Dalai Lama. I realized immediately that the BCCI had not anticipated the political repercussions of the Dalai Lama's presence at the ground. Within a short while, Dalmiya telephoned me to confirm that the Dalai Lama had decided not to attend the match.

I began to appreciate that the somewhat bizarre scheduling of the Pakistan team's tour of India was due to the need for Dalmiya – the long-standing king of Indian cricket – to bolster his support in the BCCI at the September election for the BCCI leadership. A strong anti-Dalmiya cabal had begun campaigning against him, accusing him of maladministration and corruption. This group had promoted the powerful Maharashtra strongman, Sharad Pawar, as their candidate. Viewed in geographic terms it was Kolkata's supremacy being challenged by Mumbai. Dalmiya had therefore to keep provincial heads pacified by allotting them lucrative matches against Pakistan in their domains.

Once again high-level diplomacy was required to resolve these sensitive political issues. Left to bureaucrats in the respective boards and foreign offices, a solution may not have been forthcoming. On both sides there were experienced hands that had good personal relations with each other that helped overcome the difficulties.

The team selected for India by Wasim Bari and his co-selectors omitted Shoaib Akhtar ostensibly for fitness reasons, but his indiscipline and regular tantrums had led Bob Woolmer and Inzamam to conclude that his presence was detrimental to unity and spirit in the team. He had hardly been a match-winner over the past few years and tended, after his first furious spell, to lose speed and accuracy in the longer game with frequent niggles and breakdowns. Of the other pacers, Khalil was retained but Asif dropped from the squad that had been gone to Australia. Rana Naveed had progressed well and the tall Rao Iftikhar was included for his accuracy and reliability. A slightly controversial inclusion was the 36-year-old off-spinner Arshad Khan, who had never let the side down with his tight off-breaks that he bowled from a high action. He was needed to keep an end closed when dealing with rampaging Indian batsmen like Tendulkar, Sehwag, Yuvraj and Dravid.

As regards the new manager, I had tapped a few retired Test and first-class cricketers who could manage the diplomatic as well as the cricket side of the tour, but had not found a suitable person. I had in mind some senior cricketing civil servants, but the Presidency was not in favour of detailing civil or military officials for such assignments. Finally, the ad hoc committee decided at one of its meetings to request one of its own members – Director of Cricket Operations Salim Altaf – to take on the assignment. Salim Altaf was a Test cricketer, a former senior official of PIA and had recently been appointed Director of Cricket Operations in place of Ramiz Raja. The experiment did not turn out to be a success.

On this tour, the three Test matches were played before the

ODIs. The First Test at the beautiful ground in Mohali took the predictable course of Pakistan's brittle batting collapsing on the first day and India building up a huge lead of over 200 runs during the next two days. Against all expectations, Pakistan mounted a remarkable match-saving rearguard action in which Razzaq and Kamran Akmal ensured a draw through a valiant seventh-wicket partnership. This showed a new fighting spirit in the team. In the next Test at Kolkata, India scored 407 in their first innings, but Pakistan came back strongly with Yousuf and Younus scoring not-out centuries with expectations of a first innings lead. On the third day, however, Pakistan lost their remaining eight wickets for 110 runs, a disastrous single day which led to an unexpected defeat. There was no rearguard action as at Mohali. The third and final Test was a triumph for Pakistan. Inzamam and Younus scored heavily, taking a significant lead in the first innings and, after a carefully judged declaration, bowled out India to square the series.

By sharing the Test series, Pakistan had shown their competitive spirit and a high level of performance in batting, bowling and fielding. Except for a poor third day at Kolkata that lost them the match, Pakistan had silenced its critics by determined cricket, with several young players rising to the challenge.

The six-match ODI series was a triumph for Pakistan. After losing the first two matches at Kochi and Visakhapatnam, Pakistan were emphatic victors in Jamshedpur, Ahmedabad, Kanpur and New Delhi. There were some stirring performances, especially Afridi's rapid century at Kanpur and Rana Naveed's 6–28 at Jamshedpur. Pakistan's supremacy in the ODIs seemed to demoralize India and by the time the sixth and last ODI was played in New Delhi in front of President Musharraf and Prime Minister Manmohan Singh, the result was regarded as a foregone conclusion. It was, and Pakistan won the match by 159 runs, sending Musharraf and the 5,000 Pakistan fans home elated and triumphant.

The New Delhi match had seen another example of cricket diplomacy. Informal discussion and leaders getting to know and assess each other's personalities is an important part of diplomatic negotiations. Being on an upward curve in cricket rivalry, as Pakistan was in New Delhi, does provide a favourable backdrop to these negotiations. Musharraf and Manmohan Singh seemed to have begun their relationship on a cordial note and Musharraf used his stay in New Delhi to call on Sonia Gandhi, and to hold a magnificent reception for India's elite in a happy mood of cricketing supremacy.

The hall at the hotel for Musharraf's reception was filled to capacity as the President was delayed at his informal discussions with Kashmiri leaders, who had flown to New Delhi from Srinagar to meet him. At the reception everyone from Pakistan was bushy-tailed and in good spirits after our historic ODI series win in India. As my wife, Minnoo, and I entered the hall that was teeming with guests, we noticed three venerable religious leaders seated on the sidelines. The first was Imam Bukhari of the Jama Masjid whom I had met, the second was a senior Buddhist monk dressed in traditional saffron robes and the third obviously a Christian dignitary who wore a white robe and large conical hat normally worn by the Christian Orthodox Church archbishops. Their presence at the reception was a reflection of India's secular, multi-religious background. As we passed the splendidly dignified triumvirate, I asked my wife if Yousuf Youhana should be presented to the Christian Archbishop. She thought it was a great idea and a search was made for Yousuf Youhana. Yousuf could not be found. We then increased the tempo of the search with green-blazered players, officials, Pakistani diplomats and waiters tasked to find Yousuf. Eventually, a bewildered Yousuf was traced and brought huffing and panting to the Chairman. Minnoo excitedly informed Yousuf of the presence of the Christian Archbishop and told Yousuf to go and pay homage to him, and not to forget to refer to the dignitary as 'Your Grace' or 'Your Eminence'. Manifestly elated at this opportunity, Yousuf was led to the presence of the religious dignitary. After a few minutes, he came back to us looking rather

138

crestfallen and remarked: 'Sir, woh to Musalmaan nikla. Woh Bohri Jamaat ka Maulvi tha jo ke lambi safaid topi pehentey hain' ['Sir he turned out to be a Muslim from the Bohri sect. They wear those high white conical hats']. Minnoo and I nearly collapsed with laughter at our faux pas. Even Yousuf saw the funny side of it.

After the setback against Australia, Pakistan had regained morale following the success of the Indian tour. Even better results were to follow in the series against the West Indies in the Caribbean and against England at home.

Pakistan returned home to a warm reception and all-round plaudits for squaring the Test series and winning the ODI series. Special mention was made of Pakistan's fighting spirit and its team unity, for which credit was rightly given to Bob Woolmer and Inzamam. The successful tour of India was completed, without the services of Shoaib Akhtar, with harmony and unity prevailing in the dressing room. There was not a single incident on or off the field, and the large crowds watched the games in a sporting spirit. The absence of a large contingent of Pakistan fans was noticeable as compared to the invasion of 20,000 Indian fans to Pakistan in 2004 that created such an atmosphere of public goodwill. This was due to most of the matches being played in the distant south, in destinations like Visakhapatnam, Kochi, Jamshedpur and Bangalore. Only in Mohali and New Delhi could Pakistani supporters gather in numbers. Nevertheless, the tour was an emphatic cricketing and public relations success. Woolmer had presided over nine victories as against two losses to India in the last 11 ODIs and had passed the ultimate test for the Pakistani public.

By the time these tours were completed, Bob Woolmer had been in the saddle for over a year. Since taking over as national coach there had been some negatives like the heavy defeat in Australia, the inability to groom an opening pair and the patchy, substandard fielding. The positives included the inculcation of a fighting spirit as was apparent in Mohali, Bangalore, Colombo and later in Kingston, the continuity and stability in the team that saw unity and spirit develop under Inzamam's leadership, the curtailing of extras (38 in the Karachi ODI against India in 2004!) and the emergence of four genuine all-rounders who could make the difference in ODI contests. As Pakistan climbed up the ICC rankings, Woolmer was satisfied with the progress, though he realized that the upward graph needed to be maintained by addressing our weaknesses.

Bob, who had become a friend as well as a colleague, would drop by at my house to have long discussions on the direction for the national team. It was clear that there was hardly any cultural or language gap between him and the players. He had quickly picked up the character traits of every individual player and had honed his coaching skills to help each player. Woolmer's manifest dedication to the team's welfare, his simple unostentatious living in the National Academy and the care he took to address faults individually, always supported by his computer, made him a respected coach, popular with the team, especially its middle and junior members.

Bob, who was a stickler for fitness, used to complain that senior players like Inzamam, Yousuf, Afridi and Razzaq – though not Younus – were laggards when it came to fitness and fielding. It was common for senior players not to field in first-class games but for substitutes to field in their place. Shoaib Akhtar was a rebel and a maverick for whom Bob had less and less respect. Bob felt that Shoaib's presence in the dressing room was detrimental to team spirit. He pointed to the fact that Shoaib had hardly been a match-winner in recent series and that we had performed splendidly in India, Sri Lanka and the West Indies without the services of the Rawalpindi Express.

On the issue of technique, particularly for opening batsmen, Bob felt that Pakistan had not done enough to prepare bouncy sporting pitches, with the result that our batsmen were brought up on slow, low-bounce wickets with scarcely any lateral movement. As a result, batsmen would tend to play across the line and fail to negotiate bowling with bounce, swing and movement that they encountered abroad. Bob told me that he had played all over the world for England and Packer, and considered Adelaide the finest pitch that he had encountered in terms of bounce and a fair return for bowlers, both fast and slow, and batsmen. Then, to my surprise, he added that the practice pitches at the National Academy were as good as Adelaide. Why could not our curators be asked to prepare similar wickets for first-class venues in Pakistan? This remark led me to invite New Zealand experts to advise on pitch preparation in Pakistan and for the institution of a curator/groundsman technical wing in our National Academy. We began new courses for curators and groundsmen, handing them diploma certificates, as in coaching courses. With commitment and expertise a beginning could be made in venues like Lahore, Faisalabad and Multan to provide us with better pitches. Admittedly, it was a long haul given the lack of experienced curators and groundsmen, but a start had to be made.

Woolmer complained of slow movers and unathletic fielders in the Pakistan team. Inzamam and Yousuf were supreme batsmen whose status in the team could not be disturbed. Of those on the fringe, Bob was reluctant to include fielding laggards like the plucky Asim Kamal. He preferred the likes of Younus Khan, Shoaib Malik and Mohammad Sami, and among the fringe players, Salman Butt, Mohammad Hafeez and Faisal Iqbal. Younus Khan, through his sharp fielding, dedication and galvanizing ebullience, was a special favourite and though Bob favoured Inzamam's continuation as captain, he felt that Younus Khan would be an excellent successor when Inzamam decided to call it a day.

Another source of concern that Bob discussed with me over our long sessions was the inability of the players to implement in the middle the coaching lessons that Bob imparted to each individual player. They were attentive in listening to Woolmer's advice but, in practice, repeated the errors that they had been warned against. For example, Imran Farhat had been caught at third man in an ODI series flashing at a rising ball outside the off-stump. Bob took Imran Farhat aside and worked on him to eliminate this fault, as opposition sides would invariably set a trap for him. Lo and behold! in the next match, in the very first over, Farhat played the same shot with the same result! The same was true of Imran Nazir, who kept attacking from the word go and getting out cheaply, but he too failed to heed Woolmer's advice.

I told Woolmer that I had experienced the same syndrome when I was manager during the World Cup of 2003, when Richard Pybus had made detailed plans for each match only to find that, in the middle, the plans went unheeded. I told Bob that the inability to absorb coaching advice was due to the lack of education, which led to advice not being thoroughly assimilated and implemented. This also explained the loss of focus when our players faced crisis situations, when they either froze or became frenetic in achieving manageable targets. I told Bob that he needed to keep hammering away for the penny to drop. Moreover, the prevalent coaching culture drawn from a wider environment is strongly hierarchical in terms of age and authority. Elders and coaches are to be listened to without question. This means that any constructive discussion is unlikely to occur, with most players nodding in agreement with whatever the coach suggests.

In August 2005, the President held a briefing session in which the PCB was required to make a presentation on the team's preparation for the World Cup in 2007. I took Bob Woolmer and Inzamam to the presentation that was attended from the President's side by a bevy of former Test players and experts.

In our briefing to the Patron, Bob Woolmer and I pointed to the strengths and weaknesses in our build-up. The team's recent performances had shown an upward graph, leading to a steady climb on the ICC ladder. It had also shown unity, a fighting spirit and cricketing discipline. We had won nine out of 11 matches against arch-rivals India and I mentioned Woolmer's contribution to our success, as also the advantages of stability and continuity in the team's leadership. We now had an established and strong middle-order comprising Younus, Inzamam and Yousuf. Our challenges lay in finding an opening pair, and improving fielding and cricketing discipline. There was also the question of mental strength at critical times, which had led to the team 'freezing' in crucial situations in the past.

The President chaired an extensive two-hour discussion and I could see that he was especially impressed by Bob Woolmer's briefing on the task ahead. It was evident that, though a sportsman, President Musharraf did not grasp the finer points of cricket. Often his cricketing generals like Munir Hafiz and Tauqir Zia had to intervene to save him embarrassment. He gave his blessings to us and urged us to iron out the flaws, and maintain fitness and discipline, in focusing on winning the World Cup.

THE ARMED SERVICES' ROLE IN CRICKET

Considering the fact that cricket had such a central role in national affairs, the armed services played an unexpectedly peripheral role in cricket issues. For instance, the army had played a major role in hockey, winning several national championships and producing stalwarts like Brigadier Hamidi and Brigadier Manzur Atif. The army was also the main promoter of athletics in the country, with stars like the sprinter Abdul Khaliq, the hurdler Ghulam Raziq, the hammer thrower Mohammad Iqbal and recently, the Asian sprint queen Naseem Hameed spearheading the army's role in the sport. The Pakistan Air Force became the promoter of Pakistan squash and reaped the indirect reward of 50 years of international supremacy. Even after cricket had achieved special importance in the hearts of the Pakistani public, the armed services did not appear to be keen on promoting cricket and played first-class cricket only intermittently, when the combined services team participated in one of Pakistan's first-class championships. They were soon knocked out and were content to play cricket at a lower, secondary level. Cricket was not their game, perhaps because it took too much time and was too complex and esoteric.

The armed services did, however, enter the cricket arena as

managers. At least four army generals and air marshals were nominated as Chairmen of the PCB during the long years of military rule. Among the generals, only General Tauqir Zia was a cricketer and understood the lifeblood of the game. The others were successful administrators and organizers who were given the tasks of bringing order and efficiency to the cricket field. These appointees learnt their trade on the job but were never part of a cricketing ethos. The rationale for their appointment was that Pakistan's martial law leaders recognized the importance of cricket in the political and morale-building image of the country, and felt comfortable nominating one of their senior colleagues to oversee cricketing affairs rather than leave them to civilians who were regarded as incompetent and corrupt. Thus the armed services' dalliance into cricket remained limited to the appointment of mainly non-cricketing generals, who hardly understood the complexity of the game. Typical of this attitude was the appointment of the polo-player Brigadier Gussy Hyder that I have described in an earlier chapter.

General Musharraf was no different to his military predecessors Ayub, Yahya and Zia-ul-Haq. He immediately appointed his military colleague, General Tauqir Zia, as Chairman of the PCB. His choice, however, was a good one because Tauqir Zia was a genuine cricketer with cricket flowing in his veins. His only problem was that as a serving general he could not devote enough time to running the PCB. It was only after four years, when the aura of military rule began to pale and Musharraf was heavily criticized for planting military nominees to nearly every civilian ministry, that he accepted Tauqir Zia's resignation and looked around for a civilian nominee. Several acquaintances have since claimed the 'credit' for having me named Chairman, but I believe it was due mainly to the advice of my predecessor who I had come to know playing club cricket in Islamabad and as manager of the national team.

The only occasion that Pakistan's powerful intelligence agency, the Inter-Services Intelligence or ISI, intruded on the cricket scene was during the Pakistan tour of England in 2006. The ECB had invited Nawaz Sharif, who at the time was living in exile in London, to its VIP Box at Lords. I had played no part whatsoever in prompting the invitation but, to my surprise, I received a telephone call from the ISI representative in the Pakistan High Commission in London enquiring how Nawaz Sharif had received the invitation, which he could exploit in his favour with the Pakistani media. The ISI Brigadier assumed that I, or even my wife, had helped in Nawaz Sharif's invitation to the box. He went so far as to suggest that I should use my good relationship with the ECB to cancel its invitation. I brusquely informed the ISI Brigadier that I had no hand in the invitation and had no contact with Nawaz Sharif, my former boss. I told him that Nawaz Sharif was well known in English cricketing circles as a keen cricketer and that his invitation to the box had been made independently by the ECB. I told the Brigadier that it was ridiculous to expect the ECB to withdraw or cancel its invitation to a former Prime Minister. This intrusion was more in the context of political intrigue than a cricketing issue.

All in all, the military limited its role in Pakistan cricket to managerial oversight. It did not attempt to mould cricket's vital role in national life to its advantage.

MY PERSONAL ACQUAINTANCE WITH MUSHARRAF

Over the years, I had developed a distant but affable relationship with President Musharraf, mainly because of his father, who had been a colleague in the Foreign Office. Brigadier Musharraf led an army team to Jordan while I was Ambassador in Amman, and I had got to know him better over his week's stay, playing squash with him and having him over for an informal meal. Several years later, while I was High Commissioner in London, General Musharraf attended the Royal College of Defence Studies (RCDS) course in London and again came to dinner at my residence. While I was Ambassador in France, Musharraf had presided over the disastrous Kargil adventure and later mounted a coup against the elected civilian Prime Minister Nawaz Sharif in 1999. I immediately resigned my Ambassadorship but was told to stay on for the present. President Musharraf paid a brief official visit to France on his way to the Non-Aligned Summit in Havana.

During my tenure as Chairman, I met President Musharraf about six times a year at briefings, receptions and cricket matches. He was invariably affable but I recognized that, though a sportsman, he had only a superficial grasp of cricket. He was advised by a coterie of army officers – some generals who also did not have a deep understanding of cricket and junior officers in his secretariat who were active club-level cricketers. I found Musharraf impulsive and often shooting from the hip without assessing issues in depth. For instance, after the disastrous tour of Australia, during which some unsavoury shenanigans by our players had been reported in the media, President Musharraf told me that discipline had been lax and that the manager, Haroon Rashid, should be replaced by a strict disciplinarian. I told the President that though the results were unquestionably disappointing, we had played by far the strongest side in the world on their home soil.

PAKISTAN SERIES AGAINST THE WEST INDIES AND ENGLAND, 2005

Pakistan now embarked on the tour of the West Indies, satisfied and confident after their success in India. Shabbir Ahmed, whose action had been passed after corrective training in Western Australia under the guidance of Daryl Foster, was included, as was Yasir Hameed and Bazid Khan. Shoaib Akhtar was excluded on grounds of continuing unfitness.

The ODI Series

On the Caribbean tour, three ODIs were to be played before two Tests. The first ODI, at St Vincent on an awkward wicket, saw

Pakistan victors in a low-scoring match by 59 runs. In the second ODI at St Lucia, Pakistan won again by 40 runs. In the third ODI, again at St Lucia, Pakistan's first five batsmen scored over 40, with Bazid Khan top scoring with 66, and built up a total of 303. Chris Gayle made a hurricane century but the remaining batsmen subsided to a total of 281, giving Pakistan a morale-boosting whitewash in the ODIs.

The Test Series

In the First Test at Bridgetown, Brian Lara was back for the West Indies. Edwards, the round-arm fast bowler, was also included.

The West Indies won the toss and reached 345 after a brilliant century by Lara. Then Edwards tore into the Pakistan batting in a ferocious spell. Pakistan was without Inzamam and collapsed for a total of 144. By the end of the innings, Edwards had limped off, which probably led to the West Indies not enforcing the follow-on. The West Indies made 375 in their second innings with Chanderpaul scoring 153 not out. Pakistan went in again without having to face Edwards but again succumbed to some probing bowling by Gayle (5–91) for a total of 296, handing the West Indies a thumping victory by 275 runs. Afridi, who had gone in at six instead of opening, made his second Test century and Asim Kamal (55) was the only other batsman who made a score.

Meanwhile, the Pakistan press was going to town about an altercation in the dressing room between Younus Khan and Shahid Afridi because the acting captain had instructed Afridi to open the batting. Both players apologized claiming that, between two hot-headed Pathans, such exchanges were not unusual. I had, however, to intervene and warn both players not to engage in undisciplined behaviour.

For the Second and last Test in Jamaica, Inzamam returned as captain. Pakistan made a good score of 374, with Younus Khan scoring a fine hundred. In the West Indies first innings, Brian Lara again showed his class by scoring a magnificent 153. In Pakistan's second innings Inzamam played a superb captain's knock of 117 not out. With a fourth innings target of 280, it was anyone's match, much depending on Lara's brilliance. For the first time on the tour Kaneria came into his own and captured Lara's wicket for a duck. There was scarcely any resistance from the remaining West Indies batsmen so that Pakistan squared the series, emerging comfortable winners in Jamaica.

As in India, Pakistan had squared the Test series after being one down and had emphatically won the ODIs. The team's fighting spirit was generally acclaimed at home, as was Inzamam's calm and mature leadership. The problem of the opening pair was even more acute and there was a question mark over Pakistan's strength of fast bowlers not producing the required high-speed breakthroughs. Shoaib was erratic and Sami had been dropped because of lack of form and pace. Altogether, Pakistan returned home with heads held high and a further climb up the ladders of Test and ODI ranking. We now had a long summer off to rest and prepare for the cricket tours to Pakistan by England and India later in the winter of 2005–6.

At the end of the tour, Bob Woolmer told me of a classic remark by Brian Lara after Pakistan had lost the First Test at Barbados. They met after the match in the hotel swimming pool and as Bob and Brian had been good friends, Woolmer asked Lara for his advice on our openers who had been failing regularly in matches against the West Indies. Lara replied spontaneously: 'Man, the bowling is from North to South but your openers are playing from East to West!'

ENGLAND IN PAKISTAN, 2005

England arrived triumphant from their Ashes success against Australia in the summer. The Ashes series had seen a huge success, especially in bringing Test cricket back to centre stage. Enthusiasm for cricket in England had rocketed in public support and the entire cricketing world was agog with the downing of the mighty Australians by their traditional rivals. England landed in Pakistan full of confidence with superstars Flintoff, Pietersen, Vaughan and Harmison ready to display their capabilities to the Pakistani public. Pakistan were also confident and in high gear, so the series promised a real contest between two sides on a roll. Inzamam had also silenced his critics and the next two series would be a culminating test of whether he should lead the team in the World Cup – a year later – or give way to a younger successor in Younus Khan. England and Pakistan were to play three tests and five ODIs.

The Test Series

In an exciting match at Multan, the Ashes winners gained a seemingly impregnable lead of 150 runs in the first innings. Pakistan then set England 198 runs to win, which on a good cricket surface appeared relatively easy. However, Shoaib Akhtar and Kaneria bowled England out 14 runs short of the target for a famous victory. For the Second Test at Faisalabad, the wicket was dull and lifeless as usual, leading to huge scores from both sides for the inevitable draw.

England won the toss and elected to bat at the Gaddafi Stadium at Lahore in the Third Test. They got off to a good start with both Cook and Trescothick scoring 50s. The English batting then gradually subsided with only Collingwood (96) standing in the breach. England were all out for 288 on a good wicket that was livelier than Faisalabad and Multan. After early shocks, the newborn Muslim Mohammad Yousuf, sporting a long beard, played the innings of his life. He ensured a series win for Pakistan with a magnificent 223. Inzamam reached 97 – his fifth consecutive Test 50 – and Kamran Akmal also weighed in with a century on his home ground, enabling Inzamam to declare at 636. Thoroughly demoralized, England could not avoid an innings defeat and except for Collingwood (80) and Bell (92) were all out

149

for 248. Shoaib Akhtar took five wickets and Danish Kaneria four to seal England's fate.

The Pakistan innings saw an unusual incident when a fielder flung the ball to the wicket but Inzamam who had regained his ground hopped out of the way to avoid being hit by the throw, which hit the wicket with the batsmen out of his crease. The TV umpire gave Inzamam out, when the rules clearly state that the batsman having regained his ground is not out if he strays out of the crease to avoid a throw striking his body. According to the rules, Inzamam was not out and the field umpires Hair and Taufel should not have referred the decision to the third umpire. It can be argued that when the ball hit the stumps Inzamam was out of his crease, but having more time to examine ICC rules, the TV umpire should also have given the batsman not out and explained to the field umpires his reasoning for the decision.

During the Lahore Test, Shahid Afridi was caught on TV deliberately scuffing up the pitch by turning his heel where Kaneria normally pitched the ball. It was a shocking example of petty chicanery and the PCB immediately hauled up Afridi. He admitted his misdemeanour and the PCB punished him with a ban. Malcolm Speed rang me the next day and said that the ICC had been shocked at Afridi's conduct but as the PCB had already taken disciplinary action, the ICC felt that no further action on its part was necessary. The ICC was satisfied that the PCB had taken adequate disciplinary action for a deplorable lapse. It was gratifying that the ECB took the incident as a childish prank by an undisciplined player and did not allow it to affect team relations for the ODI at Lahore.

The ODI Series

In the ODI series, the first ODI was played according to Pakistan's insistence that in our home ODI series both umpires would be neutral. Secondly, we had agreed with England's approval on the playing hours that avoided the dew factor in the early morning and late evening, giving both sides a more even playing field and negating the trend of the toss virtually deciding the result of the match. Play therefore started at 11:30 am, after the early morning dew had evaporated, and ended around 7:30 pm in floodlights for its last hour or so before the dew set in.

Pakistan won the ODI series 3–2, England winning the first and last contests. Vaughan had returned home after his knee injury. For Pakistan, Kamran Akmal scored heavily, while Shahid Afridi returned from his ban and was given a memorable reception in Karachi.

Pakistan had defeated the Ashes conquerors emphatically in the Tests, denting England's high morale and improving further Pakistan's rating in the ICC standings. Pakistan was thus full of confidence in facing their Indian rivals in early 2006. Shoaib Akhtar had returned with vigour to the team while Inzamam had been the outstanding batsman on either side. Kamran Akmal had scored two centuries as an opener and Salman Butt had also scored heavily in Tests and ODIs. Everyone else had contributed effectively and Pakistan's efforts were ascribed to the unity and fighting spirit engendered by Bob Woolmer and Inzamam-ul-Haq.

Pakistan's cricketing relations with England had a history of testiness from the early days of the dunking in a swimming pool of umpire Idris Beg by Donald Carr in 1952 to the Gatting–Shakoor Rana incident in 1987. Ian Botham's quote that he would not send his mother-in-law to Pakistan, and Imran Khan's frequent brushes with the English cricketing establishment, typified the angst between the two establishments. Inzamam, Woolmer and I set out to bury this antipathy and turn a new page. I found David Morgan and the English cricket establishment fully supportive of this aim. The England team, despite security concerns, was given a warm welcome and every care taken for their comfort and security. English Board members and their wives were treated with high protocol, dedicated transport and hospitality so that they openly drew a stark contrast with the treatment they received in India where they were not received at airports, had to fend for themselves and were not allowed access to boxes. On arrival, the England team made a favourable impact in its public relations when two of their leading players visited the earthquake zone in the northern areas, contributing to relief operations. Both teams agreed to dedicate the entire income from the Lahore ODI to the relief fund and, coupled with generous contributions from all cricketing countries, I was able to present a cheque for $10 million to the President for the national earthquake relief fund.

The turning point in Pakistani–English public relations was in the Pakistani public's treatment of the 'Barmy Army'. We knew that because of negative perceptions of Pakistan, which was seen abroad as a hostile, terrorist-oriented place, only a few hundred diehard cricket supporters would make it to Pakistan rather than the thousands that traditionally flock to India, Sri Lanka, South Africa, the West Indies and Australia. These English supporters found Lahore a most welcoming and culturally interesting city and when they moved to the smaller towns of Multan and Faisalabad, the cricket-mad public warmly received them.

Two images symbolized the Pakistani public's friendly response to British visitors. In Multan, where the stadium is 40 minutes away from the city centre, English fans made their way to the stadium from their two-star hotels in rickshaws and buses, but the return journey at close of play posed problems. English fans making their way on foot were frequently stopped by Pakistan car owners and given rides back to the city centre, a gesture that raised their spirits and resulted in a relaxed mood when they made their way to the eateries around town.

In Faisalabad, one of the Barmy Army had a heart attack and died at his hotel. When I came to know of the tragic incident, I went personally to his hotel and organized a proper funeral with the help of the local church. The dead man's parents decided to fly out to Faisalabad so I arranged for their reception at Lahore and transport to Faisalabad. I presided over a simple commemorative function, which the parents and a large element of the Barmy Army attended at the hotel. A plaque was put up in memory of the cricket fan and I know that this gesture was appreciated not only by the parents, but also by the entire Barmy Army and the British High Commission, which had sent a representative. The parents were so grateful that they instituted a special prize for sporting conduct whenever the two teams play each other. The following year, when Pakistan played England, the parents came to the Oval from the Midlands to meet me and to thank me again.

The England players were also relaxed in the friendly, hospitable atmosphere, and after the match in Karachi several players maintained that never in their cricketing lives had they witnessed such a welcoming atmosphere, especially the tumultuous welcome to Afridi in Karachi. Both in Pakistan and in India the relationship between the players and indeed between the two sets of spectators had been exemplary. The result of Inzamam's efforts and the commitment of the two Boards led to a healing of the former antipathy between the two sides.

By the time the England tour ended, Pakistan was riding the crest of a wave. Woolmer had completed 18 months and serious cricket lovers approved his cricketing methods. Even the anti-Woolmer and anti-PCB guns were silent as Pakistan rose to second and third positions in the ODI and Test ratings respectively. We were ready to enter the last year before the World Cup with a stable team and leadership that had shown discipline, fighting spirit and commitment.

Following the goodwill generated by the series, England took the lead in attempting to break Pakistan's isolation from international cricket. Giles Clarke, president of the ECB, offered to host Pakistan's matches against Australia on English grounds and to repeat the process in the following years. England also hosted a Pakistan series in 2010. Giles Clarke was nominated as chairman of an ICC Task Force aiming to assist Pakistan cricket. The MCC also chimed in with its President stating that he would promote an international team to tour Pakistan. During this period the responsible English press was generally sympathetic to Pakistan.

It therefore came as a rude shock, after the spot-fixing scandal in August 2010, when the PCB accused English players of cooperating with the betting mafia. This irresponsible statement also led to English players refusing to play the remainder of the series. The ECB demanded an apology. Better sense prevailed but the earlier goodwill between England and Pakistan had been gratuitously damaged. An apology was duly forthcoming and the PCB was roundly criticized for its irresponsible conduct by the Pakistani media and public.

CHAPTER 7

INTERNATIONAL AND BILATERAL CRICKET DIPLOMACY

Cricket diplomacy required international, regional and bilateral interaction between cricket-playing countries. In this task my 40-year experience as a career diplomat was helpful and I felt comfortable in a diplomatic role. My stints as manager of the Pakistan team in India (1999) and the World Cup (2003) had also given me a valuable insight into the need for diplomacy at the sensitive bilateral level. There was not much difference between UN Security Council discussions and attending an ICC Board of Directors meeting, an Asian Cricket Council meeting and SAARC deliberations, or indeed in negotiations at the bilateral level. In each domain it is important to master one's brief, to lobby for support with other participants, to articulate one's brief succinctly at the opportune moment, to establish personal goodwill with other participants, even one's adversaries, and to employ tact and good humour at all times.

The ICC's Executive Board of Directors comprises all ten Test-playing countries that are represented by the heads of their respective cricket boards. It also has three rotating members from the Associate countries (second tier). It has some similarities with the UN Security Council, with its permanent and rotating members. The Board of Directors is international cricket's main decision-making body. Below this governing body is a committee of chief executives that basically prepares the agenda for the Directors' meeting. The ICC has a permanent secretariat, headed by a rotating President from the Board of Directors serving two-year terms, and a permanent Chief Executive heading the ICC secretariat. The ICC's specialized committees include the Anti-Corruption Unit (ACU), the management and governance committee, the cricket committee, drawn from celebrated cricketers, and the umpires' committee.

I hurriedly attended my first Directors' meeting in Christchurch as it coincided with the arrival of the Indian team. By the time I attended the next annual conference at Lords, I had a picture of the atmosphere in the ICC. Ehsan Mani from Pakistan was a superb and efficient President, dealing diplomatically with hurdles and potential problems that made up the ICC agenda. He worked in tandem with the Chief Executive, Malcolm Speed, who was highly efficient, able and had a complete grasp of detail on every issue. Though direct in style in the Australian manner, Malcolm Speed was widely respected for his integrity and frankness. The Executive Board was dominated by its two heavyweights, Australia and India, who brought with them their financial and cricketing clout to the meetings. Bob Merriman, the Australian chief, was a delightfully friendly and affable man who carried his iron fist in a velvet glove. After completing his term, Bob was replaced by Creagh O'Connor, an equally affable and upright administrator. Jagmohan Dalmiya of India was an effervescent and immensely friendly person who had formerly been Chairman of the ICC. He seemed to have an in-built calculator in his head, which led to a stream of figures and calculations being quoted in seconds, long before anyone could even grasp their initial impact. Dalmiya was replaced after a bitter struggle within the Indian Board by Sharad Pawar, an Indian Cabinet Minister.

Sir John Anderson, the New Zealand representative, was the most experienced and long-serving member of the Board. He had held high executive office in New Zealand's financial sector and

Figure 9   Seated (right–left): Thilanga Sumathipala (Sri Lanka), Bob Merriman (Australia), Malcolm Speed (CEO of the ICC), Tunku Imran (Malaysia), Ehsan Mani (chairman of the ICC), Percy Sonn (South Africa, vice-chairman of the ICC), Shaharyar M. Khan (Pakistan), Peter Chingoka (Zimbabwe), David Morgan (England and Wales). Back row (right–left): Ray Mali (South Africa), three ICC senior officials, David Richards (Israel travelling on South African passport), Martin Snedden (CEO New Zealand), ICC senior official. Absent: Jagmohan Dalmiya (India), Teddy Griffith (West Indies).

though a man of few words, his counsel, usually made at the end of a debate, was wise, balanced and usually carried the day. Sir John's experience of cricketing and commercial issues was invaluable to the Board. David Morgan of the England and Wales Board, like me a relative newcomer to the Board, was a quiet, almost shy man who soon earned everyone's respect for his brief, incisive and pertinent comments. David Morgan never spoke unless he had to. He was pragmatic, tactful and perspicacious in his comments. David Morgan and I became good friends partly because we were both Welsh rugby fans. David was to play a crucial role during and after the 2006 Oval Test, discussed in detail in Chapter 10. Ray Mali of South Africa was a most dignified and genial personality whose interventions, based on supreme common sense, were universally appreciated. The West Indies Board was represented initially by Teddy Griffith, the only Test player (one Test) amongst us. Teddy Griffith was brief and relevant in his interventions, expertly promoting West Indian interests in the Board. The urbane Ken Gordon later replaced him. Zimbabwe consistently faced crises in the Board because of its political problems and internal challenges. Its poor performance in the cricketing arena also put it on the defensive in maintaining its Test-playing status. Zimbabwe was represented by Peter Chingoka, who handled the slings and arrows aimed at it with immense dignity and skill. It was mainly due to Chingoka's deft handling of these thorny issues that Zimbabwe cricket has survived relatively unscathed. The Bangladesh Chairman Ali Asghar was another charming personality who rarely intervened but effectively steered Bangladesh interests on the agenda. Sri Lanka had several Chairmen on the Executive Board during my three years on it, as there was constant turmoil in Sri Lankan cricket circles, which did not help unity of command in their representation. Among these representatives was the ebullient and combative Thilanga Sumathipala, who was later succeeded, through a government edict, by Kumara Dharmasala, a dignified and highly personable nominee.

There was a general impression in the Western press that, on critical issues, the Board would divide itself into regional factions. The two Africans, the four South Asians on one side, and three Anglo-Saxon representatives on the other, formed two distinctive groups. The West Indies acted as a crucial 'floater', especially when a two-to-three vote was required to pass a resolution. This impression was not totally valid as, for instance, when the T20 World Cup was initially proposed, India and Pakistan voted against it, while Sri Lanka and Bangladesh voted in favour. There were differences on other issues also, clearly dividing the Asian vote on cricketing issues.

Another impression that I gained was that some Directors placed primary importance on commercial and financial matters relating to the ICC and their own countries, while others focused on the ICC's cricket-ing authority as the guardian of the sporting traditions of the game. I firmly belonged to the latter group while others, notably Dalmiya and Merriman, were leaders of the former cabal. Ehsan Mani and Malcolm Speed brought to bear their immense wisdom and diplomatic skills in smoothly tiding over these differences of approach.

India's commercial and financial clout within the ICC was demonstrated in the ICC's contrasting attitude towards Pakistan and India on the selection of umpires. In 2005–6 Pakistan had consistently requested that Darrell Hair should not be appointed to its future series, a request that fell on the ICC's deaf ears, culminating in the Oval Test fiasco. In contrast, when Steve Bucknor gave a poor decision against Sachin Tendulkar during India's tour of Australia, leading to a furore in India's cricketing circles, Bucknor was removed from duty in the following Test and was soon pensioned off from the elite panel. On the same tour, Harbhajan Singh was accused of misbehaviour and was hauled up by the Match Referee. It was expected that he would be banned from the next Test but after pressure from the BCCI, the ban was delayed so that Harbhajan could play in the succeeding matches. More recently, the experienced Australian umpire Daryl Harper accused India of 'bullying' and retired one Test before his planned farewell as a protest.

The ICC has also given its blessing to India's highly commercial T20 IPL programme, allowing it to muscle in on the ICC's extremely congested international calendar. The ICC raised no questions when Pakistan players were excluded from IPL franchises, ostensibly on security grounds. Nor was the high risk of India's betting mafia having a field day on 'spot-fixing' in the IPL ever allowed to surface in ICC discussions. Ironically, a few years earlier, the ICC had virtually banned the ODIs in Sharjah because of the high risk of betting.

NEUTRAL UMPIRES

My first attempt at introducing improved cricketing regulations for international matches was to propose an extension of neutral umpires in all international matches. I recalled that Pakistan had spearheaded the neutral umpire concept under its PCB Chairman Air Marshal Nur Khan and captain Imran Khan. The ICC has since accepted this concept for all international tournaments (World Cup, Champions trophy and so on), and for bilateral Test matches. Only in bilateral ODIs was one 'home' umpire to accompany a neutral umpire. The rationale for this exception was that 'home-based' umpires needed to be given exposure at the international level to assess their competence. Also, the increased cost of appointing two instead of one neutral umpire for ODIs was a factor in favour of maintaining only one neutral umpire for bilateral ODIs. I argued that exposure of home-based umpires who were not on the international elite panel could now be assessed at the numerous international, African and Asian tournaments like the under-19, Associate Member and Affiliate (third tier) championships, to which they were regularly appointed. More importantly, I cited the recently concluded Pakistan–India series that had generated immense public goodwill and improved relations between the two countries. This goodwill risked being jeopardized if a home umpire gave a manifestly incorrect decision in favour of the home team. I referred specifically to two such decisions in the 2005 India-Pakistan final ODI in Delhi, which could have led to a public furore in Pakistan. As it happened, Pakistan had already taken an unbeatable lead in the ODI series and eventually also won the Delhi ODI, so that there were no adverse repercussions over the home umpire's errors. On the other hand, a mistake made by a neutral umpire would be accepted as human error. I underlined the risk – through home umpire error – of jeopardizing cricketing and bilateral relations that had been achieved by immense commitment and hard work by players and administrators on all sides.

My proposal was fairly debated in the Board, which finally decided to maintain the decision of appointing two neutral umpires in Test matches to the hosts and only one in bilateral ODIs. However, they agreed to two neutral umpires by the host country even for bilateral ODI series if the visiting team agreed. The home team would have to bear the extra cost of the second neutral umpire. Otherwise, the current regulations of appointing only one neutral umpire would stand. My proposal was therefore only a partial success and Pakistan proceeded to appoint neutral umpires for future home series against India and England. No other cricketing country has followed suit, but I personally remain committed to the concept of neutral umpires in international bilateral ODI series.

HOURS OF PLAY

In central and northern Pakistan, between November and February, the light fades quickly after 4pm. Usually play is called off for bad light around 5 pm so that an hour is lost every day. A five-day Test match is reduced to 25 hours instead of 30. In order to circumvent this problem, I decided that the PCB should give priority to developing Test stadiums in southern Pakistan (e.g. Sindh and Baluchistan), where Karachi was the only city in winter where play could be ensured for six hours a day. Hyderabad and Gwadar could be developed as Test centres in the south of Pakistan.

Though my proposal for a five-hour six-day Test in these months was not accepted, the ICC commissioned experimentation with a pink ball that could be used under floodlights. I was, however, successful in gaining ICC approval for scheduling hours of play for ODIs in Pakistan that would provide a more even playing field to the contestants and prevent the winning of the toss becoming a decisive factor. In our all-day ODIs, play normally began at 9:30 am or 10 am, which meant that early dew on the pitch gave the bowling side a significant advantage as the ball tends to deviate sharply from the pitch. As the dew evaporated, around midday, batting became much easier. This condition invariably led to the team winning the toss opting to bowl first to gain a decisive advantage.

Rescheduling hours of play from 11:30 am until 6 pm, when floodlights would be switched on for the last hour, was a success, especially with the visiting English team in 2005.

THIRD UMPIRE REFERRALS (DRS)

My third intervention in cricketing issues related to the proposal whereby a batsman or fielding side could appeal against an umpiring decision with a referral to the third umpire, who would, after consulting technology, give his verdict. The rationale for this proposal on third umpire referral was to ensure that a correct decision was handed down both to batting and fielding sides because a crucial error by the field umpire could decide a match, even a series.

Against this referral proposal, based on technology, was the argument that around 95 per cent of international umpiring decisions had been assessed by the ICC to be correct. The remaining 5 per cent were considered part of human error and a central principle of accepting the umpire's decision as final.

Referral to third umpires had initially been put to the test in some ICC-approved series. For instance, the proposal had been given a trial in the 2005 Super Series between Australia and the Rest of World and in first-class cricket in England. In both cases the initial conclusion was that the referral experiment required further refinement. It undermined umpire authority, interrupted the flow of play and devalued a vital principle of cricket – and of life – that an umpire's decision, even if incorrect, had to be respected.

At the 2006 annual meeting at Lords the referral proposal had been vigorously debated in the ICC Cricket Committee and approved. The Chief Executives' meeting had also debated the proposal and endorsed it with a bare majority. So the Executive

Board was poised to approve the resolution when I intervened against the proposal on the grounds already stated in the above paragraphs. I emphasized the demoralizing effect on umpires at the lower levels where, particularly in Third World countries, player indiscipline was rife and the example of international umpire decisions being questioned by players would lead to increased fraying of umpire control. The issue was extensively debated and I found some directors who were in favour of the experiment, especially David Morgan (England) and Ray Mali (South Africa), came round to my reasoning. Eventually the directors voted to delay the proposal.

My central point is that DRS debases – humiliates is too strong a word – the role of the field umpire by allowing the overturning of his judgment through player appeals. Almost certainly it affects the ability of the umpire to give a marginal decision that could be challenged and overturned. Since then, in an eminently sensible statement, Andy Flower, the English coach, has favoured a review of the DRS to be limited to particular dismissals. Basically, I feel that the umpire's dignity and honour need to be preserved and it should be left to the umpire to send decisions up to the third umpire, and not through appeals for a review by players.

Secondly, the DRS system prevails in some series and not in others, depending on the financial ability of the host country to mount the expensive DRS technology. In my view this uneven application of DRS is disconcerting and the ICC should implement it across the board in all series, preferably after a review of its flaws.

TEST CRICKET VS TWENTY20

Although I was recognized as a diehard conservative supporter of Test cricket and the longer game, I was conscious of the need not to stand in the way of Pakistan's financial interests through the growing commercialization of cricket through the shorter versions – notably the spread of the Twenty20 (T20) phenomenon. At the

ICC meetings, I supported measures to maintain the primacy of Test cricket despite its obvious lack of public support in most ICC countries where T20 was spreading like wildfire. Initially, India and Pakistan declined to participate in the first T20 World Cup in South Africa, quoting lack of experience in domestic T20 competitions, but later relented – as described earlier in this chapter – in order to gain African support for South Asia's bid for the 2011 World Cup. Ironically, India and Pakistan emerged as finalists in the T20 World Cup.

Once started, T20 competitions were a raging public success in Pakistan and India – leading to huge commercial bonanzas for the Boards. T20 competitions became part of the cricketing calendar of both countries, leading to India's ICL and IPL tournaments. I used T20's popularity to garner sponsorships for cricket in all forms of cricket, notably domestic first-class cricket. By lumping all three forms of cricket together, the PCB was able to obtain lucrative sponsorships from potential sponsors who were anxious to invest in T20 as opposed to first-class cricket.

At ICC meetings, I pleaded for a balance between Test cricket, which all members recognized as the supreme part of cricket, and T20 cricket, which I considered to be the bane of traditional cricket. The ICC set in motion studies on how to sustain Test cricket and I am glad to note that in its meeting in October 2010, the ICC approved a Test Cricket league, which will culminate in a Test cricket hierarchy of four teams that will contest the Test cricket crown. In this way bilateral Test series, so far played for honour and prestige, will have a competitive meaning in deciding which four countries reach the finals. (While this league was originally planned for 2013, it has regrettably been postponed to 2017 due to financial constraints.)

I regret, however, that the ICC's exhortations to support Test cricket appear to be mere lip service in the face of the landslide commercialization of the game by the T20 mania. Of course it is in the ICC's interest to profit from the T20 syndrome, but not at the expense of the traditions and balance of the game. After the IPL and the T20 World Cup, it now appears that an India-backed T20 cup on IPL lines is on the cards in Australia. My fear is that Test cricket, instead of being revived, will be submerged in the floodwaters of T20 on the grounds of public demand and rank commercialism. Personally, I would favour the ICC sending clear guidelines to member boards insisting that all bilateral series schedule three Test matches at least, a maximum five ODIs and two T20s. The Pakistan team's tour of New Zealand in December 2010 had two Tests, six ODIs and three T20s!

ICC HEADQUARTERS

Another issue relating to the traditional versus commercial values was the location of ICC Headquarters. Up to 2005, England had served as ICC Headquarters. England was regarded as the home of cricket with the MCC serving as the forerunner of the ICC at Lords. The ICC was housed in an inadequate building located in an outhouse at Lords. Clearly the ICC required a proper building in London with financial support if England was to continue to serve as ICC Headquarters. Initially, England made a bid to retain its image as the home of cricket. The ECB proposed a new building at Lords and financial benefits through British tax reforms. Meanwhile, Malaysia and the UAE (Dubai) had offered substantial financial support to the ICC in order to induce it to move its headquarters to Kuala Lumpur or Dubai. Generally, ICC Directors were reluctant to move its headquarters to a country that had little or no background in the traditions of cricket. They decided to give England a year to offer a package that would strengthen its claim to retain Lords as ICC Headquarters.

A year later the ECB reported that no tax relief amounting to a saving of about a million dollars was acceptable to the British Parliament. ICC Directors therefore assessed alternative sites for ICC Headquarters. Financially, Dubai's offer was found to be superior. Dubai offered free land for a new custom-built building which would be financed by Dubai, use of a temporary building and other financial support, amounting to substantial advantages over Malaysia's bid, which led to an ICC decision to move to Dubai. ICC Directors also noted that Dubai was located mid-way between the main cricketing countries and was the hub of worldwide airline connections, and also provided excellent hotel facilities. Thus ended the search for a new location for ICC Headquarters in 2005. As a sop to the ECB, the ICC decided that the annual meeting of the ICC family would continue to be held at Lords in summer.

SOUTH ASIA'S BID FOR THE 2011 WORLD CUP

Perhaps our most important diplomatic intervention occurred during South Asia's bid for the 2011 World Cup. There were two sets of contestants – South Asia and Australia/New Zealand – who were competing for the World Cup. Significantly, India had, in December 2005, voted in a change in its Board, with Sharad Pawar replacing Jagmohan Dalmiya as Chairman of the BCCI in a fractious contest. The Indian Board had barely taken over when the South Asia Directors met in New Delhi to finalize their joint bid. While the Sri Lanka, Bangladesh and Pakistan Boards had completed their copious and complicated documentation for the bid, India was nowhere near compliance, and though Sharad Pawar mandated his officials to work overnight to complete their bid, when we arrived at ICC Headquarters in Dubai to make our presentation, South Asia's bid was found to be non-compliant.

Meanwhile, Australia and New Zealand had prepared a superb presentation that South Asia could not have matched. I lobbied hard inside and outside the Board to explain the genuine difficulties that India faced in completing the documentation. I urged Sharad Pawar to clear the air with the African delegates, who had been upset by India's decision to cancel the Afro-Asia series that provided them with significant funding, and to work on the West Indies delegate.

With great difficulty we managed against stern opposition from Australia/New Zealand to have our presentation postponed by a month. This gave the South Asian contestants, especially India, time to prepare a worthy presentation for our bid. Meanwhile, India and Pakistan had reversed their stand on South Africa hosting the first T20 World Cup in 2007 to ensure their support. To secure a favourable vote, I urged Sharad Pawar to offer financial cooperation to the cash-strapped West Indies in hosting the 2007 World Cup. All these suggestions were aimed at obtaining the maximum vote for South Asia's World Cup bid, which was accepted 7–3, with Australia/New Zealand confirmed as the succeeding hosts in 2015. The South Asia bid had nearly fallen out of our grasp and required a supreme negotiating and diplomatic effort, first to postpone the decision when we were found non-compliant and a month later to secure enough votes to succeed.

THE ISRAELI DILEMMA

In 2004, the ICC Associates elected Israel as one of their rotating Associate Members to the ICC Board. This selection posed a problem for Pakistan whenever the Board decided to meet in Pakistan as it did not recognize Israel, and could not issue a visa to an Israeli national or have the Israeli flag or its plaque placed formally at the table. Yet, Pakistan would be denied the honour of holding an ICC Board meeting on its soil if the Israeli representative was not allowed to be present at the Board meetings.

In the Foreign Office, I had experience of such dilemmas when Israel or Taiwan were competing with Pakistan in international sporting events like the Davis Cup. Usually, a way was found by referring to Taiwan as 'Chinese Taipei' and requesting Taiwan not to fly its national flag on Pakistan soil. Fortunately, the Israeli associate member – a Dr Richards – had dual nationality, Israeli and South African, and held two passports. He was an extremely personable man and fully appreciated his sensitive status when it came to Pakistan. I used my diplomatic experience to overcome the problem when the ICC Board meeting was held in Lahore in 2005. I assured Dr Richards of full security and requested him to travel to Pakistan on his South African passport. His visa entry was discreetly arranged at Lahore airport and at the ICC Board meeting, national flags and plaques were not placed but replaced by 'Associate Member' plaques. The meetings went through smoothly with appreciation from Richards and the ICC high command.

The general atmosphere at ICC Executive Board meetings is extremely civilized, urbane and friendly, and even the most contentious issues are debated without acrimony or tension. No assessment of ICC Executive Board Meetings can be made, however, without mention of the towering personality of its long-standing stalwart – HRH Tunku Imran of Malaysia – who has represented the interests of ICC Associate Members on the Executive Board for over a decade. Tunku Imran, himself a noted sportsman, is a delightful, genial and balanced personality whose interventions at Executive Board meetings were highly respected. His major contribution to Board meetings lies, however, in bringing harmony and joy in the deliberations of the Board. Invariably at Executive Board dinners and social gatherings, Tunku Imran entertains the gathering with his vast array of songs and ditties in which other members and their wives join in, creating an atmosphere of joyous abandon. Tunku Imran is also a witty raconteur, entertaining social gatherings with his anecdotes and sometime risqué stories. He is invariably the life and soul of any social gathering, which produces a delightfully relaxed atmosphere among the delegates in and outside Board meetings.

The role of diplomacy in bilateral cricketing relations is perhaps even more important. Pakistan's relations with India and, to a lesser extent, with England were especially relevant, as these were sensitive in the political, public relations and national framework. The first requirement for bilateral diplomacy was to achieve a friendly and equable personal relationship between the interlocutors. Despite the tense political climate between Pakistan and India, I was able to achieve this status with Jagmohan Dalmiya and later with Sharad Pawar. This relationship depended on mutual respect based on frankness and courtesy. The numerous cricketing and political vicissitudes that we faced – and overcame – are amply described in Chapter 3. They led to immense success of bilateral tours between the two countries from 2004 to 2007. With England, Pakistan's relations had been coloured by a history of controversies and angst. Here again, a warm personal friendship between the Boards with a guiding influence on respective captains and players led to a successful healing process.

Another issue that required high-level personal diplomacy arose in 2005 when our TV partners – TEN Sports and ARY – had a major falling out. There was acrimony between the two partners and there was a serious danger of the forthcoming series in Pakistan not being televised at all. This would have been disastrous for the PCB, as the government and public would place the blame squarely at the PCB for signing a faulty contract with TV partners. Regrettably the contract did not include a clause to settle *inter se* differences and disputes between the contracting partners. The stand-off had become so serious that ARY had presented TEN Sports with a suit before the Lahore High Court.

I attempted to resolve the dispute by talking to both parties to find a compromise. Again, the need to have good relations with both leaders was important in negotiating separately with each party, as the partners now refused to talk to each other. Later, meetings were held between all three sets of lawyers, the PCB's led by Asghar Haider and Ahmad Hosain and the two partners fielding the best lawyers in Lahore. The discussions went through the night as we attempted a temporary compromise or ceasefire so that the televising of the series could proceed the next day. It was touch and go until 5 am when a compromise was ironed out after an all-night session. Our lawyers then proceeded at 9 am to the Lahore High Court to inform the Court of the compromise.

The televising of the series was saved! Later, in London, I discussed with the principles of ARY and TEN Sports a more permanent compromise. Abdul Rahman Bukhatir and Zahid Noorani of TEN Sports and Haji Razzaq and Salman Iqbal of ARY agreed to this fragile compromise that lasted through to the end of the five-year TV contract.

CHINA AND AFGHANISTAN

Cricket and diplomacy intertwined in Pakistan's dealings with Asian countries and particularly with encouragement to its two neighbouring countries – China and Afghanistan – who had recently taken up the sport. Neither country had a history or tradition related to the sport, and it was difficult to conceive of cricket flourishing in countries where it did not flow in the blood of their citizens, or at least in a part of the population, such as the Commonwealth settlers in USA, Canada, the Gulf or Europe. As Foreign Secretary I had engaged in diplomatic negotiations with Chinese and Afghan representatives and had a good understanding of their temperament and work ethic.

Visit to China

Between 20 and 24 September 2006 I met a long-standing commitment to lead an ACC delegation to China to encourage cricket in that country. An enthusiastic Malcolm Speed and his charming wife Alison accompanied the delegation to Beijing and Shanghai, where we visited grounds and training camps and watched cricket matches in which both boys and girls participated. Cricket in China was being organized by a dedicated committee. The committee ran up against the handicap of cricket not being an Olympic Sport and, therefore, were denied substantive funding from the government that was available for all Olympic sports with an eye to preparing China for the 2008 Olympics. China was virtually starting from scratch but was committed to improving standards. I advised the Chinese Cricket Association to give priority to training its women and under-15 squads, where the gap between them and other associate countries was narrower, than in the men's teams. In our report, my delegation recommended cricket being accepted as an Olympic sport by playing T20 cricket at future Asian, Commonwealth and Olympic Games. This decision would provide an important financial resource base for China. I left China convinced that in 20 to 30 years time, China would take its place among important cricketing countries, given the fact that the Chinese government has decided that in three major Eastern provinces, cricket was to become part of its sports curriculum.

Afghanistan

Afghanistan's relationship with cricket began with the 4 million refugees who had sought shelter in Pakistan after the Soviet invasion in 1979. These Afghan refugees were settled in camps run by the United Nations High Commission for Refugees (UNHCR) mainly in the Frontier (now Khyber Pakhtunkhwa). About half of these refugees have returned home, but the remainder are still in Pakistan with jobs, contracts and restaurants even in more distant cities like Karachi, Lahore and Islamabad. These refugee families felt at home in Pakistan as they belong to the same Pathan tribes and share a common culture and language. The Afghan refugee arrival virtually coincided with the burgeoning of cricket fever in the Frontier region that had previously not taken to cricket, but had produced brilliant squash, tennis and football players. From the 1980s onwards the Pathan people had caught the cricket epidemic that raged across Pakistan and soon were winning national trophies at all levels. The Afghan refugee children living in their camps were infected by the cricket bug and, like other young people, they began playing cricket by turning up at nets, playing some club matches and generally absorbing the complexity, tactics and traditions of cricket from their Pakistani colleagues.

These strapping young Afghan refugees were encouraged by

local cricketers and gradually started joining clubs in Peshawar, Mardan, Kohat and in the Tribal Area. From these curious beginnings began the stirrings of an Afghanistan cricket team. These refugee players banded together and began to play local club sides as Afghanistan representatives. The enthusiasm spread as they gained success through coaching, more organized cricket and some recognition from the Afghan government.

The district and regional organization of the Khyber province had helped and recognized the Afghan youngsters. When I took over charge of the PCB I officially encouraged the Afghan team by arranging representative matches, coaching through a national coach and financial support. So began the emergence of an Afghanistan team comprising essentially Afghan players raised in the refugee camps. The PCB supported Afghanistan's case at Asian and ICC conferences and continues its support to Afghan players. They were helped by an enterprising President of the MCC – Robin Marlar – who sent an MCC team to Afghanistan to help organize cricket on the mainland. They found that there were hardly any facilities for playing cricket in Kabul, but helped in supporting the core of Afghan cricketers now returned to their homeland, and arranging basic facilities like playgrounds and coaches. The progress of this Afghan team has been spectacular. From the lowest echelons of Asian cricket they have risen among the Associate Members to defeat established teams like Kenya, Ireland and the Netherlands. In the 2010 Asian Games T20 competition, Afghanistan defeated a third-string Pakistan in the semi-finals. They now aspire to Test-level cricket, though given the paucity of facilities this is unlikely to be accepted by the ICC. For the time being Afghanistan is likely to engage in extra-territorial competitions where their performance to date has been remarkable.

Cricket continues to gain support in the Middle East region, where essentially South Asian players represent countries like Oman, the UAE, Qatar and Saudi Arabia. It is less prominent in countries like Thailand, Malaysia, Singapore, Indonesia and Iran, where the South Asian influence is not so strong. However, Nepal is making significant progress and their national team is strong enough to challenge leading district teams in Karachi where they were invited to play. In time, Nepal is likely to emerge as a prominent cricket-playing nation with an indigenous base, in contrast with Asian teams that rely upon South Asian expatriates. In these countries progress is likely to be limited unless indigenous players, as in Afghanistan and Nepal, enter the cricketing arena.

CHAPTER 8

THE CONTROVERSIAL FACE OF PAKISTAN CRICKET

Over the years individuals and teams have gained reputations in terms of their on- and off-field behaviour. Pakistan's cricket and its cricketers have often come under the spotlight for breaches of discipline – some minor and some far more serious. Pakistan's lack of discipline has become part of its defining feature. Put cricket indiscipline into Google and every entry on the first page is concerned with Pakistan. This criticism began with biased umpiring and gathered momentum with accusations of ball tampering, match- and spot-fixing, boorish anti-social behaviour, indiscipline, drug abuse and petty cheating such as deliberately scuffing up the pitch or claiming catches that had clearly been grounded. These controversial acts have given Pakistan cricket the tag of the ugly ducklings of international cricket. And yet a closer look at the criticism reveals a far more complex picture.

This chapter will focus first on more general issues that have sullied Pakistan's reputation – namely biased umpiring, the general corruption in the domestic game and the more recent and controversial issue of the growing religiosity within the team. From there it will move to the more specific 'player'-related incidents such as indiscipline, ball tampering, match-fixing and the recent scandal of spot-fixing.

BIASED UMPIRING

In the early days, visiting teams, notably the Indians, complained of bias by Pakistani umpires. This may have been due to the lack of proficient and experienced umpires in Pakistan as distinct from Indian umpires, who had long experience of officiating in Indian first-class cricket. Pakistani umpires were evidently prone to making decisions in favour of a young nation aiming to establish its credentials in the cricketing world. This 'nationalist' approach was obviously a factor in the visits of foreign touring teams. In Peshawar, the MCC team dunking umpire Idris Beg in the swimming pool and the stand-off between Mike Gatting and umpire Shakoor Rana are now events part of cricket's history. In Pakistan–India matches the tension on umpiring boiled over at times, as for instance when Pakistani umpires refused, for 11 minutes, to go out on the field in protest after Sunil Gavaskar's remarks. In India, Pakistani captains were equally vocal in criticizing Indian umpires. In 1987, Imran Khan opposed the appointment of English umpire David Constant in the England–Pakistan series, only for the ECB to turn down that request and have Constant stand in the final Test match.

Of course, charges of biased umpiring were not limited to Pakistani umpires, except that other countries seemed subtler in concealing their bias. I recall watching an England–Australia Test series when top Australian batsmen like Neil Harvey were given out lbw (leg before wicket) when the ball was clearly missing the stumps. Conversely, top English batsmen were often given the benefit of the doubt. English umpires frequently 'compensated' by reversing their marginal decisions relating to tailenders. English umpires are the best in the world but when it comes to crucial decisions relating to top batsmen, there was evidence of a subtle bias in favour of the home team.

Australian umpires have also been accused of national bias not only by Pakistan but by most visiting teams. The West Indies felt extremely hard done by Australian umpires when they were on the verge of victory with tailenders Ring and Johnston chasing 30 runs for the last wicket, only to have several valid appeals turned down. In his autobiography *Whispering Death*, Michael Holding records his deep frustration at the consistently biased decisions of Australian umpires. The same was the case in New Zealand where at one point the West Indies team refused to take the field for 15 minutes after tea in protest (shades of the Oval in 2006). They subsequently decided to take the field but not to appeal to the umpires. Similarly, Pakistan, in a dominant position against Australia at Hobart in 1999, saw a loud appeal for caught behind against Justin Langer turned down, which the Australian press described could be heard around the ground! Langer went on to score 100 and win the match. In an earlier chapter, I have described how Bob Woolmer had highlighted that out of 29 marginal decisions during Pakistan's 2004 series in Australia, 25 had gone in favour of Australia and only four in favour of Pakistan. In the West Indies, too, Pakistan came close to a series victory in 1988, only to be undone by a catch not given when 'the snick could be heard in the stands'.[1]

Instances of national bias were prevalent when the host country provided umpires for Tests and ODIs. Now ICC regulations require Tests to be umpired by neutrals and one neutral umpire for ODIs. This measure has significantly reduced accusations of home country bias, as has the advent of technology that helps umpires make the correct decisions in certain specific cases. Pakistan has insisted, however, on having neutral umpires even for ODIs as a follow-up to Imran Khan's path-finding insistence in 1989 on neutral umpires, which the ICC introduced a decade later. Altogether, criticism of biased umpiring has virtually been banished from international cricket, and when neutral umpires make mistakes they are seen as human error and not part of country bias.

During the past decade, Pakistan has implemented a campaign for improving umpiring standards. Written and oral examinations are held, followed by regular workshops and seminars. Experienced

Figure 10   Aleem Dar (left) and Asad Rauf, two outstanding umpires who have reversed Pakistan's earlier poor reputation of umpiring.

Match Referees and Regional Development Officers are required to assess umpire performance on the field. An umpiring unit in the PCB, headed, in my time, by the excellent senior umpire Khizer Hayat, oversees the training and performance of umpires. As a result, the general quality of umpiring at all levels has markedly improved, with umpires having financial incentives to graduate to the higher tiers in the umpiring hierarchy. Testimony to the success of this campaign is symbolized by Pakistani umpires Aleem Dar and Asad Rauf being nominated to the ICC's elite panel. Aleem Dar has now won the Best Umpire award for four years in succession, which speaks volumes for the improvement in Pakistan's umpiring standards.

CORRUPTION

The corruption that had sullied the reputation of Pakistan cricket and which I was determined to stamp out can be seen from the following examples. In 1971, in a first-class match between Rawalpindi and Faisalabad, the umpires had decided to call off the game because of rain, frustrating the ambitions of the home team. With the complicity of teams, umpires, scorers and match officials it was decided that a 'ghost match' would be recorded, with the interested team emerging as winners. The scorecard of a match that had been aborted was concocted and sent in to the PCB in a match that had not been finished. This deplorable act of corruption came to light later but no action was taken nor any penalty imposed.

Another example of a cricketing racket related to mediocre club players seeking first-class status by playing in a minimum of five first-class matches in a season. This would entitle them to British cricketing visas. Therefore, intense pressure was placed on local selectors and officials to include these mediocre players to play first-class cricket – obviously at the expense of players selected on merit – so that they could proceed to the UK to play in one of the more obscure British leagues where standards were low. These cricketers, armed with cricket visas, would then proceed to Wales, Scotland or Northern Ireland to play for a team with a pittance for a contract.

They would earn money not from their clubs but by living with and working for local Pakistanis who owned small business enterprises, where they would obtain a temporary job. In this way, by the end of the season, the mediocre cricketer would collect a tidy sum to return home with pockets full. This racket led to a lowering of first-class cricket standards at home and the misuse of the visa system. I contacted the British High Commission and explained that the five-strike system was being misused for bogus cricket visas. At the PCB, controlling this racket was one of the main reasons why Ramiz Raja had insisted that national selectors, rather than locally appointed selectors who were susceptible to extraneous pressures, should select first-class sides. I felt Ramiz was right in coming down hard on such an obvious racket, even though he collected a lot of flak from the district associations.

A third racket was the playing of overage players in our junior teams. Soon after I took over as Chairman, I found that most of the selected players for a junior (under-17) team clearly appeared overage. I immediately ordered medical tests, which found that 11 of the 17 selected players were definitely overage. They were dropped forthwith, but even five of their replacements were found to be overage! Eventually a team was selected, but I recall the junior selectors asking me to relent on the age issue as, according to them, other teams regularly fielded overage players. I declined and to my joy the genuinely underage team won the tournament for Pakistan. The message went out loud and clear that doubtful overage players would not only be kicked out, but the concerned association would be held responsible for proposing the players' name and duly penalized. It is gratifying to note that Pakistan has since been winner of successive under-19 ICC World championships and the racket of fielding overage players has been substantially overcome.

A fourth corruptive influence was the monopolistic hold that major clubs in all cities and regions exercise over their players. It has already been noted that club cricket in Pakistan is in decline. This meant that in every region only a few clubs were operating. These clubs are the main feeder belt for players aiming to graduate into higher levels of cricket such as the district, junior and regional squads. It is evident that competition for belonging to and playing with the major clubs is intense. The clubs are usually managed by local politicians, entrepreneurs and feudal barons, employing compliant cricket managers who run the clubs with their patrons' political influence and financial clout. These clubs are bent on preserving their power and influence over players by monopolizing the advancement of their own players to higher levels. It follows that activity at the club is fraught with corruption.

Nepotism, offer of bribes in return for promoting a player (at least one current Pakistan player bought his way into a club team) and keeping out players of less fashionable and smaller clubs becomes the daily routine of the patron and his henchmen. The major clubs' monopoly has to be maintained for the sake of local political patronage and financial gain.

For example, over the last two decades, Lahore has been dominated by the monopolistic hold of four clubs, all coming under the patronage of a prominent politician. Of the current national cricketers from Lahore, Kamran Akmal and Salman Butt are products of one of those four, whereas Abdul Razzaq played for one of the other four. It has almost become a prerequisite to representing Lahore that one has to be from one of the four named clubs. Graduating to the national team is one step further though the path remains the same – from club to Lahore to Pakistan.

Many independent observers note that this monopolistic hold has led to a sharp deterioration of cricket in Lahore. Previously, Lahore's best cricketers used to come from 'Minto Park' (now Iqbal Park). Minto Park was the site for the earliest cricket grounds in Lahore and the three grounds that were situated in that locality attracted cricketers from the nearby densely populated areas even before partition. The great Indian all-rounder and captain Lala Amarnath was one of those cricketers who graced the grounds of Minto Park prior to partition. It was the traditional nursery of cricket in Lahore. Since the 1980s the power of the four clubs has meant that many a deserving cricketer has failed to make the grade because they represented a lesser club. Club cricket suffered significantly as other clubs – including those based around Minto Park – lost interest, and a culture of fake records of matches and 'buying' spots in teams became ingrained.

Many major clubs adopt ghost clubs in order to increase their voting power at the time of district elections. These bogus clubs aim to promote the major club's representation on the district and regional boards. Now, after two decades, the president of the Lahore City Cricket Association has been dislodged, perhaps leading to a change in the existing power structure. Corruption at club level is therefore widespread and has far-reaching consequences for cricket in Pakistan.

Even Mohammad Yousuf, arguably Pakistan's most talented batsman, was unable to find a place in the Lahore team and had instead to start his first-class career by representing Faisalabad. Mohammad Yousuf's experience is a typical example of the pernicious influence of monopolistic clubs. The following is another. The story was related by a young student and cricketer Hissan ur Rehman, who had been part of the under-19 trials arranged in Faisalabad in 2003–4. At the trials it was the unanimous opinion of all the players at the camp and the PCB national selectors sent to evaluate the talent on show that the young leg-spinner Shafqat Hussain was an outstanding talent. Hissan related how he had heard the selectors, Mansoor Rana and Ehteshamuddin, excitedly say to one another that Hussain could walk into the Pakistan team. He apparently had modelled himself on the great Australian leg-spinner Shane Warne and had the ability to turn the ball appreciably with both leg spin and googly variations. At the end of the trials Hussain was named part of the under-19 Faisalabad squad. It therefore came as a shock to Hissan when three months later he found out from the Faisalabad captain that Hussain had been declared overage and had been disqualified. The reason apparently was that the young leg-spinner was from a club that had major differences with the clubs of the position holders in the Faisalabad Association. As a result, the Faisalabad Association conspired to ensure that he was declared overage. Hissan returned to Faisalabad a year later to find that Hussain had quit cricket and started working in a local shop.

There are numerous examples of major clubs who have the patronage of their masters exercising an overbearing influence on the selection of players, even before regional or district selectors come into the picture. These clubs decide which player will be available for selection. In this way, like the deserving leg-spinner in Faisalabad, talent is squeezed out of the frame.

GROWING RELIGIOSITY IN PAKISTAN CRICKET

The next issue that has been seen as having 'tainted' Pakistan's cricketing reputation as controversial is that of growing religiosity. Clearly, as with corruption, growing religiosity is something that has become intimately associated with Pakistan as a country. The image of Pakistan as an intolerant, extremist, Islamic country clearly has had ramifications on the image of Pakistan cricket (and beyond). However, while there is no denying the fact that both country and cricket have increasingly been influenced by a religious discourse, the image of militant Islam and its pervasive influence has, in my opinion, been overplayed.

The issue of growing religiosity in the Pakistan cricket team has been the subject of critical comment. This was especially true during Inzamam-ul-Haq's tenure as captain. But the seeds of overtly religious behaviour had begun to take root earlier. This trend needs explaining, especially as after Inzamam's retirement, overt religiosity has almost vanished from the national cricket team.

The first explanation is that the spread of overt religious dedication reflects a national trend in Pakistan, indeed in the Muslim world as a whole. Beards, veils, vocabulary and TV programmes have sprouted up all over the Muslim world, and in Pakistan the trend has been especially pronounced after General Zia-ul-Haq – a religiously-oriented leader –presided over a decade of Islamization in the country between 1978 and 1988. Moreover, the success of the Khomeini revolution in Iran had a dramatic influence on the politics of the region. The religious mould tends mainly to affect the middle class, lower middle and underprivileged elements of the social spectrum. Most, if not all, of the current Pakistani players are drawn from this segment of

Pakistan society unlike the past, where cricketers came from more affluent and better-educated backgrounds. Imran Khan, Majid Khan, Ramiz Raja and Javed Burki were products of Aitcheson College – Pakistan's Eton – and even 10–15 years ago, the national team had substantial representatives from Government College, Lahore, and Karachi University. This is no longer true and with the change comes the greater influence of religion.

Secondly, cricket, unlike hockey and other sports, found an exaggerated reflection of its Islamic make-up. This was due to certain individual influences. As manager of the Pakistan team in India in 1999, I found the flamboyant opening batsman Saeed Anwar to be a normal cricketing practitioner, but by the time the 2003 World Cup came around, Saeed Anwar had tragically lost a young daughter, become a born-again Muslim and joined the Tableeghi Jamaat, the least politicized of Pakistan's Islamic parties. Saeed Anwar sported a long beard and was clearly the self-appointed mentor of the team.

Already, Inzamam, vice-captain, had by 2003 followed suit and so had the little leg-spinner Mushtaq Ahmed, by then living in England and no longer a member of the World Cup squad. All three – and several others – had been hauled up before the Malik Qayyum betting tribunal that had investigated match-fixing and had been penalized with fines. Was the revival of Islamic fervour and their new way of life a genuine act of remorse and penitence? Was it a turning over of a new leaf in front of the adoring public? Or was their new image a cover for the shame and opprobrium that they faced – in other words, an act of redemption. We cannot, of course, make a judgement on these inner feelings by looking deep into their hearts. Certainly there was consistent commitment from all three to play their role in projecting not the aggressively evangelist jihadi groups but the soft, persuasive face of Tableeghi Islam. More recently, Salim Malik, the principal offender named in the Qayyum report, has also joined the Tableeghi Jamaat.

I had come across these Tableeghi groups when I was posted

abroad as a diplomat in Islamic countries. The Tableeghi groups comprised about 12–15 persons, usually retired civil servants, doctors, businessmen, teachers and engineers, who toured Islamic countries and would arrive at a local mosque where they would sleep and be fed by the local Muslim community. Their dress and ways of life were frugal and they would profess to me when calling at the Embassy that their task was making ordinary Muslims into better Muslims. They would not convert non-Muslims and their only method, they said, was to preach by example and persuasion. I found the Tableeghi groups to be non-aggressive, humble and fairly innocuous. It was for this relatively passive attitude to religion that the Tableeghi Jamaat was seen as non-political, drawing the largest annual gathering in Pakistan at their Headquarters just outside Lahore in Raiwind. I was surprised therefore when I noted that the Tableeghi Jamaat had been placed on the terrorist watch list by Western countries. Possibly this vast Islamic party had been penetrated by more aggressive Islamic parties, like the Lashkar-e-Jhangvi or Lashkar-e-Tayyaba. I was disappointed, however, that the Tableeghi Jamaat made no public pronouncements condemning the criminal suicide attacks, bombings and killings that have become a weekly occurrence in Pakistan. Privately, Tableeghis will tell you that their Jamaat is against such criminal acts.

Of course, for cricketing stars and popular rock singers to join the Jamaat is considered a major public relations coup. The Tableeghi Jamaat has always targeted celebrities as a means of swelling their following and this explains the support that the Jamaat gives to converting individuals in the public eye. Yousuf Youhana becoming Mohammad Yousuf was one of their greatest prizes to date. It eclipsed the conversion of pop star Cat Stevens, who changed his appearance and his name (to Yusuf Islam) to become a Muslim.

On our coach ride into Johannesburg before we started our World Cup campaign in 2003, Saeed Anwar announced on the coach microphone that this time Pakistan was bound to win the

World Cup because 'Allah would send down his angels to ensure victory for us and that the prayers of millions of believers were with us'. This announcement generated enthusiasm and applause from the players. Rather mischievously on the way home after we had been eliminated in the first round, I privately asked Saeed what happened to the angels who were to help us. Pat came the reply: 'it was all because we were not good Muslims'.

During the tour of South Africa, I noticed that many players were being influenced by the Tableeghi message. In every city, the well-organized Saeed Anwar would contact the local Tableeghi Jamaat and take willing listeners with him to their meetings. Among the players so inclined were Saqlain Mushtaq and perhaps clandestinely, Yousuf Youhana, about whom there were rumours that he was shortly to convert to Islam from Catholicism. Some players, like Younus Khan and Azhar Mahmood, were practising Muslims but were not part of Inzamam's Tableeghi (evangelist) movement. They said their prayers regularly in private and not in public view. They remained clean-shaven and did not take on the garb of a Tableeghi Muslim.

When Inzamam took over as captain and dominated the team as a cricketing colossus, his religious influence spread quickly in the team. Many more became camp followers and even though Saeed Anwar was no longer a member, he was Inzamam's constant invitee to the team's hotel and even to the team's dressing room. It appeared that the Tableeghi Jamaat had given Saeed Anwar the licence to tour wherever the team went, to organize Tableeghi sessions in places like Durban, Manchester, Cardiff, Bristol and Birmingham, where Pakistan nationals were settled in fair numbers. By the time the England tour took place, Saqlain Mushtaq, Shahid Afridi and bowling Coach Waqar Younis were sporting beards. Mushtaq Ahmed had also been around in Pakistan as Deputy Coach to Bob Woolmer and not surprisingly many aspirants on the fringes of the national team grew beards and publicly joined players in performing their praying rituals to gain favour. Amongst the more prominent who grew beards at that time were the fast bowler Rana Naveed ul Hassan and the opening batsman Yasir Hameed, who has since been embroiled in the *News of the World* spot-fixing scandal. Incidentally, both have reverted to being clean-shaven today.

The case of Yousuf Youhana's conversion to Islam is of special interest. He was at the time the only non-Muslim in the team. Earlier, Hindus, Parsis and Christians had represented Pakistan. I believe that the selection of these minority members had been purely on cricketing merit with not a whiff of religious prejudice against them. Yousuf Youhana was no exception. In 1999, when we toured India, I found Yousuf a committed Catholic. In every Indian city I would arrange for our hotel to locate a Catholic church and order a taxi for Yousuf to attend service every Sunday morning. Yousuf was grateful for the consideration I showed, allowing him to miss team practice on Sunday mornings. On the 2003 tour of South Africa I again asked for a taxi on Sunday mornings to take Yousuf to church, but I found him to be less enthusiastic about attending services. As time passed, I found Yousuf almost reluctant to attend church, which was the time when press rumours circulated that he was contemplating becoming a Muslim. I used to rib Yousuf about his diluted enthusiasm for Catholicism and would tell him that I would have to report him to his Mother Superior.

Yousuf had represented a beacon of tolerance in at least one segment of Pakistan's increasingly polarized and intolerant society. He was a public hero with his Christianity that the public appreciated. He made the sign of the cross every time he went into bat and whenever he scored a 50 or a century. His conversion came as a shock to his Christian community and his family who briefly ostracized him, before the presence in their midst of a national hero and rich benefactor led to a degree of acceptance.

Knowing that the international reaction was likely to be negative I was concerned at Pakistan's image after Yousuf's conversion to Islam. Fortunately, Danish Kaneria, a Hindu, was by then a member of the national team.

Yousuf's conversion seemed to give him an inner security and confidence as he began to score heavily in Test matches, overtaking Vivian Richards for the highest number of runs in a calendar year (2006). Since then the wheel has turned for Yousuf, with nasty controversies with the PCB and with the unofficial breakaway T20 Indian Cricket League (ICL) and the Indian Board. His cricketing achievements have also declined after a disastrous tour of Australia in 2009–10 as captain, followed by accusations of promoting player indiscipline. Rather than face an inquiry, Yousuf retired but was recalled for the England tour of 2010.

Yousuf's defining act of conversion to Islam deserves scrutiny from religious, personal and social points of view. What made him jump? Broadly, three reasons are given by analysts. Firstly, that Yousuf was inspired by the message of Islam and found leading figures around him encouraging him to convert; secondly, that Yousuf, though highly successful as a batsman, found his path to captaincy blocked by being a non-Muslim; and thirdly, that in Pakistan – though much less so than in India – the caste system has a powerful influence in society. Yousuf was not simply a Christian but was from the lowest social caste – the sweeper or Jamadar caste, which has suffered social ostracization in India. Many believe that persons from the Hindu-scheduled castes of India became Christian or Muslim to shed the stigma of being of the 'chamar' or 'choora' caste that was still despised in a caste-influenced society. Conversion to Christianity or Islam provided a cleansing of this stigma.

Clearly, no single motivation from those outlined above formed the reason behind Yousuf's conversion. It was probably a combination of at least two of the above three factors. Yousuf was basically a simple, not very educated, and impecunious boy when he took the first steps into the cricketing arena. He was meek and compliant of character, and foreign coaches such as Bob Woolmer and trainers Dan Kiesel, Murray Stevenson, Dennis Waight and Darryn Lifson found him easily impressionable.

It is for this reason that I feel that Yousuf's conversion was primarily due to his seeing the light as projected by his Tableeghi colleagues – Saeed Anwar, Inzamam-ul-Haq and Mushtaq Ahmed. Others in the team, like Afridi, Waqar Younis and Saqlain Mushtaq, were in the process of converting. The combined influence of these fellow cricketers on a receptive mind and malleable character played a decisive role. I do not believe that blockage to the captaincy was a factor at all. Yousuf Youhana had been appointed vice-captain as a Christian. Provided his cricketing and captaincy abilities were not found wanting there was no reason why Yousuf could not graduate to the captaincy when the time came, especially as seniority-wise he was the obvious choice. Yousuf also knew of my personal, liberal attitude and would have known that religion would not be a barrier to his captaincy.

My sense is that the third motivation – the caste factor – may have partially influenced Yousuf's decision. He was the son of a railway sweeper, but he was now rich and a benefactor of his Christian community. No doubt he had achieved public adulation as a cricketer and had gained the immense respect of the Catholic Church in Lahore. Yousuf Youhana had attained wealth but his social prestige remained questionable. In fact, there are reports of Yousuf stepping onto the cricket field only to be greeted – albeit by a small section of the home crowd – by taunts of 'choora aa gaya, bhangi aa gaya' ('the sweeper has arrived').

Many such persons adopted Muslim names to escape the daily derision, wore Muslim dress but remained Christians. Others converted to Islam, losing the sympathy and protection of the Christian church and community without gaining a commensurate advantage with the Muslims. Being a member of the scheduled caste, even as a Christian, was a heavy cross to bear and converting to Islam was one way of escaping the stigma. Respectability was only possible through conversion.

I did not, of course, discuss Yousuf's religious feelings with him as I felt that this was a deeply personal matter. I only sought assurance from him that in making his choice he had not been under any coercion or pressure. He assured me that his decision had been his own free choice. I left it at that. As a precaution I told Kaneria that I respected his being a proud member of the Hindu community and that he should continue to feel proud of his association with the Pakistan team. Kaneria is an upper caste Hindu and his only difference from the rest of the team is that he is not a co-religionist. So whereas Youhana was always open to insecurity because of his status as a low-caste Christian convert, Kaneria would not have faced the same social stigma.

All this time, I had been viewing the upward graph of overt religiosity in the team with some concern, though not of alarm. The reasons for my tempered approach were two-fold. Firstly, I was convinced that this overt religiosity was skin deep and would die down after Inzamam's retirement, expected after the 2007 World Cup. I felt opposing this trend head-on would be counterproductive for team morale. It would be better to limit and control the outer edges of the Tableeghi influences. Secondly, I felt that the influence of praying together was beneficial as a unifying and uplifting factor for the team, which had won Test series at home and abroad. Except against Australia we had performed well, and for the public and media this counted for more.

An incident with Bob Woolmer illustrated the second point. Sometime in late 2005, Bob came to my office and told me of his exasperation at the constant and lengthy prayer sessions that the team held, which gave him no time to strategize or advise the players. At lunch the team prayed together for 'zohar' prayer, at tea it was 'asr' and at close of play 'maghrib' prayers, followed by a sermon, dinner, more prayers – 'isha' – and bed. Bob said there was no time for discussion and for him as coach to do his job. I told Woolmer that he should not raise this issue with Inzamam and the players, as being a foreigner and non-Muslim his comments could be taken amiss. I said I would take remedial steps myself. About three weeks later Bob returned to my office and asked me to disregard his earlier remarks because on closer examination he found that praying together was greatly beneficial to team unity and spirit. It also meant that there were no disciplinary problems because the team refrained (with one notable exception) from attending restaurants and nightclubs, avoided razzmatazz associated with sporting stars, went to bed early and were fit and bright-eyed in the morning. Bob therefore wanted the prayer regime to continue. Nevertheless, I had a quiet word with Inzamam to avoid overt displays of religiosity. I told him that the Tableeghi Jamaat had recently been on the banned list of terrorist organizations and open association with its cells could lead to embarrassment.

As things turned out, my prediction that after Inzamam retired this issue would fade away proved correct. Under Younus Khan, Mohammad Yousuf, Shoaib Malik, Shahid Afridi, Salman Butt and Misbah-ul-Haq, overt religiosity has vanished from the Pakistan cricket team, as the Urdu saying goes, 'like antlers from the head of a donkey'. However, in hindsight I could see that Inzamam's religious regime may have begun to affect the team's performance more adversely, namely during the 2006 tour in England. There were also murmurs from the 2007 World Cup that the excessive focus on Tableegh may have diluted the team's focus.

However, I firmly believe that the international media, particularly in England, Australia and India, did not take an accurate reading of this temporary phenomenon in Pakistan cricket. There was an exaggerated and unfocused assessment of Pakistan cricket, particularly following Yousuf's conversion. The English media were prone to accept the fact that Pakistan cricket reflected an extremist point of view, which had seen the army take on the Taliban in Swat, Malakand and Waziristan. The Pakistani public was anti-West, anti-US and anti-NATO, which found reflection in our cricketers. This was a huge and culpable misreading of the political barometer. Cricket has always reflected middle-Pakistan attitudes that are moderate, tolerant and abhor extremism.

In India, the misreading of cricket's temper was more self-serving, condescending and political. Pakistan has always been intolerant of non-Muslims, they claimed, which made Yousuf convert to Islam. In India nearly every team had several Muslim players who were loyal and proud cricketers for India. There was a condescending attitude to Pakistan's religious extremism epitomized by Inzamam and his bearded colleagues against 'shining India's' secular mix. The Indian press found it particularly difficult to stomach Inzamam's religiosity, questioning time and again the captain's frequent reference to Islam and 'Almighty Allah' and the team's collective prayers. And yet very little is made of the Buddhist ceremonies that often precede Sri Lanka's important tours. Neither in India nor in the Anglo-Saxon cricketing world was there a serious attempt to sensitively analyse cricketing attitudes in Pakistan. Instead, Pakistan's dominant image as a hostile, fundamentalist Islamic state was underlined.

Some questions had been raised, particularly in India, at Pakistan's attitude towards non-Muslims. For instance, in India some Muslim players like Abbas Ali Baig and Azharuddin had been criticized in extremist Indian circles for not giving of their best when playing against Pakistan. No such pressure or bias was discernible, with minority players turning out for Pakistan. For instance, Justice Cornelius, a Christian, was the first Chairman of the PCB, with K. R. Collector, a Parsi, its first secretary. Prominent Parsi players Behram Irani and Rusi Dinshaw were members of Pakistan's early teams to Sri Lanka and India. Later, Christians Duncan Sharpe, Wallis Mathias and Antao D'Souza were regular members of the Pakistan team, as were the Hindus Anil Dalpat and Danish Kaneria. As a radio commentator, Jamsheed Marker, a prominent Parsi, became a public icon. Of the minorities, Yousuf Youhana achieved star status and was made vice-captain as a Christian. His conversion to Islam was a personal decision, and not meant to gain cricketing advantage. He had already made his mark in Pakistan cricket and its public. I can state without hesitation that minority cricketers never felt prejudice against them when playing cricket in the Islamic Republic of Pakistan.

The growing influence of religion in Pakistan cricket may have increased Pakistan's 'otherness' from rival teams – partly due to the stereotypes held by others and partly due to the Pakistan players not being able to partake in activities such as 'traditional' end-of-play drinks. Overall, a cultural mismatch (including language) appears far more important than the religious element that has been highlighted by the media.

All the above issues – biased umpiring, corruption and the issue of growing religiosity – have worked together to give Pakistan cricket a negative image. Some of it is clearly warranted, as in the case of corruption and to an extent umpiring, at least in earlier times. However, it also works negatively at the level of perception wherein the perception is more severe than the reality. This was certainly the case with the issue of growing religiosity where the country's image as an increasingly fundamentalist Islamic state worked to paint the cricket team in the same light. In fact, religion played a largely positive role, instilling discipline in a disparate team. There were undoubtedly darker aspects as well, but as Bob Woolmer found these were outweighed by the benefits. Following Inzamam's retirement, the role of religion has receded and one of the disadvantages has been the decline in cohesion and discipline within the team. Younus Khan, Inzamam's successor, tried to instil a strict work ethic through personal example, but was ousted by a group of senior players not willing to adhere to the new regime. A vacuum has followed leading to further changes in captains, further cases of indiscipline and serious charges of match- and spot-fixing.

PLAYER INDISCIPLINE

More than any other country, instances of specific on-field and general player indiscipline by Pakistani players have damaged its reputation in cricketing circles. Over the years Pakistan's cricketers came under international criticism for devious and boorish behaviour. This was especially true after graduate cricketers of the early days like Mian Saeed, Hafeez Kardar, Javed Burki, Majid Khan, Imran Khan, Asif Iqbal and Zaheer Abbas had left the scene.

During my stint as Manager and Chairman, I was aware of this tendency towards player indiscipline. Shoaib Akhtar had been the worst culprit, having been sent home from an 'A' team tour of England, followed by ugly confrontations with coach, manager and captain. He constantly broke curfew, partied unashamedly and was accused of feigning injury and not conforming to fitness discipline. Seemingly, the final straw was when he struck a colleague with a bat. Inzamam, a generally cool and wise man, had once waded into the crowd to settle scores with a spectator who had regularly sledged him. Inzamam had also engaged in a physical scrap with Younus Khan during a practice session at the 2003 World Cup, witnessed by journalists who sent their sensational reports across the globe. Afridi also engaged in a physical encounter with his captain Younus Khan in Barbados and was seen on television trying to deliberately scuff up the pitch with his spikes when fielding against England in 2006. He infamously 'bit the ball' in Australia in 2010. Rashid Latif and Salim Yousuf, both wicketkeepers, claimed catches that they had clearly dropped. Latif was banned for five matches and Yousuf famously berated on the field by captain Imran Khan for unsportsmanlike behaviour.

However, I believe that in the case of player indiscipline, Pakistan's overall negative image has made things appear worse than they are. When reassessing the situation it appears that compared to other international teams, Pakistan's disciplinary record is surprisingly good. On the field, as mentioned, there have been petty infractions aplenty – but none of the over-the-top aggression that has bedevilled Australian cricket in particular. Off the field, Pakistan are awkward and reserved, signalling a cultural disconnect more than anything else. Wasim Akram and Waqar Younis may have been caught smoking marijuana in Grenada, and Shoaib Akhtar may be a serial offender as far as extracurricular activities are concerned, but these instances pale in comparison with the antics of – amongst others – Mike Gatting, Shane Warne, Ian Botham, Andrew Flintoff, Stephen Fleming, Jesse Ryder, Harbhajan Singh and Herschelle Gibbs.

DRUG ABUSE

The taking of performance-enhancing drugs has blighted international sport. Athletics, cycling, swimming and rowing have featured prominently, with players penalized by international drug control agencies in attempting to prevent the intake of performance-enhancing drugs. Cricket has not been deeply affected by drug abuse but in order to take pre-emptive action, the ICC mandated member countries to implement stringent measures to avoid drug abuse. The ICC's own tournaments require participating teams to undergo spot checks and a number of countries have implemented their own drug-prevention measures based on WADA guidelines.

One of the more prominent drug abuse scandals related to Shane Warne, who was sent home in the 2003 World Cup on the morning of Australia's first match with Pakistan after he had tested positive for a banned substance commonly used for masking steroid use. Warne protested his innocence saying that his mother had administered a diuretic to assist in weight control but the Australian Board banned him for a year. In 1986, Ian Botham was the first cricketer banned for recreational drug use after being caught smoking cannabis and in 1995, a 22-year-old Stephen Fleming – future national team captain – who had just broken into the New Zealand Test side, survived controversy when he was caught and admitted to smoking marijuana with teammates Matthew Hart and Dion Nash at their hotel while on tour. In 2001, captain Wasim Akram and vice-captain Waqar Younis were caught along with team members Saqlain Mushtaq and Mushtaq Ahmed allegedly smoking marijuana in Grenada.

The Pakistan team went through its spot checks at ICC tournaments without any qualms but doubts began to surface regarding Shoaib Akhtar's condition in 2005 and 2006, when he was frequently incapacitated by muscle injuries to various parts of his body. He tended to break down and lose speed after early spells and spent weeks out of the team, unable to perform regularly for the national side. Bob Woolmer and his colleagues shared with me their concern at Shoaib Akhtar's fitness because he barely followed the regime that they prescribed for him to return to full fitness. Instead, it was known that he regularly consulted his private doctor, whose recipe for fitness was known to be unorthodox. With the passage of time, Woolmer's fear that Shoaib was using the wrong prescriptions to regain full speed and fitness became more apparent. Shoaib's muscles appeared to bulge out of his torso, accompanied by a telltale loss of hair. Before the England tour Woolmer confided his serious concern about Shoaib taking prohibited drugs. I shared Bob's concern, but singling Shoaib out would have sensationalized the issue and so I told Bob that drug tests would need to be carried out on all the players so that no one would feel discriminated against.

Meanwhile, the ICC had also given high priority to this issue and urged all the Boards to strictly follow ICC guidelines on drug abuse and to align their respective Boards to WADA regulations. Therefore, at my briefings to the team before every series, I made it a point to emphasize the importance of avoiding drug abuse and avoiding any contact with the betting mafia. I made this issue top of my list of priorities and warned the players in Urdu of the dangers of drug abuse. At the team meeting before the England tour, I circulated to the team a list of medicines and drugs that needed to be avoided. There was no question, therefore, of the players not having been warned of the dangers of drug abuse.

When the drug scandal broke during the 2006 Champions

Trophy in India, with Shoaib Akhtar and Mohammad Asif being found exceeding nandrolone limits, Pakistan again faced damaging repercussions internationally and nationally. The first inquiry committee headed by former Governor Shahid Hamid found both players guilty, and penalized them with two-year suspensions. Subsequently, an appeal committee headed by Justice Fakhruddin Ebrahim overturned the first committee's verdict, essentially on the grounds that the players had not been warned specifically about the intake of drugs, some of which could be obtained over the counter without prescription. The appeals committee's verdict was not unanimous as the expert on drug abuse recorded a dissenting opinion, while the third member made a public statement to the Voice of America stating that the two players would be exonerated as proper procedure for WADA testing of urine had not been observed. Surprisingly, this rash revelation, long before the committee reached its verdict, did not lead to the members' resignation but earned a rebuke from the Chairman of the Appeals Committee. In fact, both the Chairman of the Committee and the PCB Chairman publicly accepted that the urine testing had been correctly carried out. The Appeals Committee's final verdict was, however, based on the lack of specific notice to the two players for taking banned drugs.

I found the Appeals Committee's verdict bizarre. Neither committee had sought my views on the issue, particularly as Chairman of the PCB at the time I had played a major role in implementing the PCB efforts to conform to anti-drug disciplines. I would have informed the committees of my efforts to stamp out drug abuse as described in earlier paragraphs, making it evident that the players had been warned specifically of the need to avoid drugs and a circular prepared indicating precisely the drugs to be avoided.

After the Appeals Committee's exoneration of the two players, the ICC and WADA questioned its verdict. Shoaib Akhtar and Mohammad Asif were included in the team to South Africa but were both sent back, ostensibly because of injuries, but it was evident that the nandrolone levels in their bodies was still above acceptable limits and they could not be risked taking the tests again. Eventually both were left out of Pakistan's World Cup squad causing a huge drop in morale, as our attacking spearheads were not available for the World Cup campaign. Controversy raged in the national press regarding the PCB's handling of the drug issue and the black mark against Pakistan's cricket. Since then, Mohammad Asif has again been found to have exceeded nandrolone limits during the Indian Premier League (IPL) matches. He was also arrested at Dubai airport for carrying a drug potion in his wallet and detained for 19 days. Asif cannot enter Dubai now, as he would be arrested. The PCB, however, briefly suspended him but later cleared him on appeal.

BALL TAMPERING

The ball-tampering issue was brought to a head at the Oval Test in 2006 and is analysed in detail in the chapter on the Oval Test. Unfortunately, Pakistan has been associated with the ball-tampering issue since the days when Sarfraz Nawaz scuffed the seam and surface of the ball when playing for Pakistan and Northamptonshire. Other teams and players followed suit, shining the ball with illegal substances (John Lever in India), scuffing up the seam with long fingernails and dust (Michael Atherton), and weighting the ball on one side with sweat and saliva. All these methods allowed the old ball to reverse-swing after the new ball's shine had worn off. The ICC has ordained a series of guidelines to umpires to prevent the 'doctoring' of the ball such as regular inspections of the ball by umpires during an innings, but it is also accepted that 'shining' one side of the ball is now regarded as legitimate. Therefore, line is drawn between shining the ball on one side and the deliberate scuffing of the rough side of the ball to make it reverse-swing. Interestingly, the person credited with inventing reverse swing was a club cricketer by the name of Salim

Mir. Mir played for the Punjab Club in the 1970s and passed on his 'expertise' to Sarfraz Nawaz, who would occasionally play for the same club.

Pakistani bowlers have regrettably been frontline suspects in the ball-tampering saga mainly because of the remarkable success of its fast bowlers. Sarfraz Nawaz was followed by Imran Khan, Wasim Akram and Waqar Younis, who were all penalized by the ICC. More recently, Shoaib Akhtar, Umar Gul and Mohammad Asif have been accused. Of course, fast bowlers from other countries now regularly reverse swing the old ball, most notably Zaheer Khan, Jimmy Anderson and Jacques Kallis. Despite this general trend, I was aware of the feelings beneath the surface in cricketing circles that the Pakistan team was adept at the deliberate doctoring of the ball to hasten it to reverse.

This unsavoury reputation of ball tampering has often been promoted by uneducated and crass boasts by our own players. For instance, in England, I was informed that Mohammad Asif, who had been playing for Leicestershire, had taught his colleagues how to scuff the ball unnoticed by umpires – a rumour that had spread like wildfire on the county circuit. Pakistani players have also distinguished themselves through the most ham-handed attempts at continued ball tampering – Afridi and Shoaib Akhtar are prime examples of attempting to tamper with the ball while all cameras on the field are trained on them. Part of this brazen behaviour may simply stem from the fact that ball tampering is rife in club and first-class cricket in Pakistan and is considered a legitimate method of gaining an advantage. A further explanation may lie in what Sharda Ugra has pointed out in her article on 'What makes sportsmen go corrupt?' – the idea of personality types. Ugra refers to the personality types on a psychological questionnaire, referred to as the Hogan Development Survey as including 'colourful' (seekers of attention, productive, with ability in crises, and possessed of belief in self and ability), 'bold' (overly self-confident, arrogant, with inflated feelings of self-worth) and 'mischievous' (charming, risk-taking, limit-testing and excitement-seeking). Akhtar and Afridi would certainly fall in the bold and mischievous mould – those who are more prone to making 'intuitive decisions motivated by pleasure'. Such players can 'overestimate themselves and their ability to get away with ill-advised risks. In addition, they typically fail to learn from or admit their mistakes and can also intimidate others, be demanding, aggressive and overbearing'.[2]

In the final analysis, deliberate tampering of the ball is no longer a viable pursuit, as wary umpires are required to inspect and keep the ball when play is suspended. It is generally accepted that minor ball tampering continues to occur in cricket, but the fact that Pakistani cricketers continue to get caught shows nothing less than stupidity. What is particularly damaging is the fact that this illegitimate ball tampering detracts from the skill of the bowlers and the fact that most of the time Pakistani bowlers work extremely hard on the ball to legitimately employ reverse swing.

MATCH-FIXING

Much more damaging than ball tampering, drug abuse and player indiscipline was the rise, in the 1980s, of match-fixing in cricket. For instance, the off-shore matches between India and Pakistan in Sharjah were often regarded as 'fixed'. When touring South Africa, members of the Pakistan team – Rashid Latif and Basit Ali – accused their colleagues of fixing matches and walked out of the touring party. In the 1999 World Cup, Pakistan's surprising defeat at the hands of Bangladesh was generally regarded as a fix, especially as Pakistan had already qualified for the semi-finals. Of course, Pakistan was not the only country tainted by the scourge of match-fixing. In India, Mohammad Azharuddin, Manoj Prabharkar and Ajay Jadeja were tarred by this brush. Hansie Cronje, the South African captain, admitted to a fix against England. Shane Warne and Mark Waugh admitted to betting on cricket matches, and players from the West Indies, Sri Lanka and New Zealand were suspected of having links with the betting mafia that operated mainly from India, UAE and Pakistan.

In this sensationalist background, Pakistan appointed a high court judge, Malik Qayyum, to investigate allegations of match-fixing. Justice Qayyum scrutinized evidence and interviewed a large number of players and officials. He even summoned Warne and Waugh from Australia to provide evidence in his inquiry. As a result of Justice Qayyum's high-profile inquiry, one player, the then Pakistan captain Salim Malik, was found guilty of match-fixing and banned for life. Another player, Ata-ur-Rehman, was also found guilty of perjury. A number of other players were found to be suspect but no firm evidence of match-fixing could be placed at their door. These suspect players were fined and certain strictures placed against their names. Included in that list were Wasim Akram, Waqar Younis, Inzamam-ul-Haq, Ijaz Ahmed, Mushtaq Ahmed and Saeed Anwar.

On the international stage there was concern over the match-fixing scandals that had come to a head after the Hansie Cronje confession. Accordingly, the ICC took serious note and appointed an anti-corruption unit (ACU) to control and stamp out this scourge from cricket. The ACU was headed by Lord Paul Condon, former head of the Metropolitan Police, who had a bevy of experienced police and security officers in his team. Within its limited remit the ACU acted efficiently and the betting mafia became wary of the long arm of the law. From then onwards it was going to be much more difficult to contact players as their telephones and mobile phones were monitored, and cooperation with local government and police had led to the mafia's phones, addresses and so on being given to the ACU's database. Personal contact with this mafia was also monitored.

Every year at the annual ICC conference in London, Lord Condon gave a briefing to ICC directors on the ACU's attempt to control match-fixing and other suspect practices. He also invited Board chairmen to have one-on-one meetings with him to discuss country-specific issues. I found these briefings and bilateral meetings to be highly informative. The basic thrust of Lord Condon's briefings was that the ACU had now got a grip on the match-fixing syndrome. He felt it was virtually impossible for a team – or most of a team – to fix the result of a match because of the scrutiny to which the players and the mafia had been subjected. Draconian punishments that national Boards and the ICC had implemented for match-fixers were another deterrent. Lord Condon stated that the betting mafia was still active and was always looking for different ways to penetrate the ACU's control on match-fixing. Their agents had, for instance, stopped making direct phone calls to target players. Instead, the mafia used indirect means like friends, agents or relatives of players, who would act as intermediaries. As match-fixing was now difficult, the mafia was concentrating on 'spot betting', which meant placing bets on, for instance, a player getting out below 25 runs or bowling a wide or no-ball on a particular ball of his over. Spot-fixing, as opposed to match-fixing, was a less dangerous business and of course involved much less money being placed on bets. Spot-fixing was, however, much more difficult to monitor and detect. Lord Condon felt that the ACU's effort, supported by ICC national Boards, had achieved significant success in controlling match-fixing. It was now focusing on eliminating the spot-fixing syndrome.

While I was manager of the Pakistan team during the 2003 World Cup, I was able to note the range and efficiency of the ACU's monitoring network. The first occasion was when Pakistan was playing a practice match against a local South African side. These warm-up matches were played under the same conditions as real World Cup matches that were to follow. After warming up, the players had gathered in the dressing room when six police cars with police sirens blaring screeched to a halt outside our dressing room, and a dozen police commandos with fire arms bristling took up positions around it. The players were unnerved and startled at this mini-siege of the dressing room by the police commandos, whose leader marched into the dressing room and sought out the manager. He told me: 'Sir you have an unauthorized person in your dressing room and we have come here to find and arrest him.' I looked aghast at the captain, coach and players, who were having their snacks before taking the field. They were equally nonplussed at the intrusion. We could find no interloper or unauthorized person in the dressing room. While the police commander began looking in bathrooms and so on, I realized that the unauthorized interloper was, in fact, our Muslim caterer who brought 'halal' food for our players twice a day. The local South African Muslim had become a regular visitor to the team dressing room and hotel, but had not received the security badge for entry into the dressing room. The ACU had detected his unauthorized presence and had scooped on our dressing room fearing a mafia intrusion. They withdrew as soon as I explained the presence of the innocent caterer.

The second example of ACU efficiency was again at the 2003 World Cup. We had just left Johannesburg for Kimberley where we were to play Holland. There I received a phone call from the head of the ACU unit stating that one of our players had received some suspect characters in his Johannesburg hotel room. One of these suspect characters was a rent collector, another had carried a gun with him when meeting our players and the third person was also of doubtful background. The ACU were therefore driving down to Kimberley to interview the suspect player. I arranged a discreet interview in a Kimberley hotel between our player and the ACU unit head. The player gave a full explanation of his meeting, stating that the 'rent collector' was the brother of a cricketing colleague who had made a social call and that he did not know the other two visitors. Two days later, the ACU unit head telephoned me to say that the player's explanation had been checked out and he had been cleared. This incident also indicated the efficiency with which the ACU monitored visitors, telephone calls and contacts between players and possible mafia connections.

On the negative side of the ACU's performance is the impression that in all these years it has focused its role on the victims of the betting syndrome – the players – without taking action on the betting mafia who are the basic perpetrators of the betting scandals. Perhaps it is beyond their legal remit to take action against these operators but if players are monitored so meticulously, the ACU could have put the perpetrators under a similar scan. For instance, the betting mafia's agents who gather at hotels, bars and other players' watering holes could be identified and even photographed and their mug shots circulated to the cricket boards or hotel security staff. Publicity could also be given to the betting mafia's method of operations and the centres from which they operate.

Secondly, the ACU appears to be too slow and cautious for effective action. It is known that the ACU has been monitoring dubious betting activity, as for instance the Pakistan–Australia Test at Sydney that took place in January 2010, but it took a newspaper – the *News of the World* (*NOTW*) – to unearth an alleged spot-fixing scandal during Pakistan's summer 2010 tour of England.

THE SPOT-FIXING SCANDAL

On 7 February 2011, the ICC adjudicating tribunal that had been assessing the spot-fixing accusations against three Pakistani players – Salman Butt, Mohammad Asif and Mohammad Amir – pronounced the players guilty, handing them ten-, seven- and five-year bans respectively. A day earlier the English Crown Prosecution Service that had separately investigated the scandal announced that the three players would be indicted for a criminal offence in March 2011.[3] Pakistan's cricket cauldron, that had been vigorously stirred, now boiled over into shame and ignominy.

The spot-fixing scandal came to light sensationally after a *NOTW* sting operation, which implicated the three players engaging in spot-fixing during the Lords Test between Pakistan and England. The sting operation was filmed by the newspaper's reporters,

Figure 11　The three Pakistani cricketers caught spot-fixing in a sting operation
— left to right: Mohammad Amir, Salman Butt and Mohammad Asif. They were
found guilty in a British criminal court and sentenced to prison.

with the three players and their ringmaster agent Mazhar Majeed
handling large sums of cash. The scandal was perhaps the most
sensational scar on cricket's reputation as a clean gentleman's game.
In a related incident, the team's wicketkeeper Zulqarnain Haider
had done a bunk from the team's hotel in Dubai and on arrival in
London announced that he and his family had been threatened
by the betting mafia, and that he would in due course spill the
beans on players engaging in spot-fixing. Haider has since first
unsuccessfully sought political asylum in the UK and then decided
to return home to Pakistan.

In another bizarre incident around the same time, the Pakistan team lost the Hong Kong Sixes final when captain Shoaib Malik brought on the irregular bowler Imran Nazir to bowl the last over when the opposition required 48 runs to win – seemingly an impossible task. Imran Nazir proceeded to bowl five wides and conceded five sixes for the opposition to progress into the final. If any event was fraught with match-fixing, the Hong Kong Sixes presented an ideal example. Why did Shoaib Malik bring on a non-bowler for the last over? Why did the bowler concede wides and sixes for the impossible task to be fulfilled? Apart from Malik and Nazir, who else was involved in the bizarre climax? Why did the Pakistan Security Force not detain and question the two players on return from Hong Kong? What action has the ICC and PCB taken to investigate this manifestly doubtful result? Since then the PCB has not selected Shoaib Malik for the World Cup without giving a public explanation. Danish Kaneria, questioned but not charged by the Essex Police, has similarly been kept out of the Pakistan squad. Possibly, the ICC has indicated its doubts on the integrity of these players even though it does not have sufficient evidence to press charges. All these developments show Pakistan cricketers in a murky light.

The Pakistan public has received the news of the spot-fixing scandal with anger and indignation. The PCB has met its share of media criticism for allowing matters to slide towards shame and ignominy. Mazhar Majeed was obviously a shady character. He was not only the 'agent' of the three accused but of several other players in the team. He had a free run of the hotel where the team was staying, with licence to mix freely with players and officials. Why did the manager, the coach and above all, the accompanying security officer, not smell a rat when these spot-fixing deals were being concocted? The *NOTW* 'sting' caught the three players and Mazhar Majeed red-handed, but who were the other players compliant in the 'shyster's' operations?

THE ICC TRIBUNAL REPORT

The ICC Tribunal consisting of Michael Beloff, QC, Justice Albie Sachs and Justice Sharad Rao have made their report on the accused players available on the Internet. It makes compelling reading and was unearthed by the *NOTW*'s ace reporter who posed as a representative of an Indian betting syndicate. The report contains profound resonances that affect the corruption syndrome in Pakistan cricket. The report therefore deserves careful examination.

The early narrative of the report establishes that its conclusions relate to the three players' complicity in the Lords Test. 'Ringmaster' Mazhar Majeed (MM), though a central figure, is not one of the accused and his evidence is not cross-examined. It is clear that the players were complicit in attempts to spot-fix at the earlier Oval Test [18–21 August], but the Tribunal decided to focus on the accusations relating to the Lords Test [26–29 August] and dropped references to the Oval Test, probably because the Oval Test accusations were not so watertight in their evidence. It is also apparent that during the earlier West Indies tour by Pakistan, attempts by Mazhar Majeed to ensnare Salman Butt and other players had been made. The report describes how the *NOTW* reporter gradually gained the confidence of sceptical and hesitant Majeed from their first meeting at the London Hilton in Park Lane to subsequent meetings in restaurants and hotels. Majeed and the players naturally wanted to see the colour of the undercover fixer's money before they engaged in their nefarious activity. Gradually this confidence was gained. A few trial runs were agreed, with players' complicity being tested in return for relatively small sums of money. Then, the reporter delivered his main reassuring coup to Majeed by opening his briefcase and handing him £140,000 in cash. These notes were marked and were found later in Salman Butt and Mohammad Amir's rooms during a search by Scotland Yard (but not in Mohammad Asif's room). This operation was filmed in the *NOTW* sting operation.

Two vital juridical points are made early in the Tribunal's report. Firstly the players and their lawyers eventually accepted that the filmed 'sting' operation was genuine and the film with its detailed timing of no-balls had not been 'concocted' to suit the *NOTW*'s sensational story. Initially, the players had questioned the validity of the filmed sting, but after incontrovertible evidence of phone-call and text message timings, all the accused and their lawyers accepted that the sting film was genuine. In its own words the Tribunal stated:

> Para 37. The first and threshold question is whether the recordings were authentic or fabricated wholly or in part in particular were they made before those balls were bowled or after? If after, the ICC case dissolves, if before, it demands an explanation.

> Para 38. By the start of our hearing however, counsel for all players agreed that they (the recordings) were genuine. The threshold question accordingly falls away. Their provenance having been established the recordings constitute direct evidence of the conversations having taken place and what was said between the parties.[4]

This important point of evidence put paid to the conspiracy theories that stated that the ICC was out to 'get' Pakistan, that some of its members had conspired to show Pakistan in a poor light.

Secondly, the players' lawyers in their defence did not question the legal validity of the sting operation. This point is significant in that English courts considering criminal cases tend not to take into account evidence drawn from a 'sting' operation. The Tribunal states that the players' lawyers did not raise objection to the evidence from the sting. Nevertheless, the Tribunal stressed the importance of treating evidence in its stricter sense by only accepting assertions that were beyond 'reasonable doubt'.

The Tribunal's report pointed to several disturbing developments affecting betting and corruption in Pakistan cricket. In his evidence, Mazhar Majeed has referred to six Pakistan team players whom he claimed to be in his 'stable'. Who were the three other players that had not been brought before the Tribunal? Are they identified by the ICC and PCB and are they still playing for Pakistan? Mazhar Majeed was a regular visitor to the team hotel. Were not the officials aware of his shady background? What was the security officer's role? And who were the people that threatened Zulqarnain Haider? Were they connected with other team members? The spot-fixing syndrome appears to have stretched back to the West Indies, possibly even earlier.

Then there is the broader question of the central hub of the spot-fixing mafia, seemingly in India. While the players have been accused and found guilty, what measures are being taken to root-out the perpetrators of this evil from its source?

Finally, reading through the Tribunal's report, any reasonable person would accept that it is manifestly judicious and fair. The players and their lawyers have been given every opportunity to plead their defence and their pleas have been carefully examined. The laying out of incriminating evidence – timing of phone calls, text messages and so on – has been meticulous and compelling, leaving no doubt that the Tribunal's conclusions have been honest and every consideration that could have aggravated or mitigated the players' guilt has been carefully examined. For instance, the players showed no signs of remorse nor was there any attempt to 'come clean' on the issue. Salman Butt has been seen as the principal cog in organizing the fix. Mohammad Amir's youth and gullibility was recognized but placed against the basic tenets of justice. The following quote from the Tribunal's report summarizes their conclusions of the players' guilt:

[Para 221] The fact is that they did nothing to assist the ICC in helping to stamp out a blight that threatens to take the lustre out of the very game that has given them a generous income and extraordinary status and corroborated the fact that acting as a group, they added to that blight.[5]

As for Pakistan cricket's tarnished image over corruption and match-fixing, the Tribunal's judgment has left the Pandora's Box only half-open. There is much more to be investigated and set right. Are the PCB and ICC willing to take these essential steps?

Subsequently, in a criminal prosecution by the Metropolitan Police, a British Crown Court found all three players and their controller, Mazhar Majeed, guilty of fraudulent conduct. The court sentenced Salman Butt, Mohammad Asif and Mohammad Amir to prison sentences ranging from two years to six months. Amir had changed his plea before the ICC Tribunal from not guilty to guilty in the Crown Court.

After reading the Tribunal's report, our conclusion of the spot-fixing scandal is that the three players were guilty. But that is only the tip of the iceberg. Much more has to be done to clean the swamp. Secondly, we consider the three players to have been badly advised by their lawyers. A different approach involving showing regret and remorse, helping to uncover the betting mafia and questioning the legality of a sting operation as evidence would have led to lighter sentences, especially for the inexperienced village lad Mohammad Amir.

Immediately after Bob Woolmer's death, when all sorts of rumours regarding match-fixing being a motive were flying about, I made a statement that I was convinced that the Pakistan team was not involved in match-fixing and that if Woolmer had the slightest suspicion that his players were involved in this heinous activity, he would have shared his concerns with me. My conclusion was not only based on my close association with the team but from the knowledge that the ACU had achieved a firm grip in eliminating the spectre of match-fixing from cricket. From my briefings by the ACU, I added that as distinct from match-fixing the practice of spot betting had not been eliminated. It appears that it is the latter, spot-fixing, that has more recently raised its ugly head in the team.

All the issues that have so far been examined – from player

indiscipline to ball tampering and match-fixing – need careful analysis. The reason why a player gets involved in ball tampering or match-fixing have common features, but in the end it is a combination of factors that pushes individuals to indulge in the kinds of behaviour that we have looked at above. These are analysed in the next chapter.

CHAPTER 9

THE REASONS FOR PAKISTAN'S CONTROVERSIAL IMAGE

At the time of Bob Woolmer's tragic and controversial death – described later in Chapter 11 – a plethora of controversies was unleashed in the international press, with the British tabloids taking the lead in sensationalizing the forensic experts' initial verdict that Woolmer had died in suspicious circumstances. Had he been strangled? Had his drink been spiked with poison? These suspicions pointed primarily towards the Pakistan team itself. Had some religious bigots in or around the team gained access to his hotel room and punished the 'unbeliever' for leading the team to ignominy? Was Woolmer about to blow the whistle on a betting scandal resulting in the betting mafia or the guilty players silencing him? All these suspicions of criminal intent pointed the accusing finger towards the Pakistan players, and it was no surprise that the team was quarantined in a Jamaican hotel for weeks during which they were questioned and cross-questioned by the Jamaican police, confirming the tabloid impression that the players were the prime suspects. They were seen as capable of performing criminal acts that had led to Woolmer's controversial death. It was only after foreign experts had reviewed the evidence that the coroner decided that Woolmer had probably died through natural causes. The team was then allowed to return home.

No sporting team in the world carries the tag of criminal behaviour as was the case with the Pakistan players, who were seen to be capable of committing a criminal act – even murder. What are the reasons for this presumption of criminal behaviour? Or were there racial undertones to the media campaign against Pakistan, an upstart Muslim nation that aspired to reach the cricketing summit? Was it – as mentioned earlier – the aura of religiosity? Were there social and economic reasons for the players to be suspected of malice? Was the history of being associated with the betting mafia a reason for this suspicion? The reasons for the dark suspicions that swirled around Pakistan cricket need to be examined in greater detail. This chapter looks not only at issues such as education and poverty but also at wider socio-cultural and political influences that have moulded society in Pakistan.

THE EDUCATION GAP

A closer look at the player indiscipline record shows a series of petty on-field indiscretions usually borne of a domestic structure that sees ball tampering, scuffing the wicket, appealing hysterically and claiming catches as part of the game. Much of this has been promoted by the fact that many of the current players have not completed even a basic formal education before entering the cricketing arena. This means that they often have no idea of the traditions, history or rules of the game. Most of them leave schooling early and are drawn from the '*maidaan*' where they learn their cricket starting with tape ball and night cricket under street lamps, gravitating towards recognition by clubs and local associations. The more gifted players then graduate to first-class and national levels, where they find financial reward. Most of the first-class players that I came across were obviously from underprivileged backgrounds and were school dropouts. For them and their families cricket provided a rare opportunity to ensure a secure future – a decent house, a car or motorbike, a television set, jobs for themselves and family members. Moving up to first-class cricket meant security for the player and his family. For the few that achieved star status this meant public adulation, living in luxury with gleaming Mercedes or BMW cars and financial fulfilment. Some of these stars, like Shoaib Akhtar, achieved notoriety by indiscreet behaviour. Others found sudden riches, compared with their previous near-penury, emotionally difficult to handle.

Over the decades the education levels of the Pakistan team and its first-class cricketers have been falling compared to earlier teams, in which graduates, college students and matriculates would figure prominently. The current Pakistan team did not include a single graduate – until Misbah-ul-Haq arrived on the scene and was later appointed captain. The recent teams have included a few with school matriculation, but the majority (who may have attended school) were essentially dropouts.

In the decade of the 1970s, we saw in the raft of Pakistan players Oxford and Cambridge graduates like Javed Burki, Majid Khan and Imran Khan, Government College graduates like Ramiz Raja and Wasim Raja, Karachi graduates like Zaheer Abbas, Asif Iqbal, Haroon Rashid, and a large number of players who had their grounding in English county cricket like Javed Miandad (Sussex), Salim Malik (Essex), Sarfraz Nawaz (Northamptonshire), Wasim Akram (Lancashire), Waqar Younis (Surrey), Aqib Javed (Hampshire), Mushtaq Mohammad (Warwickshire), Sadiq Mohammad (Gloucestershire) and Mushtaq Ahmed (Sussex). These players had learnt the traditions of cricket, its social mores and conversational English in their long apprenticeships on the county circuit. Though some of them may not have completed a formal education, their cricketing personalities and learning process had been considerably enhanced by long experience of county cricket. Most of these players were also drawn from Karachi and Lahore but the process of expanding Pakistan's cricketing net was growing. Waqar Younis came from Burewala, a village in Punjab, Aqib Javed from Sheikhupura and Mushtaq Ahmed from Sahiwal.

This education gap has negatively impacted on the image of recent Pakistan teams. Its social conduct has been tellingly criticized by Ian Chappell, when he remarked that Pakistan was the only team the Australians could not engage with socially after a day's play. Lack of spoken English is of course a factor in this syndrome. Woe betide the winner of the man of the match award who strides over to the interviewer and pieces together in broken phrases rehearsed answers to questions. He usually ends up parroting phrases like 'definitely it was a team effort' or Inzamam's famous, perhaps apocryphal, reply to a question on how his unborn child was progressing. 'Praise be to Allah the benevolent and merciful', he replied, 'all credit goes to the boys'.

The cultural differences between a Pakistan team and most other sides have not been fully understood or appreciated. An essentially Muslim team like Pakistan (or Bangladesh) does not embrace the culture of a shared beer after close of play. Their players feel awkward in this culture, even though some players are not averse to imbibing alcohol. There is a greater need by the other nations to be sensitive to the different cultures of other teams.

Whereas other teams have successfully managed to use their cricketers as ambassadors, Pakistan have had more problems except in India, where language and culture are less of a barrier. Often the player's social etiquette is awkward. Intekhab Alam, in his manager's report of the 2010 Australia tour, stated that several players were not properly toilet-trained. This social awkwardness translates on to the field also, where Pakistan have had trouble striking up a rapport with players of the opposing team or with officials and umpires. Taken in conjunction with theatrical appealing, misuse and misunderstanding of the English language and a cultural disconnect, it explains why Pakistan players are seen as inward-looking outliers in the set of international teams.

In my experience as team manager I had to work hard on training players in their social behaviour. For instance, at receptions by Ambassadors or their hosts the players tended to gather together in a corner talking among themselves. I told them not to stand slouched with hands in pockets in some remote corner of the reception hall but to mix with the guests and circulate with the invitees. I told them that most guests wanted to meet Pakistani players and have a brief chat with them. I reminded them that they should not appear bored and on penance and to thank the hosts at the time of departure. My coaching worked briefly but I got the feeling that they would slip back into their old ways as soon as my back was turned!

Nevertheless, these were, in my view, peripheral matters that did not lead to fundamental flaws in the make-up of Pakistan teams. The national academy set up behavioural lectures for the national, 'A' and under-19 teams to attempt to educate our players, but these lectures merely scratched the surface of the problem. Their personalities had been moulded by deeper influences on their childhood and adolescence.

The cricketing arena, where the education gap left its mark more emphatically, showed the inability of these lesser-educated players to filter, absorb and implement the coaching and other experiences that had been conveyed to them by coaches, managers and so on. They were eager listeners but their ability to synthesize and rationalize was inhibited by not developing an educated mindset; for instance, our habitual inability to respond to cricketing crises in a steely, calm and mature manner like Collingwood, Dhoni, Hussey or Bevan, who were known for holding their nerve and surmounting crises by measured steely aggression. Pakistan players tend to go for glory by hitting out when nearing a difficult target, and inevitably perish. Not for them the sharp ones and twos that gradually take the team to its target. I consider the gap of education as the main reason for our lack of cricketing maturity in a crisis and the inability to think rationally to surmount a crisis.

Another domain where the education gap affects the Pakistan cricketer is the inability to grasp the complexity of cricket's labyrinth and detailed rules. The prime example was during the Oval Test, when Inzamam failed to grasp the impact of Darrell Hair's rulings and forfeited the match. The inability to think through the disastrous repercussions for Pakistan when Inzamam adamantly refused to play the succeeding ODIs – supported by his gang of 'four': Yousuf, Razzaq, Afridi and Waqar – was another example of this education gap. Emotion and a false sense of pride overshadowed the need for rational thought. Contrast this attitude with Sri Lankan captain Arjuna Ranatunga keeping one foot in the playing area while he took his team off the field after the same Darrell Hair had no-balled Muralitharan for throwing. Ranatunga had protested but he was not going to be penalized for forfeiture!

The intelligentsia in Pakistan often criticizes the team's lack of education as the principal cause for its downfall. As recently as the return from the ill-fated 2010 England tour, the coach Waqar Younis mentioned that better education would help the team overcome its multiple problems. I do not fully agree. I feel the education gap has been overstated as the reason for Pakistan's woes – cricketing, social or worse. The gap definitely affects social behaviour patterns, it may also affect cricketing issues, but I feel that when it comes to hardcore problems like betting, corruption, cheating, financial greed and other such critical issues, lack of education is a marginal issue. The more educated players have been just as culpable. There are other influences at work that are much more complex, particularly when the issues of match-fixing and spot-fixing are analysed.

THE POVERTY TRAP

About 400 players a year play first-class cricket in Pakistan. Far too many. As we have seen from earlier chapters, these first-class players no longer belong to the educated middle class but are from underprivileged homes with minimal education. There is no luxury of school coaching, proper umpires and scorers, and manicured grounds, as in Australian grade and junior cricket, English and South African schools, or even the superb schools' cricket system of Sri Lanka.

Cricket in Pakistan, as in the whole of the subcontinent, is a madness, an obsession especially for the youth. They play the game anywhere and everywhere in the open spaces and in the most unlikely arenas. My most memorable venue was when I visited the FATA (Federally Administered Tribal Areas) region in the North West Frontier Province (now called Khyber Pakhtunkhwa). In one of these fiercely independent regions, cricket is surprisingly more popular than anywhere else in the country. The region also abounds with immense talent. I was conducted to some local matches by the local hero, Riaz Afridi, who had distinguished himself in first-class cricket and had a Test match under his belt. Riaz Afridi took me to the 'ground' where he had learnt his cricket. This ground was in fact a large flat rock situated on a hilly plateau. The rock was surrounded by high mountain cliffs on all sides. Riaz Afridi told me that when his local village played a team from another village, Afridi tribesmen, with their long beards, turbans, traditional dress and rifles slung across their backs, would gather on the cliff sides and applaud the two teams. Usually about 4,000 spectators would witness these matches, enjoying the entertainment that they barely understood. The enthusiasm even in this 'fierce land' (currently the theatre of Army–Taliban battles) was amazing. It demonstrated the extent to which cricket had permeated the least privileged and remotest areas of Pakistan. It also showed the importance of cricket to a public that has precious little – of late – to keep up its spirits. The loss of international cricket to Pakistan will have ramifications beyond simply the arena of cricket.

In a country of 180 million, these 400 first-class cricketers feel they have reached the gates of Valhalla. The key to relative prosperity was in their hands. They could build a house and move away from their simple environment of cramped accommodation, no modern sanitation and hand-to-mouth existence. They could buy a motorbike, television set, a mobile phone and the basic accoutrements of a middle-class existence. For these 400 players perhaps the next vital step would be to represent Pakistan at the national level. This step would land the 20–30 players in the lap of luxury and should they become stars like Shoaib Akhtar, Mohammad Yousuf, Wasim Akram, Shahid Afridi, Inzamam and so on, there is no limit to the fame, money, the fast cars, the watches and the designer clothes that they would possess.

Of course the number of players who qualify for first-class cricket and higher leagues is an infinitesimal percentage of the millions of young people who hope that cricket would take them out of the misery and penury that surrounds them. They are desperate to succeed and would go to any lengths to make the grade. Sheer talent helps but is usually not enough, and a player looks for a helping hand to make him graduate to the next level and the next.

Some of these stars that make it to the next level are unable psychologically to handle the transition from near penury to luxury, bearing in mind also that many are young, under the age of 21, and have little or no education. Surprisingly, most of them remain level-headed and modest. Their main concern is to make as much money as possible while the sun shines. Into this mix enters the element of greed. Having lived through poverty and experienced the luxury of plenty, even the most humble and modest seeming player faces greed and insecurity. The motive for match-fixing and spot-betting comes into the frame. It is for this reason that stars like Wasim Akram, Inzamam, Waqar Younis, Ijaz Ahmed and Mushtaq Ahmed were hauled up and penalized by the Malik Qayyum commission. In the recent spot-fixing inquiries, Mohammad Asif is reported to have acquired several mansions in Lahore. Salman Butt is from a well-off, middle-class family and was educated at an English-medium school. Salman Butt was also questioned by Scotland Yard. So in matters of greed it is not necessarily the education gap or the rags-to-riches syndrome that motivates these players towards making a fast illegal buck.

CRICKET – A REFLECTION OF NATIONAL POLITICS, MORES AND SOCIETY

Cricket is not insulated from society itself. Unrestrained capitalism has driven the idea that 'greed is OK' the world over. In Pakistan itself, sections of society have made impressive financial gains over a short period of time whether in business, real estate, through the drug trade or political connections. These 'role models' drive the feeling of relative deprivation for others, including cricketers.

It is also probably a truism to state that a country's history, politics and character is reflected in its cricket team. India and Pakistan were one country prior to 1947. Now as three separate countries does their cricket reflect the different social, political and cultural influences that fashion a nation's character? Maybe partially, but there are other influences at work in this respect, notably the extraordinary role of a captain in cricket, which is far greater than in any other sport. Jardine's tenure during the bodyline series influenced national attitudes of two peoples, and not vice versa. Imran Khan's imprint on Pakistan cricket was spectacular and imperious but perhaps not typical of the Pakistan psyche. The same could be said of the influence of Frank Worrell and Clive Lloyd on the West Indies. Perhaps these stalwarts went against the grain of national character.

It can be argued, however, that a country's cricket would, in large measure, reflect its political, cultural and social environment. Taking Pakistan as an example, with its lack of focus on education, its political experience of dictatorial military rule for most of its 63-year-old history (as contrasted with neighbouring India's consistent democracy), its religious orientation as opposed to secular influences of India, Sri Lanka and Bangladesh, the degree of corruption that currently pervades its society and its ethnic mix is bound to find a certain reflection in its cricket. For instance, today, Pakistani teams are drawn from the *maidaan* experience and not as in the past from elite schools and universities. No wonder they are awkward at speaking English and interacting socially with Anglo-Saxon teams. On the other hand, despite the political tension and arch-rivalry, Indian and Pakistani players get on famously at a personal level. They speak a similar language, they appreciate the same songs, films, TV, pop stars, have similar taste in fashions, eat the same food and enjoy each other's earthy humour. Harbhajan Singh and Shoaib Akhtar are special favourites in each other's dressing rooms. There is no cultural clash between Pakistan and Indian teams.

Given the social, historical and cultural background reflecting itself in a nation's cricketer, it comes as no surprise that a religious tinge appears in a Pakistani cricketer's composition. Briefly it was excessive and damaging but, as expected, reverted to normal after a period of excessive fervour under Inzamam.

In general, Pakistan players do not read books – and with precious few books being published or translated in Urdu what options do they have? The traditions and folklore of cricket are not absorbed by reading about them but by picking up oral scraps provided by senior players. Is it any wonder that in a country where corruption, nepotism and fraudulent dealing is rife from top to bottom, where there is no accountability and even if you are caught someone is likely to get you off the hook through graft, Pakistan cricketers feel encouraged to take bribes, fix matches and generally behave in an undisciplined manner? The fact that they come from poor families is beside the point, irrelevant. They know as national players that even if they are not superstars they will make enough for themselves and their families. It is the poor man that realizes that one large town house is not enough and he wants to have even larger town houses. This is the greed syndrome that is currently in vogue with politicians, bureaucrats, some crooked bankers and the private sector. They are all out to make a fast buck while the sun shines. Hardly anyone pays taxes, a fair number of parliamentarians have lied under oath about being graduates and when discovered showed no remorse – simply a stratagem that did not work! Too bad, try again by another route! Cheating is acceptable, so long as you do not get caught. And even if you are caught, some godfather will come and save you.

Eminent sports psychoanalysts like Mike Brearley, Rudi Webster, Maqbool Babri and Dr Sandy Gordon have expressed their views on the impulses that have led sportsmen on the threshold of fame to risk their careers through corruption and betting. For these psychoanalysts greed is too simplistic an explanation for errant behaviour. Brearley refers to the 'doomed fatality' of the first step for a sportsman when he gives even casual assistance on the wrong side. Once in, it is very hard to get out. Dr Sandy Gordon, a well-known Australian sports psychologist, has referred to 'derailers' that have induced great athletes like Mike Tyson, George Best, Diego Maradona or Tiger Woods to stray into gambling, drugs and violence against women. Gordon states it is about 'character meeting opportunity'.[3] Temptations come in many disguises. What stays constant is the powerful lure. Gordon states that individuals overestimate themselves and their ability to get away with ill-advised risks.

Dr Maqbool Babri, the Pakistani sports psychologist who worked with the Pakistan cricket team before their 2009 ICC World Cup T20 win, believes a team develops a micro-culture that kicks in one way or another. Babri feels that a team needs role models who could be the captain, coach or a senior star. Their role is of an adult figure among a group of ambitious, highly strung young players. Obviously, after Imran, such a figure was not present with the Pakistani team. In fact, it was quite the contrary.

It is apparent that Pakistan – in its cricket and more widely, in the national arena – has thrown up few mentors and its more recent heroes have been deeply flawed. Pakistan's demographic structure – a large and young population – will throw up talented young people, and without responsible leadership or mentoring, this group of young people almost always end up behaving badly – rock stars, film stars and the like are prime examples. Keep in mind also that according to psychologists the pre-frontal cortex (PFC) of the brain, an area that deals with planning, forethought, motivation, impulse control and the modulation of emotions, is also not fully developed until the youth reach their mid-20s. Professional sport has strong visible and invisible institutions for mentoring, but despite that sportsmen have often been those who have been hauled up for misconduct – Mike Tyson, George Best, Diego Maradona and Tiger Woods are only a few examples.

Maqbool Babri has been quoted in an article by Sharda Ugra as saying 'that teams need role models within their own structures. It could be a senior figure – the coach, say, whose role is not merely that of a technical instructor but also a counsellor and psychotherapist who players can go and talk to without fear'. The coach's role is that of the adult figure among a group of young, ambitious, highly strung men on a high wire of ambition and expectation.[1]

In Pakistan the mentoring function has almost evaporated and this omission is made more acute by the minimal impact of education. The exception was Imran Khan, who moulded a team of young players and infused them with discipline and a competitive self-belief. Woe betide the player who stepped out of line with Imran. Such was the force of his personality that team colleagues and often the opposition remained in awe of him. Since Imran retired Pakistan has had 16 captains – Australia have had four, England eight and India six[2] – and none has played the role of mentor to a young team. Wasim Akram and Waqar Younis, Imran's heirs, were said to discourage young fast bowlers in the team. No effort was made to groom them. To some extent the combination of Inzamam and Bob Woolmer filled the mentoring gap, but even here Inzamam used his religious morality to hold sway over the team, mistaking piety for morality. It means the tough job of maturing morality is taken lightly, as though almost mechanically done. Moreover, despite his seniority and position in the team, even Inzamam felt insecure – often blocking entry into the team of promising middle-order batsmen. In contrast to Pakistan, Anil Kumble recently stated what important roles senior players have played in the Indian team. He mentioned his own role along with that of Srinath, Dravid, Laxman, Ganguly and Tendulkar – all highly respected, educated senior members of the team who ensured that the younger members of the team matured and followed their example. Pakistan, in contrast, have recently included in their team management Waqar Younis and Ijaz Ahmed, both players who were prominently mentioned in the Qayyum report.

Maybe the most destructive recent impact of the lack of positive mentoring appears to be the example of Mohammad Amir, the young fast bowler at the centre of the spot-fixing scandal. Did his captain order him to overstep the line? Was his senior partner Mohammad Asif a contributing influence? Amir comes from a desperately poor background, but his meteoric rise has seen him move from a small town in Punjab to owning a town house in an expensive area of Lahore. Asif, of course, has been on the scene much longer but has been no stranger to controversy. In Amir's case the combined influences of poor mentorship, lack of education, a rags-to-riches rise and a corrupt and criminal environment have jeopardized the career of one of cricket's most exciting prospects.

Inzamam did stamp his authority on the team. On assuming the captaincy, he seriously set about arresting the trend of indiscipline, bringing to bear his seniority and dignity on the players. He sought unity in the team, and as a highly respected elder, emphasized the importance of avoiding incidents on the field that could spiral out of control, of reducing sledging and ensuring correct behaviour on and off the field. In addition, Inzamam inculcated respect for religion and encouraged players to pray together, avoid the bright lights and maintain curfews. Inzamam, assisted by Bob Woolmer, was largely successful in this endeavour, particularly during the India and England home series that had previously been noted for player angst and a tradition of antipathy between the teams. It is highly unlikely that match-fixing or even spot-fixing would have been possible during Inzamam and Woolmer's reign.

I could not help feeling that Inzamam discouraged the induction of players with educated, middle-class backgrounds like Bazid Khan, Misbah-ul-Haq or Hassan Raza. Often they were discounted with labels like 'poor fielder', 'too old' or 'scared of quick bowling'. Inzamam preferred players who were prepared to conform.

Regrettably, corruption, graft, nepotism and political dealing permeate every layer of society in Pakistan; it starts at the top and goes to the lowest levels. Of course there are exceptions like the Motorway Police and the Supreme Court that are recognized as bastions of integrity, but these are exceptions to the rule. Moreover, Pakistan's poor image overall appears to have disproportionately sullied its on-field image.

Pakistan's negative image is a powerful factor in influencing how people view its cricket team. Simultaneously, the trigger images of the 'world's most dangerous place', the hub of Islamic terrorist activity, a volatile, intolerant, illiterate, corrupt and hostile country that increasingly seems to want to disengage with the global community, prevail across the globe.

The role of poverty and education appears to be important but has been overemphasized, particularly if other important factors are kept in mind in the overall environment. Rudi Webster, a renowned sports psychologist and former cricketer, who worked on performance enhancement in Australia and with many of that country's best athletes and sports teams, wrote in an article:

> A player's behaviour is an interaction between him and the environment. The conduct of players found guilty of wrongdoing should therefore be judged not just in the context of their own environment but also in that of broader society.[4]

Webster's article also argues that a recent set of experiments in the Harvard Business School showed that even the brightest and most privileged American students would cheat if they were given the opportunity, and once tempted to cheat, the students did not seem to worry about the risk of being caught.

This appears to bear out the facts that have been discussed thus far. Neither low levels of education nor poor economic backgrounds by themselves should be a defining factor of why individuals are tempted to cheat. But when taken with a wider environment of graft, lack of mentorship, corruption and non-accountability, education levels and poverty can combine to have a decisive role. This will be all the more important in those areas that are seen as petty offences – including ball tampering, player indiscipline, drug abuse and even spot-fixing. These are, for individuals, far easier to 'rationalize', usually through recourse to explanations such as 'everyone does it, we did it for the team, or even we deserve better pay as everyone else earns more than us'. The last issue has been compounded recently with Indian cricketers earning so much more than their Pakistani counterparts and because Pakistani cricketers have for two years been barred from the earning frenzy of the IPL.

Match- and spot-fixing, however, are qualitatively different offences – ones that involved criminal elements and behaviour. Moreover, those that enter this murky world find it very difficult to extricate themselves. Spot-fixing appears to be the start of that slippery slope that can end with players finding themselves in this criminal quagmire with no way to free themselves.

Cricket is thus a reflection of this environment. No wonder Pakistan languishes at the bottom of the ladder in the corruption syndrome. The most recent example of this was the PCB's inquiry into the conduct of players accused of match-fixing, indiscipline and player power, after the disastrous tour of Australia. Seven of these players were found guilty and penalized. Nearly all of them were let off through political graft and reinstated, obviously for the sake of future performance. The moral of the story was that you may be caught and penalized but you can get off scot-free by pulling strings! The PCB must be held responsible for promoting an environment where accountability has been reduced to a farce as in the case of the country at large. The Qayyum report – at

30,000 words – is a substantial and important document. Ignoring the report has allowed those tainted by match-fixing to take on positions of influence. The exceptions have been Salim Malik and Wasim Akram. Similarly, Mohammad Asif and Shoaib Akhtar's doping bans were overturned. In another instance that was related to me, former Test captain Aamer Sohail, then captaining his departmental team Allied Bank, accused the opposing bowlers of tampering with the ball. Instead of corrective action being taken Sohail found himself banned by the PCB for an international series. These incidents clearly show that accountability counts for little.

A further contributing factor is Pakistan's obsession with conspiracy theories. Generally, conspiracy theories are those that inhabit the fringes of a discourse. In Pakistan, aided by the media and a largely illiterate population, the conspiracy theory has come to inhabit the centre of political discourse. As a result, the suicide bombings that take such a heavy toll on society are the work of America or India or Israel, sometimes all three! The attack on the Sri Lankan cricket team in Lahore was immediately said to involve the ubiquitous foreign hand. Even wicketkeeper Zulqarnain Haider's sudden and recent disappearance from the team hotel in Dubai and subsequent defection to London was said to be the result of foreign influences out to destroy Pakistan cricket. Zulqarnain Haider's recent defection reflects yet another controversial element of Pakistan cricket. The actual reasons for Haider's slinking away from the team hotel will probably unravel in time, but his stated reason was that he was threatened by the betting mafia and feared for his life.

Most other cricketing issues have followed this pattern. Ball tampering, poor umpiring, allegations of match- and spot-fixing have all been seen as a massive conspiracy against Pakistan cricket. This viewpoint is deeply ingrained and spouted as an explanation by both the self-employed fruit seller to the English-speaking banker. What this siege mentality has led to is a complete lack of self-reflection and the inability to put in place remedial measures.

226

Moreover, the constant recourse to conspiracy theories weakens Pakistan's case where genuine injustice has taken place.

It was not always the case that Pakistan and Pakistani cricket held such a reputation. In the early decades of its existence, Pakistan was the unexpected success of the region – a country that made remarkable economic progress in the 1960s and had friendly ties with the West as well as with China and the Islamic world. In the 1970s and 1980s Pakistan saw a continued if artificial prosperity as the United States pumped aid in an effort to drive the Soviet forces from Afghanistan. For cricket, Zia's decade was also somewhat atypical because of the influence of Imran Khan. The 1970s and 1980s were a honeymoon period for Pakistan and its relations with the West. A staunch ally against the Soviets, Pakistan was a safe and welcoming destination and had a cricket team with the glamour of Imran Khan, Zaheer Abbas, Majid Khan and Asif Iqbal. But from the 1990s a decline had set in in the country's fortunes. For a while cricket remained one of the increasingly rare bright spots, but in time the malaise in the country infected Pakistan's cricket. In some ways the fall of Pakistan cricket has been mirrored by the rise of India as a cricketing superpower – economically and in cricketing terms. Gone are the days of Indian teams collapsing mentally even before Pakistan stepped on to the field. Now the insecurities and fragility are on the other side.

So if the whole country is steeped in corruption, graft and the get-rich-quick syndrome, why should cricketers be excluded? Many in Pakistan have complained about cricketers hauled up for controversies and the recent spot-fixing scandal has seen an outpouring of scorn on the three accused players. But what is rarely noted or admitted is that while it is often stated that the accused have tarnished Pakistan's image, the reality is that it is society that has failed these players not the players who have failed society. Essentially, it is a reflection of the lack of morality and principle that is the norm in Pakistan's social and political environment. Every layer of society is involved. Make a fast buck while the going is good. Principles, moral issues, possible disgrace and public opprobrium are relegated to the back seat and the feeling is that even these can be managed usually by pulling political strings! Moreover, however dysfunctional Pakistan may be, its image is even worse. Perceptions are reality.

But cricket in Pakistan has suffered a brutal blow and in effect the chickens have come home to roost. The spot-fixing scandal has highlighted all that has gone wrong in society and reflected it in a cricketing debacle. Mohammad Asif and Mohammad Amir, two supremely talented cricketers, who rose from humble backgrounds to become amongst cricket's most compelling performers, are banned from the game, their reputation tarnished forever. Asif, the repeat offender, has already survived a drug ban and other infringements. Amir, tellingly, is unable to comprehend what he did wrong or the magnitude of the deception involved. And the third banned and disgraced cricketer, Salman Butt, the young captain from a middle-class, educated family, who represented for the nation a modern image of an erudite, well-spoken and articulate leader, who promised to forge a young team together, and who had already managed to win Test matches against Australia and England in his short stint in charge. A leader who could be the modern representative of this proud cricketing nation. Pakistan wanted that. Pakistan needed that. Instead, he presided over and was instrumental in the spot-fixing scandal that has damaged the reputation of Pakistan cricket so severely.

CHAPTER 10

2006 – THE FATEFUL YEAR

INDIA TOUR OF PAKISTAN, JANUARY–FEBRUARY 2006

Returning now to the cricketing narrative, the year 2005 had ended on a high note. Pakistan were ready to enter the last year before the World Cup on a rising graph of performance, stability and continuity in the team and its management, and relative cohesion. However, 2006 was to prove a fateful year that led to my resignation being accepted three months before my term ended. The year ended with Woolmer's tragic death.

In early 2006 India's second tour of Pakistan was eagerly awaited on both sides of the border. The two earlier series had been contested with immense enthusiasm, both teams playing the game in the best spirit watched by sporting crowds with no trace of animosity. The 2004 India–Pakistan series was acclaimed as the 'friendship series' after the luminous public relations glow that it generated.

For the 2006 series I had directed the chief curator to prepare true, bouncy pitches that would produce lively cricket. Unfortunately, the weather in the preceding winter months had been unusually cold and rainy so that the pitches could not be baked in the sun. I had been assured by the chief curator that we did not, as last time, require the services of Andy Atkinson, as he felt confident that our ground staff could produce the desired results. Regrettably, this claim failed to materialize, except for the Test in Karachi.

In the PCB we were better prepared to organize the series so that accommodation, visas, security, media reception, tickets and hospitality were well in hand before the tour began. There were no major glitches before the tour even though the BCCI – under its new administration – raised objections to playing in Karachi, but we referred them to the Indian manager's public announcement after the 2004 visit to Karachi that next time India would play a Test in Karachi. Thanks to Sharad Pawar and Raj Singh Dungarpur's support, the BCCI relented and agreed to play a Test and an ODI in Karachi. This time the Test series preceded the ODIs.

Test Series

The first two Tests were dull matches played on lifeless pitches providing no help to the bowlers, fast or slow. Only eight wickets fell in five days of cricket at Lahore. Faisalabad was as bad with centuries flowing from the batsmen of both teams.

I was extremely annoyed with the chief curator and the curators of the Lahore and Faisalabad stadiums for not heeding my orders of preparing fast, bouncy wickets. Their excuse was that the inclement weather had prevented them doing so. I wished I had asked Andy Atkinson to come out again but my cricketing advisers, the Director of Cricketing Operations and the chief curator, had advised me against it. I then appointed Hanif Mohammad, who was known in cricketing circles as the finest expert on pitches, to help reverse the trend for the last Test in Karachi.

For the Third Test, in contrast to the two earlier matches, Karachi provided an excellent pitch on which grass had been left to produce a positive result. In fact, the Karachi Test provided an extraordinary turn-around with Pakistan emerging winners after being six wickets down for 39 runs in the first innings. Winning the toss, India inserted Pakistan and in a sensational start reaped immediate reward for their decision. In his first over, Irfan Pathan achieved a hat-trick and had Salman Butt, Younus Khan and Mohammad Yousuf back in the pavilion. Pathan had taken three wickets for no runs. Imran Farhat, Faisal Iqbal and Shahid Afridi soon joined the trio with the match virtually written off. Then Kamran Akmal and Razzaq, the heroes of Mohali, engaged in another rearguard stand, and with the help of Shoaib Akhtar reached a respectable total of 245. In India's first innings Mohammad Asif, Pakistan's new find as an opening bowler, blasted out the opening batsmen, with the spinners completing the job by bowling India out for 238. In their second innings, all seven Pakistani batsmen made more than 50, with Faisal Iqbal outstanding in making his maiden Test century. Yousuf and Razzaq made 90s before Pakistan declared at 599 for 7. India then subsided to the Pakistan bowlers with Asif again prominently announcing himself as a leading find.

Pakistan's series win against India provided a boost to national morale and of course to our cricketers. There were better crowds for the Test matches, strongly supported by students, who were given special facilities such as buses and packed lunches.

ODI Series

In the ODI series, that India surprisingly won 4–1, India recovered some of its prestige. At Peshawar, the only ODI that Pakistan won, a bizarre incident took place, which led to Inzamam's dismissal for obstructing the field.

An Indian fielder, noting Inzamam straying from the crease, hurled the ball at the wicket. Inzamam, who had in the England series been given run out when avoiding such a throw, this time hit the throw with his bat, and was rightly given out for obstruction. Inzamam was both furious and confused by the decision and made the highly comic comment: 'I am given out against England when avoiding a throw aimed at me. This time I hit the ball when the throw is again aimed at me, I am still given out. I don't get it!' Anyway, since Pakistan won the match there were no further repercussions of the incident that has since passed into cricket folklore.

The friendship series was another cricketing public relations success without the tension and hype associated with the 2004

Figure 12   On-field camaraderie – Inzamam and Anil Kumble walk back arm in arm at the close of play after a brief spat on the field – Lahore Test, April 2004.

Figure 13   President Bush asks Inzamam and Salman Butt: 'When can a team change the new ball?'

contest. There was not a single incident on or off the field. Typical of the spirit between the two teams was when Kumble flung the ball into the wicket narrowly missing Inzamam. The two players glared at each other and perhaps exchanged a few hot words. At the close of play Inzamam and Kumble walked back to the dressing room arm in arm.

Pakistan's series win in the Tests boosted its international standing in the ICC ranking to second. India's easy win in the ODI series was a compensating gain for them. Having defeated England and now India, Pakistan was riding the crest of a wave, full of confidence, unity and spirit.

PRESIDENT BUSH'S CRICKET NET IN ISLAMABAD ON 7 MARCH 2006

The fact that cricket is a vital element of Pakistan's ethos was recognized by a non-cricketing country – the USA – when it decided that as a public relations coup President Bush needed to be seen at a cricket photo-op during his official visit to Pakistan in March 2006.

On 7 March 2006, President George W. Bush arrived on an official visit to Islamabad. I am not a statistician and stand to be corrected but President Bush was probably the first US President to actually play cricket, albeit with a tennis ball! In 1959, President Eisenhower watched a Test match in Karachi, and George Washington once posed with a cricket bat, but I doubt if any American President has actually batted and bowled in a cricket net. It was, therefore, a momentous event in the long history of cricket when President George W. Bush engaged in a cricket experience in Islamabad, and as I was a personal witness, I feel that posterity demands that I record the proceedings in some detail. Long after the turgid minutiae of joint communiqués, nuclear non-events and compacts on terrorism have been buried in obscurity, President George W. Bush's historic step into the cricketing arena could shine like a beacon forever.

It all began three days before President Bush's official visit to Pakistan, with a telephone call from a US Embassy official in Islamabad enquiring if I could help organize a short introduction to cricket for President Bush during his visit. Could I also bring along a few national stars? For security reasons, the event would be organized on the Embassy lawns, where local schoolchildren would participate in a net session. I immediately checked with the Foreign Secretary who gave me the all-clear to cooperate with the Embassy. It was obvious that the cricket event had been scheduled at the 11th hour at the initiative of the Presidential entourage as a photo opportunity for the US President, who would be seen to engage in a sport that has a fanatical following in South Asia. I then asked Inzamam, Younus Khan and Salman Butt to accompany me to Islamabad as other national stars were engaged in the T20 finals in Karachi.

Two days before the visit, an American diplomat was killed in a terrorist attack in Karachi and I was asked, on 6 March, to put the cricket net on hold. Then at 4pm, the green light was given and we began our slightly hazardous journey to Islamabad on the day of an aggressive wheel jam strike called by the Opposition. We were to meet at the US Embassy at noon for a rehearsal and again at around 5 pm when the US President would attend the schoolboys' net. Inzi and Salman joined me from Lahore but Younus, travelling from the North West Frontier Province (now Khyber Pakhtunkhwa), was stopped by security at Attock Bridge and had to return home to Mardan.

A rather amusing rehearsal was held at noon on the Embassy lawns, where a young red-haired State Department official who did not have the first idea of cricket rehearsed our respective roles.

'You, Mr Commissioner,' as he addressed me, 'will stand here and brief the President for about three minutes on the laws of cricket.' 'The best I can do in three minutes,' I replied, 'is to summarize the differences and similarities between baseball and cricket.' 'OK, fine. Captain Inzamam will stand there with the students and you

Mr Commissioner will introduce him to the President. Salman Butt will stand there at the bottom of the net,' he explained to the three of us, adding bushy-tailed, 'aren't you guys excited?'

I remained impassive while Inzamam gave his famous vacant stare. Salman looked bemused. A few more instructions were conveyed to us by the State Department official on how the President would interact with the schoolboys while repeating his earlier comment: 'Aren't you guys excited?' A comment he repeated three times during the rehearsal to deadpan faces. He treated us like a bunch of English schoolgirls awaiting royalty.

After a five-hour wait during which the lawns, the schoolchildren and the three of us were thoroughly security-checked by metal detectors, sniffer dogs and various other gadgets, we were paraded to our appointed positions while the 20–25 schoolboys and a few girls began their net.

At 5:15 pm the Presidential media party lined themselves on the perimeter of the playing arena, somewhere between square leg and mid-wicket. It was a sign that the President was about to arrive. I then saw in the distance the Presidential group approaching the net like a swarm of bees. President George W. Bush was in trousers and a blue shirt with sleeves rolled up. Laura Bush, Condoleezza Rice, Ambassador Crocker and security personnel accompanied the President but stood back at the top of the slope. As often happens in carefully planned rehearsals, the President did not follow his cue, and instead of walking down the curved path where Inzi and I awaited him, he bounded straight down the grassy slope through the bushes and trees, leaving Inzi and I waiting at our appointed positions. Halfway down the slope, he came across the winsome headmistress of the Islamabad Model School and gave her a bear-hug from behind. Fearing that the breakdown in the rehearsal might lead to chaos, Inzi and I broke ranks and dashed over to the President, who was talking to the slightly bewildered headmistress.

I introduced myself to the President and began my three-minute

Figure 14 President Bush with students (boys and girls) of the Islamabad Model School after their net on the Embassy lawns. The US President batted and bowled with a tennis ball. The headmistress stands on the right.

introduction to cricket. I told the President that cricket's similarity with baseball was that in both sports 'the batter' struck the ball to collect runs, except that in cricket the batter ran up and down while in baseball he careered round a diamond-shaped quadrangle. In both sports, the batter could gain bonus runs by hitting the ball out of the field. In both sports the batter could be caught by a fieldsman and run-out if he did not reach base. The main difference from baseball was that the 'pitcher' threw the ball full toss at the batter, while in cricket he was not allowed to throw the ball but to bowl it. Unlike baseball, the bowler bounced the ball on the pitch on its way to the batter, hence the importance of the pace and texture of the pitch. Moreover, in cricket, play was possible behind the batsman, while in baseball, play could take place only in front of the batter.

Halfway through my three-minute introduction, the President bellowed to the gathered media: 'Listen, you guys, the

Commissioner is explaining to me the differences between baseball and cricket.' After my brief introduction, I introduced Inzamam as the national team captain, adding that he was one of the finest batsmen in the world. President Bush asked Inzi which was the best team in world cricket. 'Australia,' replied Inzi, 'but Pakistan is also a good team. We have recently defeated England and India.' I interjected that even Australian commentators felt that Pakistan posed the greatest threat to their supremacy. I added that cricket was a great unifying force in Pakistan as rich and poor, young and old were fanatical followers of the game. The recent series with India had led to a mega-burst of goodwill at the public level and had created a positive benchmark in political relations between the neighbouring countries.

President Bush, having listened attentively to our comments, then waded into the schoolchildren playing in the net. He engaged the youngsters in a warm and friendly banter that put them at ease as he sought their comments on how the game was played. Then the US President walked down to the wicket and after Salman Butt had given him a brief lesson on the correct stance, President Bush faced his first ball from a net bowler. We held our breath but the President struck the tennis ball with a straight bat, lofting it in the direction of mid-off to relieved applause from the schoolkids. The next ball was firmly struck in the direction of cover point but the third ball was a spinner that bounced high, striking the US President on the shoulder at which the bemused batsman asked, 'Was that a googly?' The President was obviously enjoying his batting stint and hit the next ball for a straight six. There was loud applause and a wide grin from President Bush. He played a few more balls and then moving to the bowlers' end, began bowling to Salman Butt. He was certainly 'bowling' the deliveries and most of them were straight on target, while a few landed in the side netting. The President's batting and bowling stint lasted about 15 minutes and President Bush thoroughly enjoyed himself in the net. He then had a long chat with the schoolchildren without interference from us or from security. He was extremely warm and gracious with the students and ended the cricket encounter by autographing each and every youngster's shirt with a felt pen.

President Bush then rejoined Inzi, Salman and me, and asked some pertinent questions, clearly indicating that he was a sportsman and an active baseball player. Looking at the new cricket ball in my hand, he asked, 'What happens when the shine goes off?' Inzi explained that the new ball swung readily in the air and was used by the faster swing bowlers. After the new ball lost it shine, the spin bowlers used the old ball more effectively. He asked: 'When do you change the new ball or do you play with one ball throughout the innings?' Inzi replied that a new ball was due after 80 overs. 'Does not the bowler get tired bowling for so long?' asked the President. I replied that it was the captain's decision when to rest a bowler and replace him with another. Slow, spin bowlers could bowl longer stints than the fast bowlers who used up more energy. Taking the new ball in his hand, President Bush enquired, 'Do you wear gloves when fielding?' Inzi replied that only the wicketkeeper wore gloves, the remaining players fielded barehanded. I asked Salman to open the palm of his hand and showing it to the President explained that through intensive fielding and catching practice, the palms had become hard. 'These players could catch cannon balls,' I added.

President Bush then enquired how long an innings lasted because it seemed that a batsman could play for as long as he liked. I told the President that the team captain needed to declare an innings closed so that he could 'bowl out' the opposing team in an attempt to win the match within the agreed time frame. President Bush then enquired if there was a World Championship and whether a US team participated. I replied that a World Cup was held every four years with the senior Test-playing countries participating alongside six qualifying associate members. The USA was an associate member but was not strong enough yet to qualify for the next World Cup, which was to be held in the West Indies early the following year. Given support from the government, the USA had the potential from its Caribbean, South Asian and Commonwealth residents to prepare a strong US team in the future.

So ended the 40-minute cricket encounter in which the US President had a net with the schoolchildren. One last gesture from President Bush showed his appreciation. Halfway back up the slope, he noticed the banner of the Islamabad Model School welcoming him. President Bush walked all the way down and autographed the banner before bidding farewell to the children.

PAKISTAN IN SRI LANKA, MARCH–APRIL 2006

The Test series win for Pakistan against India had been satisfying; only the 4–1 ODI series loss had taken the shine off Pakistan's success. Mohammad Asif had been the find of the recent series and Shoaib Malik had batted with discipline and composure. Pakistan's improved fielding, discipline and team spirit had seen it climb the international ratings to second (in Tests) and third (in ODIs). The Sri Lanka tour was to be the final test for Pakistan's strength especially as, at home, Sri Lanka were always redoubtable opponents. Inzamam had been appointed captain for the whole year and was virtually confirmed as the team leader for the World Cup. Shoaib Akhtar was not included in the squad as he had failed to pass fitness tests after a spate of injuries.

The Test Series

In the First Test at Colombo, Pakistan held out for a tense draw in a rain-affected match. Pakistan then went on to win the Second Test at Kandy, thanks to superb seam bowling by Asif and Razzaq. Pakistan thus notched up its second series win of 2006.

ODI Series

Pakistan went on to win the three-match one-day series 2–0 with the first match being washed out. So far, 2006 had seen Pakistan climb the international ladder. Even the guns of our traditional opponents were silent as we approached the series against England.

THE PAKISTAN TOUR OF ENGLAND, JUNE–SEPTEMBER 2006

Bob Woolmer considered the Pakistan tour of England to be crucial not only for team morale but because it was the last important series before the World Cup. All loose ends needed to be tied up, including the final squad, management and coach–player relations.

During the winter season, I had prevailed on the selectors to include Mushtaq Ahmed as assistant coach to Woolmer. Mushtaq had been the toast of English cricket because he had, almost single-handedly, won the county championship for Sussex and had taken over 100 wickets in the season. Mushtaq was a jolly, ebullient soul who was a born-again Muslim sporting a thick beard. My reasoning for including Mushtaq in the squad was primarily because Woolmer had come to appreciate his contribution to player management. He was a highly respected cricketer and had an excellent relationship with the players, especially with Inzamam. Bob Woolmer had great regard for Haroon Rashid, the former manager, because the players respected him and Haroon helped Woolmer organize the nets and cricket practices. In fact, Haroon Rashid acted as a bridge for Woolmer in bridging the cultural gap between the coach and the players.

After Haroon Rashid's tenure as manager had been terminated following the Australia tour, Bob had felt the need for a wise and mature cricketer to play this bridging role. Unfortunately, Haroon's successor as manager, Salim Altaf, had a poor, grating relationship with Bob, so the need of a wise moderator became all the more urgent. Mushtaq filled this vacuum perfectly and his presence among the players was of immense help to Woolmer.

My second reason for having Mushtaq around was that even

though he was in his mid-30s, his extraordinary success in the English county championship merited that he should be considered as a second spinner in the squad, not necessarily as a replacement for Kaneria but as a second top-grade spinner, in the mould of Shane Warne and Stuart MacGill, who sometimes played in tandem for Australia. Pakistan had not seen the emergence of a good second spinner since Saqlain Mushtaq's loss of form, with neither Shoaib Malik nor Arshad Khan assuming the role of a wicket-taking spinner. I accepted the view that Mushtaq would not be required for the World Cup but I considered winning Test matches equally important, for which Mushtaq's credentials could not be doubted.

My reasoning fell on deaf ears with the selectors, coach and captain. Contrary to media opinion, that saw Mushtaq's engagement influenced by Inzamam, his friend and Tableeghi companion, it was the conservative captain who was disinclined to include Mushtaq in the playing squad but was enthusiastic about his role as assistant manager and bowling coach. Inzamam maintained that including Mushtaq as a player would undermine Kaneria's confidence and would unnerve a key player. Inzi probably insisted on protecting Kaneria and was supported by Wasim Bari and Bob Woolmer, so Mushtaq was retained not as a player but as assistant manager/coach. As a matter of principle, I did not interfere in selection matters and did not press my point, though I still feel that Mushtaq's inclusion as an attacking bowler was justified.

Secondly, Waqar Younis was engaged as a bowling coach to the team, this time at the behest of Inzamam. Before appointing him I consulted Bob Woolmer, who was not enthusiastic but did not raise any objection, particularly if it helped smooth relations with Inzamam. Waqar was engaged on the clear understanding that he would train the faster bowlers in pre-series camps and would accompany the team for part of its foreign tours, in the mould of Troy Cooley, the Australian bowling coach hired by England, who rarely accompanied the England touring party. In the early period, Woolmer found Waqar's presence helpful as he assisted him in taking practice and supervised the bowlers efficiently. Later, misunderstandings developed between the two but not at a critical level.

Another issue was the appointment of a manager for the team. Salim Altaf had filled in this role after Haroon Rashid's termination, which meant that he was away for long periods from his appointed position as Director of Cricket Operations. Salim was keen to resume his official duties as Director of Cricket Operations and preferred to be released from the role of manager. In any case his stint as manager had not been an outstanding success with the players and especially with the coach. My first preference for the role of manager for the England tour was senior civil servant Shahid Rafi and alternatively, another secretary to government, Aslam Sanjrani. Signals from the Presidency indicated, however, that neither of these two senior civil servants would be spared so I turned to Majid Khan's brother – Asad Jehangir Khan – an Oxford Blue and senior police officer. He too declined. Meanwhile, Zaheer Abbas, the famous batsman and current columnist, was appointed manager for the Pakistan tour of Sri Lanka from which he emerged with credit, even though Inzamam seemed to doubt his capabilities in critical situations. Salim Altaf proposed Talat Ali, his former PIA colleague and Test opener, but I felt that Talat should first gain experience by managing an under-19 or 'A' team tour before his appointment as manager of the national squad. Eventually, the matter was debated in the ad hoc committee and though Salim Altaf pressed Talat Ali's credentials, the committee preferred Zaheer Abbas on the grounds of his cricketing fame, his affable personality and for being a member of the journalist community.

One last factor before proceeding on the tour of England was Bob Woolmer's proposal that he would, for a reasonable fee, seek the coaching skills of Alan Knott and John Snow – perhaps for a couple of days each – to give specialized coaching advice to our team before they started on the Tests. I agreed. Earlier in June, I had engaged Jonty Rhodes for a one-week fielding coaching work-out because, despite our recent success at home and in Sri Lanka, our fielding had not shown the desired improvement. Bob Woolmer did not agree with me and felt the overall standard of fielding by our team had been improving, but after discussing the issue with some Test cricketers, it was apparent that though improved, our fielding had reached a plateau.

Jonty Rhodes, a supremely committed man, arrived in Lahore in the intense heat of June for a week's coaching stint. He decided to divide coaching of the squad in groups of four, giving each group 90 minutes of intensive personalized coaching. From 10 am to dusk, I could see Jonty Rhodes from my window giving 150 per cent of his expertise to the players in the burning heat. While the groups practised, four at a time, in imbibing Jonty Rhodes's expertise, Jonty himself was out in the field all day with succeeding groups and returned every evening covered in dust and bathed in perspiration. I deeply admired Jonty's commitment and at the end of the day would ask the players if they had benefited from his coaching. They, especially the young ones like Salman Butt and Imran Farhat, reported that the fielding experience had been unique and highly rewarding. Alas, Inzamam had a cold and did not attend any of Jonty Rhodes's sessions. Yousuf and Razzaq were clearly laggards and Shoaib was still nursing an injury. I could not help feeling that the commitment of the seniors was not exemplary for the juniors.

Cricketing relations between Pakistan and England had turned the corner in the 2005 series. The recriminations of the past had been buried, and cricketing ties restored between Pakistani and English players and the public. Unlike the past, the British press adopted a sympathetic and friendly attitude towards the Pakistan team, reflecting the goodwill generated in the earlier series.

The first port of call for the Pakistan team was a visit to Glasgow to play a one-day match against Scotland. Unfortunately, the cold and sleety weather prevented practice, so the ODI against

Scotland was played in front of a sparse crowd, with frequent weather interruptions. The players were also grumpy because their hotel was uncomfortable and they could not wait to move down south to England. When they arrived in Kent, in contrast to Scotland, England was engulfed in a heatwave. Once again there were complaints about hotel conditions as players and their families found it difficult to sleep without air conditioning. Player-management relations deteriorated further when Inzamam refused to allow his team members to be routinely photographed by the tour sponsors, and raised objections to Knott and Snow providing coaching tips at practice that Woolmer had arranged and organized with his former colleagues. At Canterbury, Inzamam cancelled a practice session that Woolmer had organized and it was obvious that Inzamam was engaging in one of his periodic sulks with Woolmer. I sensed a rift between Woolmer and Inzamam with senior players supporting Inzamam. Player power was beginning to rear its head.

Strident religiosity was also affecting the performance of the players. Normally, Pakistan cricketers on tour are left to decide for themselves whether or not they say their prayers at the appointed time or not at all. In my two stints as manager I noted that players usually said their Friday prayers jointly. The more religiously inclined players would say their prayers regularly, sometimes jointly with others and sometimes on their own. After Inzamam's stewardship of the team, growing religiosity meant most players felt obliged to follow the captain's example by offering their prayers jointly and at the prescribed time. This meant that in an English summer, the morning (Fajr) prayer, which has to be performed before first light, meant getting up at around 3 am for the community prayer. Sleep was interrupted as the more religiously inclined cricketers woke up their colleagues around 3 am to prepare for the joint prayer. This meant loss of vital sleep and energy.

I had proceeded to London to attend the Annual ICC meeting and had decided to take my annual month's leave watching cricket.

This tension between the captain, coach and management was a source of concern to me, and I spoke to Bob Woolmer, Inzamam and Zaheer Abbas with a view to diffusing these minor issues that appeared to be due to miscommunication. Inzamam appeared intent on assuming total control of the team and I noted that the overt religiosity in the team had increased, with team members attending local Tableeghi sessions at mosques in London, Manchester and Leeds.

Test Series

Pakistan therefore approached the First Test at Lords slightly undercooked and they proceeded to drop six catches in England's first innings, four of them by the unfortunate Imran Farhat. Despite creditable bowling by Pakistan's seamers, their fielding lapses saw England build up a huge total of 528 with centuries from Collingwood, Bell and Cook.

Despite losing the usual early wickets, Pakistan responded with a total of 445, with Mohammad Yousuf making a sublime double century and Inzamam scoring his fifth consecutive Test half-century. In their second innings England scored 296–8 declared with Captain Strauss scoring a fine century. Pakistan saved the match comfortably with Inzamam making yet another 50 against England.

On a fast wicket at Old Trafford for the Second Test, Pakistan were blasted out for 119 by a fearsome spell of fast bowling by Harmison with only Younus Khan 44 resisting the onslaught. England went in and built up an impressive score of 461, Cook and Bell repeating their centuries at Lords and showing that the wicket was playing fast and true. In Pakistan's second innings Harmison intimidated the Pakistan batsman with sustained hostile bowling and had them all out for 222, giving England an innings victory. Some of the Pakistan batsmen were seen retreating to square leg in the face of Harmison's short-pitched fast bowling.

After Pakistan's pusillanimous performance at Old Trafford, I sensed that all was not well in the Pakistan camp. Woolmer was unhappy at the truculent attitude of the captain and the senior players. Zaheer Abbas was at loggerheads with both captain and coach, having lost control of discipline in the team. My suspicions were confirmed when for the county match against Northamptonshire two senior players – Yousuf and Afridi – were rested and two league players who were not part of the Pakistan squad included without consultation with the PCB, the selectors or me. Moreover, the players' families, who were supposed to have returned home after the Lords Test, were still accompanying the players, apparently with Inzamam's permission, and creating havoc in the hotels, where extra beds and cots for children had to be procured at short notice. The children were also out of control, keeping their parents and others awake by screaming and running around corridors until late at night. I sensed that discipline and cohesion were falling apart and that player power and overt religiosity were taking over. I was alarmed at these reports of player power and decided to motor up to Northampton, where I had sharp admonitory words with the captain and manager. I told them to pack off their families immediately and to concentrate on reviving Pakistan's performance on the remainder of the tour. Bob Woolmer was clearly unhappy at this attitude but resolved to put matters right in his usual persuasive manner.

For the Third Test at Leeds, Pakistan fielded yet another set of openers – Taufeeq Umar and Salman Butt – with the reliable Shahid Nazir coming in as the third seamer while Asif and Shoaib were still unavailable, recovering from their injuries. England batted first and thanks to three appalling errors by the umpires – two by Darrell Hair and one by Billy Doctrove – Pietersen and Bell were let off the hook and scored centuries. Even the British press acknowledged that they had been fortunate. Pakistan then responded creditably with Younus and Yousuf scoring over 150 each. Inzamam, who came in to huge cheers, was out in another bizarre manner, losing his balance and falling in a heap on his wicket. He seemed to resemble Oliver Hardy doing a comic turn in one of his films! Nevertheless, Pakistan took a narrow lead in the first innings, taming the threat from Harmison. In their second innings, England scored 345 thanks to a century by Strauss, but Pakistan collapsed spinelessly in their second innings to Sajid Mahmood and Monty Panesar, losing by 167 runs.

Kamran Akmal, who had been a sprightly and reliable wicketkeeper for Pakistan, began a progressive decline in his performance. He appeared to be wearing iron gloves as he dropped simple takes and missed catches and stumpings with regularity. His confidence was gone and his batting was affected. I mentioned his loss of form to Bob Woolmer, who admitted that it may have started from his remark at Canterbury that Kamran should concentrate on improving his wicketkeeping as Bob had informed the selectors that a reserve wicketkeeper, Zulqarnain Haider, was ready to join the team. Bob intended this remark to challenge Kamran into lifting his performance. Instead it unnerved him into a further loss of confidence. Bob admitted his error of judgement to me, which I considered to be an element of the culture gap, not realizing its effect on players who are generally insecure. Kamran's loss of form with bat and gloves affected team performance in England.

The infamous Fourth Test at the Oval is described in detail in the next chapter. Pakistan was playing for honour and had Asif back in the side. Hafeez was drafted in as opener for yet another opening pairing. Asif bowled superbly, supported by Umar Gul, so that England were all out for 173. For a change Pakistan were off to a great start, with Hafeez (95) and Imran scoring 90s and totalling 504. Mohammad Yousuf scored his third century of the series, receiving support from Faisal Iqbal. In their second innings, Pietersen and Cook made a spirited reply but were both out by lunch, leaving Pakistan in the driving seat to secure the match with a day and a half to go. Then came the ball-tampering saga which led to England being awarded the match because Pakistan had 'refused to play'.[1]

The ODI Series

In the first ODI at Cardiff, Asif and the now fit Shoaib Akhtar opened the bowling for Pakistan. Only Bell (88) stood in the breach and England were all out for 202. The threatening clouds then emptied themselves for two stoppages and play was abandoned before Pakistan, ahead on the DL system, could complete the minimum number of overs.

In the second ODI at Lords, Shoaib Akhtar and Asif pulverized the England batting, bowling them out for 166. Pakistan then comfortably made the runs, with Younus (55) and Yousuf (49 not out) ensuring a seven-wicket win.

For the third ODI at the Rose Bowl, England batted first again and this time built up a score of 271, Dalrymple (62), Collingwood (61), Strauss (50) and Bell (42) contributing to the total. Pakistan then chased successfully, with a century from Younus and steadfast support from Yousuf. Despite a late-order collapse, Inzamam stayed in like a rock and led Pakistan to victory by two wickets.

For the fourth ODI at Trent Bridge, Pakistan batted first and were 165 for eight when Razzaq, in a blistering knock off 75, saw them to a respectable total of 235. Strauss (78) and Bell (86) then led England to victory by eight wickets.

For the final ODI at Edgbaston, coming off the boil, Pakistan allowed England to square the series 2–2 by being bowled out for 154, only Younus 47 making a respectable score. England in turn made heavy weather of their task and were 118 for seven but Yardy and Mahmood saw them home.

The England tour of 2006 had led to deep acrimony as a result of the Oval Test fiasco. Though the Pakistan team's indignation towards the umpires and the ICC had been addressed, there was a negative fallout on Pakistan–England cricketing relations, particularly after Inzamam's reluctance to play the ODI series. Nevertheless, the British media remained relatively sympathetic and supportive towards Pakistan over this period.

During the England tour, player power had resulted in a breakdown in relations between management and players, as described in detail in the next chapter. Woolmer was distraught at the fraying relations between himself and the senior players. There was also a perceptible slide in the team's performance even though Mohammad Yousuf had achieved a record-breaking year by overtaking Vivian Richards's record of most runs in a calendar year. By the end of the year there were question marks regarding the performance of Abdul Razzaq, Kamran Akmal, the assorted openers, Shoaib Akhtar and Shoaib Malik. This decline did not augur well for the World Cup that was to follow six months later.

The overt religiosity issue was also getting out of hand, with strident criticism of the team's conduct from the Pakistan press and liberal public opinion. The fateful year of 2006 had begun. And now to the Oval Test fiasco.

CHAPTER 11

THE OVAL TEST AND ITS AFTERMATH

The Oval Test between England and Pakistan in 2006 was not simply a cricketing debacle. It unleashed demons of Pakistan's national psyche that had been lurking under a thin veneer of rationality. These demons consisted of a feeling that the whole world was ranged against Pakistan because it was a Muslim country and because it threatened Western supremacy! The ICC, the umpires and England were seen as part of this conspiracy to denigrate and restrain Pakistan. Conspiracy theories abounded in Pakistan – English coach Duncan Fletcher was reported to have told Match Referee Mike Procter about his suspicion of ball tampering by Pakistan players and Inzamam refused to believe that Ranjan Madugalle's delay in holding the inquiry was due to his sister's hospitalization. At the Oval, the demons of player power and indiscipline also emerged.

Examples of these attitudes abound. For instance, nearly every time there is a terrorist explosion in Pakistan, the administration in its knee-jerk reaction points an accusing finger to a 'foreign hand', meaning Indian intelligence. This helps to transfer the burden of preventing such terrorist attacks away from the police and anti-terrorist forces. The same knee-jerk accusation was made immediately after the attack on the Sri Lanka team in Lahore. Now, two years later, the anti-terrorist forces have proudly announced the arrest of home-based Lashkar-e-Tayyaba terrorists, including their mastermind, who attacked the Sri Lankan players! The foreign hand, so conveniently present, is associated with the West, especially the CIA, as well as India and Israel. The conspiracy theorists had a field day with the assassination of Osama bin Laden in Abbotabad. He was not dead – the CIA had drawn a blank and was covering up, said some. Bin Laden had been killed months earlier and was being 'preserved' for an appropriate announcement to boost Obama's electoral chances, believed others. ISI had tipped off the CIA about bin Laden's hideout and had looked the other way as they carried out their deadly raid. The subsequent furore was merely a cover-up!

All these demons have their roots in the political, historical and social mix in Pakistan: the quest for legitimacy and for parity with India, and the insecurity bred from the fact that before 1947 Pakistan did not exist on the map of the world. The break-up of Pakistan in 1971 into two countries – Pakistan and Bangladesh – gravely undermined Jinnah's 'two nation' theory that had seen the eventual acceptance of Pakistan. The undefined role of religion in Pakistan also added to the fear. Was Pakistan a theocratic Islamic state or was it a homeland for the Muslims of India? The West, India and the Jewish lobby are viewed by the Pakistani public as the principal opponents of the country. Every incident, every setback is ascribed to their pernicious role and no blame is placed on Pakistan's own failings and shortcomings. For instance, the separation of Pakistan into two countries in 1971 is seen as a conspiracy to destroy Pakistan by India, supported by the West and the Jewish lobby that influenced the world media. There is hardly any soul-searching that Bangladesh became independent because of Pakistan's own mistakes and shortcomings. The conspiracy theories prevail, consistently standing in the way of rational soul-searching and introspection.

At the Oval, Inzamam and his players saw the ICC as the epitome of the Western establishment. Woolmer, Zaheer Abbas, Dr Nasim Ashraf and I were seen as their apologists, while Malcolm Speed,

Mike Procter and all four umpires were regarded as instruments for Pakistan's attempted destruction. It is in assessing this broader perspective of the Oval Test fiasco that I have discussed the issues raised by it in considerable detail.

The infamous Oval Test will be recorded in the annals of cricket history as one of its most controversial events. I was an eyewitness to the unfolding drama almost throughout the event. Much of the behind-the-scenes negotiations have been recorded in the media but many issues relating to the controversy still remain under cover. In this chapter, I shall describe these events in detail so that an objective assessment can be made of the event.

As umpire Darrell Hair took centre stage in this drama, it is important to provide a background to his nomination to this Test match. For a period stretching almost three years before the Oval Test, the Pakistani players and management had been uncomfortable with Darrell Hair's attitude towards the team. They found Hair overbearing, condescending and downright rude. In 1995, Hair had been at the centre of the Muralitharan no-balling controversy, leading to a walkout by the Sri Lanka team in Australia. Hair had been accused of a personal bias and the ICC acted sensitively to the stand-off by not appointing Hair in a series involving Sri Lanka for eight years. Pakistan's reservation about Hair was, however, based on their own experience. Hair's brusque and admonitory attitude towards the players was complemented by a number of marginal decisions that were regarded by the players – and by Woolmer – to go against Pakistan. The end result was that Hair's appointment to Pakistan matches was unwelcome and viewed with apprehension. It needs to be stated that Pakistan had regularly supported the extension of neutral umpires even for ODIs and had never raised any doubts about the neutrality and competence of the ICC umpires panel with the exception of one – Darrell Hair.

According to ICC regulations no country has the right to object to or veto the appointment of an umpire. The only way it can convey its reservations about a particular umpire is in the captain/manager's post-match report given in writing after every international match. This did not preclude informal approaches to the ICC about a particular umpire. Normally the ICC was sensitive towards countries like Sri Lanka that had a known problem with a particular umpire, as was apparent by its not appointing Darrell Hair to a Sri Lanka series for eight years. Pakistan had willingly participated in international matches supervised by Indian umpire Venkataraghavan despite the known rivalry between the two countries. Similarly, India accepts Aleem Dar and Asad Rauf for its international matches.

Over the period when Darrell Hair's attitude towards the Pakistani team became more pronounced, I informally raised the issue of his future appointment to Pakistan matches with Malcolm Speed. His reply was usually terse and predictable: 'Shaharyar, Darrell Hair is acknowledged as a leading professional umpire. I know that he can be brusque at times but there is no doubting his competence and neutrality. In any case the ICC cannot accept countries selecting or vetoing umpires on the panel as otherwise it would lead to chaos.' Apart from indicating that we felt Hair had a 'problem' with Pakistan, I could not refute Speed's arguments.

My concern over the Hair issue became more acute when I found that he was being appointed regularly to umpire series involving Pakistan. In the period since I had taken over as Chairman, the ICC appointed Darrell Hair to the following series:

- The Champions Trophy 2004
- Pakistan–India 2005
- Pakistan–West Indies 2005
- Pakistan–England 2005
- Pakistan–England and Scotland 2006

This ICC attitude was the reverse of the sensitivity shown to Sri Lanka after the Hair–Muralitharan incident, and it appeared like punitive action against Pakistan for questioning an ICC umpire's

253

credentials. The ICC seemed bent on appointing Hair to Pakistan series as frequently as possible. The ICC defended itself from my informal remonstrations by stating it had to take into account financial considerations in appointing umpires to various series. It also defended itself of bias against Pakistan by demonstrating that two Pakistani umpires – Aleem Dar and Asad Rauf – were on the elite panel and that after Venkataraghavan's retirement, the Indians had none. However, while Darrell Hair was discreetly kept away from Sri Lankan matches for eight years, when it came to Pakistan, he was nominated in five series over two years! The Pakistan players and media perception was that the ICC, whose Chief Executive was also an Australian, did not heed the PCB's remonstrations. Would the ICC have been equally stubborn if India or Australia had been the complainants?

Questions have legitimately been raised as to why Pakistan's demarche against Darrell Hair's appointment had not been heeded by the ICC, particularly when contrasted with immediate ICC compliance when India objected to Steve Bucknor and Daryl Harper as also Hair's non-appointment after the Sri Lanka incident. Was it that the ICC gave Pakistan's request lighter weightage indicating absence of clout? Was it because of personalities at the helm of the ICC's hierarchy? Or was it that Pakistan's doubts were regarded as frivolous and lacking in objectivity?

In response to the first question, obviously Pakistan did not have India's political and financial clout. Secondly, Malcolm Speed had always been a stickler for upholding ICC rules and he believed that giving in to Pakistan's request could set a wrong precedent. An earlier administration responding to the Sri Lankan issue may have been more responsive and diplomatic in handling Sri Lankan sensitivities. These are the likely reasons for the ICC declining Pakistan's request, which, with hindsight, the ICC would rue later.

The critical point relating to Hair's nomination came during England's visit to Pakistan in 2005. Apart from several marginal decisions going against Pakistan, in the Lahore Test, Hair wrongly instructed that Inzamam was run out when he was avoiding a fielder's throw to the wicket. In the West Indies, Hair had banned Kaneria from bowling because of his following through on the middle of the wicket. He also admonished a startled Salman Butt for running on the pitch and deducted a run when Salman took a sharp single. A traumatized Salman Butt was out in the next over, obviously unnerved by Hair's punitive decision. At the end of the game, Woolmer was furious at Hair's attitude and brought me clips from his computer showing Kevin Pietersen frequently running in the middle of the pitch without any intervention from the umpires. During this Test, I again telephoned Malcolm Speed to repeat Pakistan's reservations due to Hair's attitude. I said that our apprehensions had been confirmed and that the PCB was prepared to convey these reservations in writing. Malcolm Speed advised me not to do so as it would evoke the usual rebuttal regarding a Board member not being allowed to exercise a veto against umpires. Instead, he advised sending a written comment in the post-match report at the conclusion of the Second Test, which was the correct procedure to follow. I informed Woolmer of my discussion with Speed. Bob and Inzamam duly sent a negative report on Hair's performance. According to ICC rules, a captain's negative comments were conveyed to the umpire for his response.

In the aftermath of the Oval crisis, Ehsan Mani, President of the ICC, made a statement indicating that the PCB had not shared its reservations about Hair's appointment with him, implying that had it done so he would have taken remedial steps. Normally, whenever I had issues of principle to raise with the ICC, I would discuss them informally with both Ehsan Mani and Malcolm Speed to seek their reaction and advice. On the Hair issue, I had deliberately avoided consulting Ehsan Mani because I had not wished to involve the Pakistani President of the ICC on a contentious issue that could embarrass him. Therefore, I spoke only to Malcolm Speed on the Hair issue. With hindsight my decision may have been an error of judgement as Ehsan Mani is a man of high integrity, and his informal counsel may have persuaded Malcolm Speed and the ICC's head of the umpiring panel to take a more sensitive line on the regular appointment of Hair to a Pakistan series.

Despite the written negative report and my informal reservations conveyed to the ICC, I was shocked and disturbed to note that Darrell Hair had again been appointed to the Scotland ODI and the England–Pakistan series, especially as he was by then aware of Pakistan's written complaint against him. In 2006 I had premonitions of further problems with Hair, borne out of his decisions in the Leeds Test and culminating in the Oval fiasco. There is no doubt in my mind that the ICC's lack of sensitivity to Pakistan's reservations towards Hair contributed to the crisis at the Oval.

Now to the Oval Test. I had decided to witness the Oval Test because, on the third day, the Surrey County Cricket Club and the PCB had decided to hold a function for the dedication of the Pakistan room located at the Oval's brand new stand opposite the Pavilion. Surrey County Cricket Club had developed an impressive new stand and had offered Pakistan a large room with a beautiful view of the ground that would reflect Pakistani cricketing history to those who occupied the room. The PCB had accepted the offer and with the help of High Commissioner Dr Maleeha Lodhi and overseas Pakistani stalwarts Sir Anwar Pervez and eight other Pakistani entrepreneurs, a sum of £450,000 was raised to formalize the dedication. India and Australia had already negotiated the dedication of large rooms at the new development. I had recommended to the Patron, President Pervez Musharraf, and to Prime Minister Shaukat Aziz, that they might schedule a tour of Europe at the time and take a day out to watch the Test and preside over the dedication. Both were enthusiastic but eventually developments at home prevented their being present at the Oval. The PCB had not spent a penny on raising funds for the dedication of the Pakistan Room, except in blowing up eight photographs of our cricketing icons ranging from Hafeez Kardar to Imran Khan and Hanif Mohammad to Wasim Akram. The PCB also provided some Pakistani furnishings to give the room a Pakistani ambience. I was particularly keen to seal the deal for the Pakistani Room as the Oval has a special place in Pakistan's cricketing history with the famous win in 1954, which confirmed Pakistan's status as a cricketing nation. The dedication function was a resounding success, with Sir John Major – former Prime Minister and a cricket lover himself – presiding over the well-attended function.

At the Oval Test, Pakistan was playing for honour, having lost the series with defeats at Old Trafford and Headingley. At least one of our injured spearheads, Mohammad Asif, was back in the team, while Shoaib Akhtar, though recovering, was not fit enough to make the team. Throughout the summer, the British press had been unusually sympathetic to the Pakistan team, with Inzamam emerging as a lovable, food-loving, idiosyncratic and immensely gifted player. The British public had been equally supportive, burying the acrimony that had tainted previous encounters between the two sides. Pakistan began well at the Oval by bowling England out for a low score with Asif making the initial inroads. Pakistan then built up a massive total and although England had made a spirited response to save the match, Pakistan was expected to win the Test. On the fateful fourth day, Pakistan had prised out the dangerous man, Pietersen, and the last two recognized batsmen Bell and Collingwood were batting when the drama began to unfold. The events recorded below in a log drawn from television images and confirmed in the adjudicators' judgment are, therefore, precise and beyond doubt.

ACT I

At 2:35 pm, sitting in the Oval Committee Room, I noticed the umpires changing the ball. I believed the ball had gone out of shape. Kaneria had been operating a long spell from the new stand end and with the ball 55 overs old, Darrell Hair consulted his colleague,

257

Billy Doctrove, and called for the third umpire, Trevor Jesty, to bring out a fresh set of balls. Hair had decided that the ball had been tampered with, and when Doctrove concurred, he signalled that Pakistan had been penalized five runs for ball tampering. I was sitting in the main stand and did not notice Hair's signal but Woolmer had. Hair was seen to be reluctant to show the 'damaged' ball to the captain, Inzamam, who was arguing with the umpires. He appeared to want to examine the ball but Hair turned his back on him and walked away. Jesty, who had taken possession of the ball, briefly showed it to Inzamam and walked off. Inzamam, who had also not noticed Hair's penalizing signal, appeared perplexed and angry.

A few minutes into the on-field commotion, Bob Woolmer walked up to me in the Committee Room and informed me that the Pakistan team was being accused of ball tampering. He said a huge crisis was looming and that we needed to take preventive steps. Woolmer added that he expected to be called in by the referee, Mike Procter, to be officially informed of the ball-tampering decision. I told Woolmer to register a formal protest with the referee.

At 2:40 pm Woolmer went to the referee's room and was informed of Hair's decision backed by Doctrove. He asked to examine the ball. Procter initially declined but later relented and showed him the ball. Woolmer found that the ball had the normal scuff marks that would be expected from a ball used for 55 overs. He saw no evidence of tampering. Play continued, with the Pakistan team dazed and confused. Woolmer, having studied the rules in Wisden and the ICC Manual, concluded that the umpires were the sole arbiters of ball tampering with no further recourse for appeal to the referee or the ICC. The umpires had therefore not only charged the Pakistan team of ball tampering but had unilaterally held them guilty.

At 3:47 pm, due to bad light, the umpires decided to suspend play and take early tea. The umpires then lodged their formal report on ball tampering with the referee. From TV replays, I realized that with Hair's signal, we had already been found guilty. Sensing a crisis, I proceeded to the team's dressing room. There, I found the team in a high state of indignation. Inzamam, who thought that he would have his say with the referee at the close of play, was informed that the die was cast and that he and his team stood accused and guilty of ball tampering. He insisted that as a protest his team would not go out and resume the match. His players were clearly in agreement with their leader. The team was convinced that no tampering had taken place, confirmed by Hair's refusal to show Inzamam the ball. The players were also convinced that Hair's action was part of his negative attitude towards the Pakistan team. Inzamam was mortified that the Pakistan team and the Pakistani nation were being branded as cheats, especially after he had succeeded in banishing former waywardness, as evident during the harmonious series with India and England. All Inzamam's efforts to develop a disciplined and sporting culture in the team for which he had worked so hard were being destroyed. Pakistan and its team's *izzat* (honour) were being sullied!

During the extended tea break, I addressed the gathered team in the dressing room for 20 minutes. I stated that I shared the team's anger and indignation. We had opposed Hair's appointment but the ICC had appointed him in five recent series featuring Pakistan. The PCB would not only protest but also do everything possible to expose Hair. I concluded by saying that I sympathized with the team's protest and recommended that they should hold back for 'about five minutes, equivalent to two overs' to publicly register their protest and then proceed to play. Woolmer forcefully argued that after a brief registering of a protest, the team should return to the field.

Inzamam responded that a formal protest was 'only a piece of paper' that would not salvage the team's pride and honour. A slur had been committed against the team and the nation. The team was not prepared to play unless the decision was reversed and the umpires apologized publicly.

Realizing that a prolonged delay could lead to ICC penalties, I made a more impassioned plea to the team. I stated that I knew an injustice had been perpetrated on the team and I supported a brief protest, but the team must go out and play after a brief lapse of time. Otherwise, the tide of sympathy that was flowing in our favour (evident from comments by the Sky commentary team of Nasser Hussain, Michael Atherton, Michael Holding and Ian Botham) would turn against Pakistan. We could be penalized severely by the ICC. Pakistan would be handing over the advantage to Hair and spoiling its own case. (Play was to start after tea at 4:40 pm.) Inzamam appeared unconvinced. Only one player, Shoaib Akhtar, was nodding in agreement with my appeal. Younus Khan sat in a corner head bowed. Other players seemed confused and ready to follow their captain. The junior players were in a daze. At one point, Inzi said that 'the team can play but I will not go into the field'. I immediately rejected any such proposal and with Woolmer and Zaheer's support, I urged Inzamam to return after a short period (five minutes). Woolmer even suggested that the team could show their protest by sitting down on the field for two minutes to register their protest and then proceed with the game.

At 4:40 pm, when play was scheduled to restart, the Sky commentary team was beginning to state that Pakistan would not return to the field after tea as a protest. Accordingly, Woolmer and I pointed to the television set in the dressing room and stated that the Pakistan team's protest had been duly registered and after a short delay, the team should go out and play. Apart from all the factors mentioned earlier, this action would be greatly appreciated by the large capacity crowd. At that point Inzamam agreed to take the field.

At 4:43 pm Inzamam and a couple of players actually took a few steps out of the dressing room (recorded on TV) but turned back after seeing the umpires leaving the field. I realized the situation was becoming dangerous, as the players had not actually taken the field.

Returning to the pavilion, Hair and Doctrove proceeded straight to the Pakistan dressing room. While sitting in the team dressing room, I noted Hair and Doctrove appear at the dressing-room door. I noticed that Hair abruptly asked Inzamam: 'Are you coming out or not?' Inzi retorted: 'Why did you change the ball? Why did you not show me the ball?' Hair replied brusquely, 'I am not here to answer these questions. If you don't come out, I shall charge you again,' and walked off. Inzamam was incensed by Hair's attitude and dug in his heels and decided again not to take the field.

Shortly after Darrell Hair's visit, the Match Referee Mike Procter came to the dressing room. He asked to see the captain and manager. I said I would also like to come along. Procter declined but, in the corridor, I conveyed the following to Procter:

- The team was deeply anguished by the ball-tampering accusation.
- Having registered their protest the team was ready to resume the match. This fact was admitted in Procter's written evidence before the adjudicator.

At 4:54 pm, about 11 minutes after Hair had spoken to Inzamam, the umpires walked out again onto the field with the English batsmen trailing behind. The Pakistan team did not appear.

After waiting a couple more minutes for the Pakistan team to appear, the umpires removed the bails and declared the match forfeit. Only 12 minutes had passed between the time Hair gave his ultimatum to Inzamam and the umpires returning to the field and taking off the bails.

As I left the dressing room, I saw Dr Nasim Ashraf coming towards me. Dr Ashraf, an ad hoc committee member, had stopped over in London after a visit to the USA to be present for the opening of the Pakistan Room at the Oval. He had also been sitting in the Oval Committee Room and offered to help bring sense to the team as every passing minute saw an increased danger of ICC punitive measures and enormous loss of goodwill.

Dr Nasim Ashraf and I re-entered the dressing room and found that the team had changed from whites into their tracksuits. The team had obviously veered towards a complete protest and Inzamam announced that 'we shall not play until the referee and umpires make a public apology on television and take back their ball-tampering accusations'. This hardened line was a shocking reversal of the earlier decision by the team to go out and play. It represented a total disconnection with rationality, even in the midst of a crisis.

At 5:10 pm, jointly addressing the team with Dr Ashraf, I stated once more that:

- It had won the battle of hearts and minds as the public and media were so far with them.
- However, not playing at all would reverse this trend.
- It would play into Darrell Hair's hands.
- The Pakistan team was likely to be severely penalized.
- Our moral high ground would be lost and any financial loss accruing to England would be claimed from us.

I concluded that the protest had been duly registered and that the team had a duty to the PCB and Pakistan to go out and play.

Dr Nasim Ashraf also made an impassioned plea for the team to now go out and play as their legitimate protest had been amply registered. Eagerly waiting for play to be resumed were 20,000 spectators, and the team would cede the moral high ground if it did not play. Despite the impassioned pleas of Dr Nasim Ashraf and myself, supported by Woolmer and Zaheer Abbas, Inzamam kept insisting that the umpires should apologize on TV and take back the ball-tampering charge. I told Inzamam bluntly that they would never do that and the team's interest required that they should go on the field, but he did not appear inclined to listen to our advice.

During this period (between 5:05 and 5:20 pm) Dr Nasim Ashraf telephoned President's House on his mobile phone to inform him of the brewing crisis. He briefed the Military Secretary to the

President and was subsequently connected to the President. After a few words, the telephone was passed to Inzamam who spoke to the President.

After the telephone call, slightly divergent interpretations of the President's direction appeared. Dr Nasim Ashraf stated that while the President had sympathized with and supported Inzamam's decision to protest, he had urged the captain and the team to follow rules and the management's advice. Inzamam's recall was limited to the President's support and not to the second part of the directive (follow rules). This may have encouraged Inzamam towards continued intransigence.

At around 5:15 pm, Dr Nasim Ashraf and I had a discussion with David Morgan, Chairman of the England Cricket Board, who wanted to persuade Inzamam to resume play. I took David Morgan to Inzamam. In a calm and reasoned manner, Morgan explained the importance of playing for the sake of Pakistan's image, for the guiding principles of cricket and in order to maintain the moral high ground. Dr Nasim Ashraf and I supported Morgan. As a result, Inzamam agreed to take to the field and began changing back into whites.

Morgan went straight to the referee to inform him that Pakistan would take the field. I instructed Zaheer Abbas and Woolmer to inform Procter that we were ready to take the field. I made three brief statements to the media outside the dressing room (live on Sky Sports and the BBC) stating that the team had been traumatized by the accusation, but after registering its protest the team was ready to play.

At 5:24 pm the team changed into whites and went out on the field for about five minutes. As the umpires did not follow, the team went back into their dressing room at 5:30 pm. It is important to note that in the dressing room, between 4:40 and 5:25 pm, two crises took place. The first was minor and easily overcome while the second was major and led to the forfeiture. The first crisis related to Inzamam and the team's refusal to resume play after tea

(4:40 pm). Following intensive discussion, Inzamam agreed to resume play after a brief (five-minute) protest. Inzamam and some members of the team actually came out of the dressing room but found the umpires returning from the field and stepped back. The first crisis had at that point been weathered and the Pakistan team had decided to resume play.

The second more serious crisis came when Hair and Doctrove came directly to the Pakistan dressing room. Hair, in a highly brusque and intemperate tone, addressed Inzamam and left the room. It appears that he then went (with Doctrove as always trailing behind) to the English dressing room and asked if the team was ready to play. On being given an affirmative response he told the padded up batsmen – Bell and Collingwood – to follow the umpires. Thus, against the traditional norms of cricket, the batsmen followed the umpires on to the field when normally they wait for the fielding side to precede them. It took Hair and Doctrove exactly 12 minutes after initially walking back from the middle, giving an ultimatum to Inzamam, walking back on the field with the English batsmen trailing behind and removing the bails to declare the match forfeit! No one, neither referee nor umpires, informed the captain or the manager that the match had been forfeited.

Predictably this second crisis led to Inzamam, who was already seething with anger, digging his heels in further and refusing to play after Hair's rude intervention. I was a witness to the Hair-Inzamam exchange and the immediate reversal of Inzamam's earlier decision to resume play. Even this crisis was overcome after Woolmer, Dr Nasim Ashraf, Zaheer Abbas, myself and most tellingly, David Morgan, had persuaded Inzamam and his team to see the light. At 5:25 pm the team went out on the field to resume play but by then the umpires refused to follow, maintaining that the match had already been forfeited.

I was informed that the ECB, Surrey Cricket Club and the Match Referee made several attempts to get the umpires to resume the match but they were adamant. By 6:10pm, play had been called off for the day and the Match Referee had called an immediate meeting of officials, managers and captains.

ACT II – THE ATTEMPT TO REVIVE THE MATCH. MEETING AT 7:00 PM CALLED BY THE MATCH REFEREE IN THE PLAYERS' DINING ROOM

7:00 pm

Present at the meeting chaired by Procter were the following: From the ICC, Match Referee Mike Procter, umpires Hair and Doctrove, umpires' manager Doug Cowie; from the ECB, Jesty and Hartley (third and fourth umpires), David Morgan (Chairman ECB), David Collier (CEO), Andrew Strauss (captain); and from the PCB, Shaharyar M. Khan (Chairman), Inzamam-ul-Haq (captain) and Zaheer Abbas (manager).

Mike Procter began the proceedings by stating that he had called the meeting with a view to starting the match the following day (Monday). The impasse needed to be broken and the meeting was intended to devise a move forward rather than looking back. He asked for comments.

I immediately took the floor and said that the team had felt deeply insulted by the ball-tampering accusation that was tantamount to calling the team and the nation cheats. The team had, after a brief period to register their protest, agreed to resume the match (Hair seemed to sneer mockingly at my remarks) and had informed the Match Referee. As evidence of wanting to play they had actually gone out onto the cricket field to resume play. I informed Procter that Pakistan was ready to play on Monday morning.

David Morgan stated that the ECB also wanted play to start the following day as 12,000 tickets had been sold. Commercially and financially, England would face huge losses if cricket were not resumed on Monday. In the interest of cricket, play should be resumed on the Monday.

Andrew Strauss said his team would like to play on Monday. The only issue was to find a mechanism that would ensure play. With a little flexibility he felt that such a mechanism could easily be devised.

Inzamam also stated that he wanted to play and that except for the brief period to register its protests, his team had shown its readiness to resume play.

Darrell Hair, summing up his actions, stated that Inzamam had been given enough time to take the field. He and Doctrove had also gone to the dressing room to enquire if the Pakistan team would take the field. He had not received a reply. So after 'ample' (12 minutes!) time he had taken off the bails and according to the rules of the game the match had been forfeited. The umpires' decision was final and could not be changed.

At this point, Inzamam interrupted and asked Hair directly: 'Why did you change the ball? Why did you not show me the ball? If there were scratches, why did you not tell me? It is the captain's right to be informed. You did not inform me.' Inzamam spoke in an agitated manner, presumably believing that the meeting had been called on the ball-tampering issue. I tried to restrain Inzamam. At this point Hair stood up, stating, 'I don't have to listen to this rubbish,' and walked out of the meeting. Doctrove and Cowie stayed. At a later date, Hair accused Inzamam of making a dismissive gesture that led to his walkout. I was sitting next to Inzamam and saw no such offensive gesture. Inzamam was aggressive and perhaps irrelevant but I saw no evidence of a dismissive gesture.

Procter repeated that the object of the exercise was to start the game on Monday. We had heard the umpires' verdict and no progress appeared to have been made. At this point, Morgan and I insisted that we should continue to try and break the impasse and that flexibility from both sides would help overcome the problem. The game was greater than any individual. Doctrove and Cowie supported Hair's verdict.

Around 8:00 pm, almost two hours into the meeting, Procter excused the managers and captains, who withdrew from the room, leaving David Morgan, David Collier, Cowie, Doctrove, Zaheer Abbas and myself in a restricted meeting. Procter stated that the umpires were adamant that the forfeiture issue could not be reversed and as he did not have the authority to reverse the umpires' decision, he would seek intervention from the ICC. David Morgan and I agreed that the matter was serious enough for the Match Referee to seek ICC intervention.

Procter then contacted Malcolm Speed in Dubai on the telephone from an adjoining room. After about ten minutes, Procter came back to the meeting saying that Speed had called him back, stating that he had spoken to Darrell Hair and urged him to show flexibility but Hair was adamant. Malcolm Speed also spoke to David Morgan, who confirmed that both chairmen and captains wanted the match to resume the following day.

When Procter reported the news of the continued impasse back to me, I felt determined not to give up trying to find a way forward. I quickly drafted a paragraph in which the PCB expressed its 'deep regret' at not coming out in time after tea. I felt this would act as a face-saving peg on which play could be resumed the following day – something that everyone desired. Procter showed the paragraph to Hair who again refused to alter his decision. Mike Procter then rang up Speed a second time, who again telephoned Hair only to be rebuffed. The die was cast.

By 10:15 pm Hair, Doctrove and Procter had left the Oval for the hotel, so had both the teams, and in the absence of flexibility or any agreement, the match was abandoned at 10:15 pm. I was grievously disappointed as I thought there was still some room to manoeuvre, but as all the ICC officials had left, there was no option but to accept Hair's verdict.

In my diplomatic experience, I had sat through whole nights to negotiate resolutions to break such an impasse. Here we had the Match Referee, both chairmen, both captains and both coaches willing to start the match the following morning. Malcolm Speed, the Chief Executive, twice telephoned Hair to show flexibility but he remained obdurate, sticking to the letter of the law. Worse still, instead of trying to find a solution to the impasse, Hair left for his hotel leaving us dangling, empty-handed. During Procter's absences from the meeting room, while he telephoned Malcolm Speed, I had informally discussed with David Morgan other measures for breaking the deadlock. I had offered to accept two English umpires to complete the match and even to alter my press release by replacing the term 'regret' with 'apologize', but the umpires had walked away, leaving the Match Referee, both captains and both chairmen of the respective boards to deal with a cricketing, public relations and financial disaster that was in my view entirely avoidable. I recalled the wise words of the English captain Andrew Strauss, who said that the impasse could easily be overcome with a little flexibility so the match could restart the next day.

Aside from the umpires walking away from ongoing negotiations, I was also gravely disappointed by the attitude of the Match Referee, Mike Procter's passive and weak role during the episode. Aside from holding the meeting, at which he clearly stated that it was being called to restart the match the following day, he took no firm action to translate the unanimous view around the table to persuade the umpires to alter their decision. He quickly passed the buck to Malcolm Speed and then, in the face of a cricketing catastrophe, simply shrugged his shoulders and went back to his hotel. In my brief experience as manager I had seen Match Referee Cammie Smith take an enlightened view when in 1999 the Kolkata crowd erupted after the Tendulkar run-out. Pakistan waited until the following day before the match could be resumed. I had similarly seen Match Referee Clive Lloyd take decisive measures to control a volatile situation during Pakistan's World Cup match against Australia. These Match Referees were fully in control and through firm and decisive action settled issues in the overall interests of the game. No such action was forthcoming from Procter.

Speed telephoned me at around 11 pm to say that he regretted that all four umpires had taken a joint stand on the issue. Speed added he did not believe he had the authority to reverse an umpire's decision or order them to resume play if they did not wish to do so.

Monday 21 August

On Monday, 21 August, Speed telephoned me again and said he was appointing Ranjan Madugalle Chief Adjudicator for a hearing to be held four days later on Friday. Speed said Procter was too close to the event and was likely, in any case, to be called as a witness. I agreed. Later in the day, Speed telephoned me again to say that Madugalle's sister had been suddenly admitted to hospital and that he may not be able to make the hearing on Friday. Later still, Speed informed me that Madugalle would definitely not make the hearing on Friday, 25 August but he hoped to schedule it a few days later, before the ODIs started on 30 August.

I relayed this news to Inzamam who sensed an ICC conspiracy to gain time. He wanted to have the hearing immediately so that the stigma of ball tampering was removed before the ODIs. He expressed reservations over continuing the tour until the team's name was cleared. I told Inzamam that the reason for Madugalle's delay was personal and understandable. I cautioned Inzamam that the tide of unprecedented media support would evaporate and even run against the team if Pakistan did not fulfil its remaining obligation to England. Pakistan's plaint was with Hair and the ICC and not with England, its team or English spectators.

On Monday, 21 August, I had decided to take legal advice, and Dr Naseem Ashraf, after consulting the Pakistan High Commissioner, suggested DLA Piper, a top-ranked legal firm that specialized in sports disputes. They called on me in the afternoon and I found them impressive and decided to engage them. As a leading law firm they informed me that their fees were high. Their lawyer Mark Gay was the leading sports expert in Britain.

From 21 August itself and for the next week, the British press

269

was stridently sympathetic towards the Pakistan cricket team and critical of Darrell Hair's actions, particularly after the revelation by the ICC that he had offered to retire if a large sum were paid to him. The following are some of the quotes that appeared in the media.

Simon Barnes, the doyen of British sports journalists, stated:

> He knew it was nothing like telling a batsman: look, you got a touch, you should have walked, now I'm telling you to go. He knew that it was going to cause a massive rumpus. He knew he was calling the Pakistan players the equivalent of a whore.
>
> He also knew the scandal he would cause by refusing to come out and umpire a game when two teams and several million people were ready to carry on. Was it a taste for drama in a drama-prone man? Was it demoniacal moral rigidity? Was he standing unforgivably on his dignity? Or was he right about the decision he made?
>
> Sky, not short of cameras or curiosity, was unable to find any footage of a guilty player doing some sneaky thing to the ball. All we have, then, is Hair's judgment: Hair's punishment: Hair's abdication: Hair's creation of one of the great periodic scandals in cricket history. All I can say is that he'd bloody well better be bloody well sure that he was bloody well right.[1]

The Tribunal's decision on the ball-tampering issue was that Hair and Doctrove were wrong!

Michael Atherton, speaking on Sky Sports, stated that Hair's decision lacked any historical context and common sense:

> It's bound to inflame things. It would have been best to leave it to the end of the day. He's not a man to back down. He's a stubborn character, a strong character... so even though Pakistan said they were willing to come back out [after the bails removal/apparent forfeiture] you could imagine him sitting in the dressing room refusing to come out.

Nasser Hussain, former England captain, wrote in the *Daily Mail*: 'Did Darrell Hair actually see a member of the Pakistan team tampering with a cricket ball? Has he got proof?' 'If he hasn't then he has made a massive mistake,' Hussain added:

> If I had been accused of cheating in this way then, as long as I was sure of our innocence, I would have done exactly the same thing as Pakistan.
>
> I wouldn't have come out after tea, either. People have said that Pakistan should have waited until the close of play and then gone down the right channels, but they wouldn't have seen it that way.
>
> To Pakistan, if they had carried on playing, they would have been admitting their guilt.[2]

Christopher Martin-Jenkins, in *The Times* dated 21 August, stated that the ICC arguably bore the prime responsibility for the chaos that ensued after the five-run penalty had been applied when England were 230 for three, not because the adjudication was right or wrong, but because of the umpire who took first responsibility for the decision. Hair had been a controversial figure for a long time in Asian cricket circles. It was insensitive and unwise to appoint him for the last two matches of this series, not least because he had twice incensed Pakistan during the Faisalabad Test in November.

Sir Ian Botham, writing in his column in the *Daily Mirror*, stated: 'I blame the ICC for the saddest and most serious stand-off that I can remember in Test cricket. The blame lies with the International Cricket Council.'

Dickie Bird, the famous umpire appearing on BBC Radio 5, stated: 'I think they should have finished the Test match. Pakistan have been badly hurt but the people who have to suffer are the fans. They have paid the money. After the match you can get round the table and thrash it out.'

ACT III – LAWYERS, DELAYS, FIXING OF HEARING

During the day, I received calls from Sri Lanka, Bangladesh and India conveying their support for Pakistan. They felt Hair's action

271

had been harsh and unwarranted. They conveyed their support if and when Pakistan decided to raise the issue at the ICC. Malcolm Speed also telephoned to say that Madugalle's sister's condition was worse than expected and that he may not be able to travel to London until after the ODIs. The ICC had considered other options, but in view of the high political sensitivity of the case, he felt Madugalle was the right adjudicator.

Our lawyers were keen for a delay as they wanted to prepare witness statements, forensic reports and expert witnesses and wanted at least ten days before the hearing. They were only too glad for Madugalle's enforced postponement.

On the other hand, Inzamam was brooding continuously and imagining conspiracies, mainly the ICC's attempt to delay the hearing. He kept stating that the hearing would result in complete innocence for the team and delays only meant that the ball-tampering accusation would keep hanging over the team's head.

In order to maintain the momentum of public goodwill towards Pakistan, our lawyers and their media advisers had strongly recommended that we announce that regardless of developments on the hearing issue, Pakistan would play the ODIs. I agreed totally with this view as not playing the remaining matches to which we were committed was not an issue. Yet Inzamam kept making statements that hinted at the team pulling out of the ODIs if the hearing was not held before the ODIs started on 30 August 2006.

On Tuesday, 22 August, I telephoned President's House to inform the President through his Military Secretary of latest developments on the hearing. I conveyed my views that we had to play the remaining ODIs. The President's Military Secretary rang me back to say that President Musharraf agreed entirely with my views.

On Tuesday 22 August at 4 pm, I organized a meeting between the lawyers and Inzamam at the Renaissance Hotel at Heathrow where the team was staying. Our lawyers went through the evidence and strongly advised Inzamam to make a statement confirming playing the ODIs. Inzamam seemed hesitant and I told the lawyers I would work on him.

The next day at 2 pm I met David Morgan at Paddington station and we took a taxi to the Renaissance Hotel where I was to meet Inzamam again. Morgan again spoke gently and rationally to Inzamam, telling him that he was losing support and sympathy from the British public by expressing doubts about playing the five ODIs. Inzamam kept up his irrational contention about the delay of the hearing, but Morgan and I soothingly persuaded him to drop his hesitation and come out in favour of playing the ODIs. Our lawyers had also prepared a brief press release from Inzamam stating that his team would be playing the five ODIs. Inzamam remained hesitant and noncommital.

I stayed on at the Renaissance Hotel and at 7 pm that night I met the team at maghrib prayers and made the following points:

- Our complaint was against Hair and the ICC, not against our hosts – the ECB or England players.
- Hair had been consistently against Pakistan. We had regularly asked the ICC not to appoint him.
- We would pursue the Hair issue with the ICC after the hearing – and even consider legal action.
- The delay in the hearing was due to genuine personal reasons – Madugalle's sister's hospitalization. There was no sinister reason for the delay.
- The British press had been heavily supportive of Pakistan. Not playing the ODIs would turn this attitude around.
- Not playing the ODIs was not an option.

I told Inzamam privately that I had spoken to President's House who entirely agreed with my line of action. Inzamam told me that he too had received a call from President's House and they had said that he (Inzamam) should follow my guidelines. I stayed the night at the Renaissance Hotel and returned to London convinced that the team and Inzamam were now on board.

Meanwhile, I had received a telephone call from Percy Sonn, President of the ICC, in which he had conveyed his deep concern at the Hair incident. He told me (from Sri Lanka) that he was proceeding to Dubai where he intended to convene an emergency Executive Board Meeting. I briefed him on developments. At the conclusion of our telephone discussion, Percy Sonn told me that his press release would contain 'something for Pakistan'.

At 4 pm on Thursday 24 August, David Morgan telephoned to inform me that the ECB was obliged to announce alternative arrangements if Inzamam and the PCB did not come out with a confirmation of the ODIs. I told Morgan that after his meeting with Inzamam the day before, I had spoken to Inzi and he had confirmed at prayer time that he would play the ODIs. I told Morgan that we were announcing this the following day and it would be futile to announce alternative arrangements. Morgan regretted that he was obliged to announce the alternative arrangements that night. I asked him to come over to my residence from where I would telephone Inzamam.

At 6:30 pm Morgan arrived and I agreed with the need for Inzamam to make the statement, which was our last chance to retain British goodwill. If made later, the statement would appear to be the result of ECB pressure and ICC direction, because Percy Sonn and Malcolm Speed were due in London the following day, having cancelled the emergency meeting of the Executive Board. After a 15-minute telephone discussion, Inzamam seemed inclined to support the statement but asked for ten minutes to consult his colleagues (Yousuf, Razzaq, Afridi and Waqar). After half an hour he rang back. He said that he was not agreeable to making the statement to continue with the ODIs. It seemed that Inzamam's close advisers had insisted on his maintaining his intransigent attitude. This, despite his having concurred with me the day before and the Military Secretary and the President's telephone call to Inzamam to follow my advice.

At 7:30 pm Morgan left me dejectedly, stating that he would

be obliged to issue the press release announcing alternative arrangements. Morgan told me that the West Indies had agreed to replace Pakistan in the five ODIs.

I was furious at this volte-face by Inzamam. I told him that he would do great damage to Pakistan by not playing the ODIs. I had conveyed to him the clear advice of the Patron and myself the day before to play the ODIs. I told Inzamam that I would proceed immediately to the Renaissance Hotel to hold a team meeting (it was 8 pm) that night.

Just before leaving, Asad Mustafa, assistant manager, rang and told me that many of the players had gone out to dinner and would not be able to attend the meeting. I vented my anger again at Asad Mustafa for him to convey to Inzamam, but I agreed to hold the meeting at 9 am the following day (Friday, 25 August).

On Friday, 25 August, I left early in the morning for the Renaissance Hotel for the third time in three days and arrived at 9am, and was met at the door by a contrite Inzamam who informed me that there was no need for a team meeting as he and the team had unanimously decided to play the five ODIs against England. I told Inzamam that he had changed his position twice and I wanted to be doubly certain that he would stick to his decision. The delay had lost a lot of goodwill for Pakistan. He reassured me that there would be no change.

It transpired that Mushtaq Ahmed, a mature and worldly-wise cricketer, whom I had met a few days earlier at the final of the English one-day trophy and briefed about Inzamam's strange, inconsistent behaviour, visited the Renaissance Hotel and knocked some sense into Inzamam's head. The meeting probably clinched Inzamam's decision to play the ODIs against England.

I telephoned David Morgan immediately that the ODIs were on. Friday morning's press had carried the announcement of the ECB's alternative plan for the West Indies to replace Pakistan in the ODI series. Our agreement to play had come too late.

Meanwhile, Percy Sonn and Malcolm Speed had arrived in

London. I met them at their hotel where they told me that after consulting three separate lawyers, they had decided to publish Darrell Hair's email in which he asked for $500,000 to retire. (He later withdrew his offer.)

Percy Sonn and Malcolm Speed held a press conference at 3 pm, at which the sensational news of Hair's demand was made public. In an earlier meeting with me at his hotel, Percy Sonn told me that the decision to make Hair's demand public was because the press would, sooner rather than later, obtain a copy of Hair's demand and the ICC would rightly be accused of withholding evidence relevant to the formal inquiry. Hair was roundly criticized in the British press. The hearing was set for 27 September and the immediate issue was closed. The team proceeded to play the ODIs to general relief.

Though I had planned to return home immediately after the Oval Test, I decided to stay on in London to discuss urgent issues with the lawyers and also to guide the team through the trauma of the Oval fiasco. Clearly, Inzamam had assumed full control of the team, with coach Bob Woolmer and manager Zaheer Abbas losing all influence. At the Oval, during my 20-minute harangue urging the players to go out and play, I noticed that nearly all team members listened to me with bowed heads and without making eye contact. They all waited for Inzamam's cue. Even educated and independent-minded players like Younus Khan, Mohammad Hafeez and Salman Butt would not look Bob Woolmer or I in the eye. Younus Khan, who had retreated to a corner in the dressing room during the crisis, later confided to me that he knew that what we were advocating was correct but he had to follow his captain. The only exception was the wayward but worldly-wise Shoaib Akhtar, who not only looked me in the eye but also signified his agreement with my appeal by repeatedly nodding. Shoaib was nobody's poodle and knew the stakes were high during those critical moments in the dressing room. For the remaining team, culture and tradition kicked in. You do not question your elders and certainly not if their authority is bolstered by religious knowledge.

After the team had agreed to play the ODIs and the date for the hearing had been set for 27/28 September, I had time to reflect. I am convinced that the Oval fiasco had been avoidable and was due to Darrell Hair's refusal to heed both chairmen, captains, the referee and even Malcolm Speed's attempts to restart the match on Monday. Billy Doctrove went along with Darrell Hair, but it was evident from his body language that he was uncomfortable with Hair's decision. It transpired later that he had advised Hair to wait a few overs before finally deciding that the ball had been tampered with. Significantly, after Hair's walkout from Procter's meeting, Doctrove had not followed him and stayed in the room. Clearly, Hair had studied the laws on ball tampering and forfeiture and had concluded that they gave the umpires the sole and unfettered authority to decide these issues. The referee had no specific mandate to alter the umpires' decision. Since the Oval debacle, the ICC has amended the regulations to include the Match Referee's role on these issues.

Deeply disturbing for me was Inzamam's reluctance to take his team out to play during the dressing-room crises. It could be argued that in the dressing room Inzamam was too disturbed and overwrought to think clearly of the repercussions. His long and successful endeavour to build up a sporting and harmonious approach to the team lay in ruins by the ball-tampering charge. His own and Pakistan's *izzat* (honour) had been demeaned. He could be forgiven for not heeding Bob Woolmer, Dr Nasim Ashraf and my exhortations to take the field. Eventually he agreed, too late, after David Morgan had gently reasoned with him.

Much more disturbing in the days that followed was Inzamam's refusal to play the ODIs. Base instincts and crass stupidity seemed to overtake him and at one point he told me: 'We will not play (the ODIs) and you can replace my team with other players from Pakistan.' This was player power at its worst, with a leader who seemed to be guided by a self-destructive urge to play a misguided and shallow grandstanding role to the Pakistan gallery. It reminded

277

me of the Pakistan hockey team's protest at the Munich Olympics, when the players hung their silver medals around their shoes in an act of misplaced defiance. The Pakistan Hockey Federation had to pay a huge price for this show of truculence and was banned by the World Hockey federation.

The basic reason for such attitudes is a lack of educated background that prevents our players from seeing the wood for the trees. Coupled with this lack of education is a sense of insecurity that the captain felt at the strident criticism in the national press and by retired icons like Imran Khan, Sarfraz Nawaz and Javed Miandad aimed at his defensive, non-assertive leadership. I yearned, at times, for leaders like Ricky Ponting, Andrew Strauss, Rahul Dravid, Imran Khan and Kumar Sangakarra, who were worldly-wise and had a complete grasp of ICC regulations. Inzamam had demonstrated that despite a long Test career and captaincy he did not have such a detailed grasp of regulations. In New Zealand he failed to claim the extra half-hour to secure the match and had gone into the final day knowing (or perhaps not knowing) that the weather forecast was dire. Fortunately for him, though it rained heavily, there was sufficient time to win the game. In Peshawar, he had struck a throw-in from a fielder with his bat and had rightly been given out for obstructing the field. He later complained that he could not understand the umpire's decision!

To his credit, I had generally found Inzamam a mature, dignified and level-headed person. He had a sense of humour. I had supported him as captain through the barrage of salacious criticism levelled against him. He had confided in me several times that he knew I was his strongest supporter. He quoted his father advising him that I was his staunchest ally. Yet, at the critical moment during and after the Oval Test, he chose to flout my advice. I could have forgiven his outburst in the heat of the crisis in the Oval dressing room, but his subsequent obduracy I found unacceptable and deeply disturbing.

I returned to Pakistan in mid-September with a heavy heart. Not only would the Oval incident affect the morale of the Pakistan team, but the decline in the form of our four all-rounders bode ill for our World Cup prospects. I had genuinely believed that Pakistan had every chance of success at the World Cup because of our engine room of four excellent all-rounders – Razzaq, Afridi, Shoaib Malik and Kamran Akmal. No other team in the world had such a flush of genuine all-rounders – not just bits and pieces players – that could influence a one-day match. We had a superb opening attack with Shoaib Akhtar, Mohammad Asif and Umar Gul, good middle-order batsmen, and there had been spirit, unity and commitment in our team that had led to results placing Pakistan second and third in the ICC Test and ODI rankings. Regrettably, during the England tour, these all-rounders had regressed. Razzaq's batting was inconsistent and his bowling had lost its cutting edge. Afridi had hardly made a score since his triumphs against India, West Indies and England, getting out early to undisciplined hoicks. Kamran's wicketkeeping had seen a sharp downturn in performance that affected his batting, and Shoaib Malik had been out of action after his elbow operation. We had not been able to find a reliable opening pair and our fielding had shown no improvement despite Jonty Rhodes's coaching stint. Suddenly, from robust optimism, I had found our chances of success at the World Cup diminishing sharply. All these factors, and especially the growing player power, led me to conclude that I should resign my Chairmanship of the PCB when three months later my tenure came to an end. In my mind I had concluded that if the Patron wished me to carry on for three months until the World Cup, I would do so but not beyond.

ACT IV – THE HEARING

On 24 September, I took a flight directly to London from Shanghai to attend the hearing scheduled for 27 and 28 September. Inzamam, Bob Woolmer and our excellent lawyer Ahmad Hosain had already preceded me to London. At DLA Piper's offices, we held briefing sessions with Mark Gay and prepared our evidence for both items that were to be decided – the ball-tampering and forfeiture issues. Mark Gay was a superb professional and his handling of the case had been highly impressive, giving us confidence of a favourable verdict. We were informed that Ranjan Madugalle, the official adjudicator and chief referee, would be assisted by a leading Queen's Counsel, Lord David Pannick, and that the prosecution would be led by Pushpinder Saini, a young Sikh barrister who was a member of a leading British law firm which shared the same chambers as David Pannick QC. In an informal chat in the recess, Pushpinder Saini remarked that it was ironical that one of his favourite batsmen was Inzamam-ul-Haq! On Darrell Hair's behalf, umpires Doctrove, Jesty, Match Referee Procter and ICC umpires' manager Cowie would give evidence, while the defence

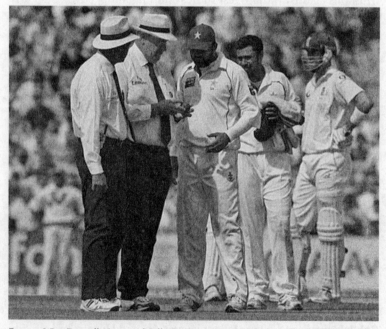

Figure 15 Darrell Hair and Billy Doctrove accuse Inzamam and the Pakistan team of having tampered with the ball, setting off the Oval crisis, 2006.

Figure 16 Addressing the press after the Oval Test decision in which the Pakistan team were found not guilty of tampering with the ball, 2006.

would produce experts John Hampshire (former international umpire), Mark Hughes (a TV expert) and the famous Test player and commentator, Geoff Boycott.

The proceedings began in a small, packed room at the Oval, with the prosecution witnesses giving well-rehearsed evidence maintaining that, in their opinion, the ball had been tampered and that the umpires had given their decisions strictly according to the rules. Mark Gay expertly cross-examined the witnesses raising doubts about their evidence. During this examination, I found Madugalle and Pannick intervening briefly with pertinent and incisive questions that showed them both to be fair and judicious in drawing their conclusions. When it came to our turn to give evidence, Inzamam was provided with an Urdu–English interpreter. Woolmer and I also gave evidence and were followed by our experts. Hampshire and Hughes made excellent, precise witnesses, Hampshire concluding that Hair should not have aborted play so abruptly, while Hughes maintained that the state of the ball corresponded to its 55-over use and that there was no evidence of tampering.

However, the tour de force came from Geoff Boycott, who tore into the prosecution with highly articulate, pugnacious and superbly crafted arguments. In his typical Yorkshire accent, Boycott decimated the prosecution's reliance on the minutiae of the laws, maintaining that the fundamental requirement for the umpires was to protect the basic image of cricket. Reading out the relevant overarching paragraph on the laws of cricket, he stated that the umpires had failed to uphold the basic interests of cricket by not showing patience and understanding of the spirit of the game and had arbitrarily aborted a match that could and should have continued. As regards ball tampering, Boycott took the offending ball in his hand and remarked that its scuff marks were totally consistent with 55-over use and at no time had 26 TV cameras noted the slightest evidence of tampering. The least the umpires could have done was warn the captain and to have consulted the referee before arriving at the precipitate and final decision. Boycott's intervention was dramatic, highly convincing and virtually carried the day for the defence. His audacious arguments even evoked guarded smiles from Ranjan Madugalle and David Pannick QC. We went home elated that after the final arguments the following morning, we could expect a favourable verdict.

On the morning of 28 September, we huddled again in the small room at the Oval for the final arguments. Pushpinder Saini took the floor and in a superb hour-long summing up for the prosecution appeared to clinically demolish the defence's case. The British Sikh averred that Hair and Doctrove had acted scrupulously within the law in deciding on the ball-tampering and forfeiture issues. His arguments were superbly marshalled, and overall Pushpinder Saini was brilliant in his advocacy. In response, Mark Gay was less impressive, rounding up the defence in a 20-minute summation. After the elation of Boycott's farrago the day before, we went into lunch in a state of depression as the young Sikh had clearly won the last round on points. Ahmad Hosain explained to me at lunch that the difference was that Pushpinder Saini was a barrister while Mark Gay was a solicitor.

After lunch, we trooped back into the Oval room where after a brief introduction by David Pannick QC, Ranjan Madugalle read out the verdict. On the first count the Pakistan team was found not guilty of ball tampering. On the second count the Pakistan team was found guilty of bringing the game into disrepute by refusing to play. Madugalle then asked Inzamam if he wished to make a comment. I told Inzamam to proceed to the dais and apologize for his misjudgement. This he did with the result that Inzamam was penalized with a four-match ban which was the minimum punishment for a Grade-III offence. After the verdict, Inzamam embraced me warmly and there was elation in the Pakistan camp that we had succeeded in overturning the slur of ball tampering that had been made against Inzamam and his team. For us and for the Pakistan public this was the basic issue of honour for the team and country and the not-guilty verdict had preserved our honour. The forfeiture verdict was seen as a minor sideshow to the main issue. Significantly, the adjudicators' verdict on the ball-tampering count was 'not guilty' and not 'not proven' which would have been weaker. That evening I held a press conference in which I welcomed the verdict without in any way gloating over it or referring to Hair's demand of $500,000 to retire, which had virtually led to his shooting himself in the foot.

I received a surprising number of accolades from Pakistan cricket lovers and the general public. They came in letters, emails, phone calls and messages. In London, Pakistani bus drivers, taxi drivers and even ordinary folk on the underground and buses would recognize me and make the V sign. The same was true when I returned to Pakistan, at airports, in shops and in hotels. The congratulations for redeeming the team's honour came simply and spontaneously. Even British cricket lovers approached me at times and praised the dignified manner in which we had handled the case.

The not-guilty verdict on ball tampering had been a great relief, but when I received the adjudicators' final written judgment, I found the penultimate paragraph to be a clear indictment of Darrell Hair and Billy Doctrove's role in deciding Pakistan had forfeited the match. Neither the British nor the Pakistani media has focused on this vital paragraph of Madugalle's judgment. It reads as follows:

> Finally, I should comment on one final matter. The witnesses agreed in evidence that player management and effective communication is an important aspect of umpiring at international level. In my judgment, a difficult and sensitive situation such as that which arose in the present case (finding of ball-tampering causing a substantial sense of grievance in, and protests from, the Pakistan team) requires handling with tactful diplomacy (as well as adherence to the Laws). This was an unprecedented situation. If (one hopes not) such a situation were to recur in international cricket, I would hope and expect the umpires would do everything possible to try to defuse

tensions in the dressing-room by explaining that a team is entitled to raise any grievance through the ICC but that it is not in their interests, or in the interests of the game, for the team to interrupt play. The Umpires and other officials should do everything possible to ensure the resumption of play. And they should not return to the field of play and then declare the match to be forfeited unless and until they are absolutely sure that the team is refusing to play the rest of the match. All other options should first be exhausted, involving discussions with the team captains and management.[3]

Based on this judgment, the following questions related to the above paragraph are pertinent:

- In a 'difficult and sensitive situation', did the umpires handle the situation with tactful diplomacy?
- In the dressing room did the umpires 'do everything possible to try and defuse the situation' and explain to the captain the implications of the team's refusal to play? (Knowing that Inzamam's English was poor?)
- Did the umpires do 'everything possible to ensure resumption of play'?
- Were the umpires also 'absolutely sure that the team was refusing to play the rest of the match before returning to the field and deciding to forfeit the match'? (It took them 12 minutes!)
- Did the umpires 'first exhaust all other options' involving team captains and management, before deciding to forfeit the match?

An important factor in this crisis was Inzamam's inability to fully understand and express himself in English, which must have been well known to Hair who had supervised five series in two years involving Pakistan.

The judgment defines the steps that an umpire is expected to take when faced with a team refusing to go out on the field. In short, the question arises as to whether or not Hair and Doctrove fulfilled any of the conditions stated in the judgment quoted above?

After reading the adjudicators' judgment, I firmly believed that a fair and honest view of Hair's role at the Oval Test and his subsequent attempt to extract money from the ICC would apportion blame, at least partly, to Hair for prematurely forfeiting the Test in favour of England. I knew that England had suffered huge financial losses on tickets, commercials and related issues as a result of the aborted Test and would want to be compensated by Pakistan as the judgment had found it guilty on the forfeiture count. The written judgment opened the way for the PCB to raise with the ICC the question of fixing responsibility for the Oval fiasco. Pakistan had not refused to play. They had been stunned and angered by the ball-tampering decision on which Pakistan had since been found not guilty and had temporarily delayed their re-entry on the field. In fact, at 4:45 pm Inzamam and some players had been seen on television to step out of their dressing room to resume play only to find the umpires walking back. There was then the fracas in the dressing room between Hair and Inzamam, which led to a further delay, Hair (and Doctrove) taking exactly 12 minutes between leaving the field, their ultimatum in the dressing room and decision on the field to declare the match forfeited.

On reviewing the relevant paragraph of Madugalle's judgment, I decided to write to the ICC requesting the formation of an independent panel that would fairly and impartially decide on fixing the responsibility for the consequences of aborting the Oval Test. This proposal was not aimed at pursuing a vendetta against Hair, but was an attempt to exonerate Pakistan for the forfeiture and at least partially sharing with the ICC the responsibility to compensate England for its loss. In my second letter to Speed, I formally conveyed that Pakistan would not accept Darrell Hair as umpire for future matches.

To my surprise, at the next ICC meeting attended by my successor Dr Nasim Ashraf, a casually appointed committee of three ICC Directors decided, with ICC approval, to remove Darrell Hair from the elite umpires panel without going through 'due process'. Predictably, Hair decided to sue the ICC on grounds of racial discrimination. The ICC decision appeared a grandstanding success for Pakistan but it left the responsibility issue undecided. England had every right to expect compensation for the financial loss for the Oval Test.

A year or so later, the ICC decided to reappoint Darrell Hair to the elite panel and to declare the Oval Test abandoned – a decision that the MCC stated was not within the ICC's competence. The ICC's latest decision smacked of a behind-the-scenes arrangement that would restore Hair and Australia's honour, while Pakistan could rejoice in the forfeit being replaced by a no-result decision. These U-turns undermined the credibility of the ICC and were widely criticized in the media. Yet another twist in this drama came when in January 2009 the ICC decided to rescind its earlier 'no result' decision and to reaffirm the 'forfeit' decision of the Oval Test. These decisions brought no credit to the ICC.

MY RESIGNATION

I returned to Karachi on 2 October and, according to a plan to meet each player individually, I met the Karachi players Kaneria, Sami, Faisal Iqbal and Younus Khan, who was in Karachi and had been nominated captain for the Champions Trophy after Inzamam's disqualification.

As always, it was a pleasure meeting Younus Khan. We discussed the forthcoming Champions Trophy and the need to avoid the decline in our spirits that saw us lose the last two ODIs. Younus was ebullient and raring to go. He made two requests. To fill Inzamam's forced vacancy, he requested one of two players – Misbah-ul-Haq or Naveed Lateef. His second request was to include Asad Mustafa as assistant manager in the management team.

I told Younus that all the names of players and support staff had already been sent to the ICC, as we had to meet a deadline. We could not now change. Only Inzamam's replacement would be allowed as a special case. The PCB had considered Asad Mustafa as manager, but since the Champions Trophy had only four or five fixtures and visits to two cities, we had after careful consideration decided against sending him. Moreover, as logistics manager, Asad Mustafa was required for the West Indies tour that followed immediately after the Champions Trophy. As regards Inzi's replacement, I said I would pass on Younus's recommendations to Wasim Bari, the Chief Selector, but I hinted that Misbah had barely been on the selector's radar and Naveed Lateef, at the age of 36, was not a candidate. I reminded Younus that I did not interfere in selection matters but I would convey his views to Bari. Younus left the meeting happy and content. He laughingly took my leave saying he was going fishing.

I immediately rang Wasim Bari and informed him of Younus's preference for filling Inzamam's place. Bari said that he and his selectors had already considered Inzamam's replacement and decided that the choice lay between Shahid Yousuf and Faisal Iqbal. Bari felt that although Shahid Yousuf had been selected for the England ODIs ahead of Faisal, Inzamam's replacement needed to be an experienced player ready to take pressures of large crowds in India. For this reason they had tilted in favour of Faisal Iqbal. He said neither Misbah nor Naveed Lateef were viable candidates as they were not serious candidates for the World Cup. I told Wasim to interact with Younus and I would accept the choice they made after mutual consultation. I then took a flight to Lahore.

On 6 October, I had scheduled a meeting at 10:30 am with a visitor sent by Governor Khalid Maqbool. At precisely 10:30 am I asked my Secretary if the visitors had arrived and on being told that they were waiting, I asked that they be ushered in. Prior to the visitors entering my office, my peon informed me that Younus Khan wanted to see me. I sent word that I had a previous appointment that would take five minutes. I requested Younus to wait a few minutes after which I would call him in.

Players and management frequently sought impromptu appointments with me and if I was free, I received them immediately, but if I was in a meeting or had a previous appointment, I asked them to wait. Sometimes Woolmer, Inzamam, Shoaib Akhtar and other players waited up to an hour before I became free.

In fact, I actually finished my scheduled meeting in five minutes and asked for Younus Khan to come in. Regrettably, unknown to me, Younus Khan stormed into the waiting press conference and in a fury announced his resignation as 'dummy captain'. He clearly acted in a fit of pique for being kept waiting a few minutes and kicked away cricket's greatest honour – being captain of one's national team. It was also Ramadan and Younus was fasting, which sometimes leads to a short fuse.

For two hours – from 10:45 am to 12:45 pm – various messages were sent to Younus Khan but he would not relent. Eventually, his mentors – probably former captains Rashid Latif and Imran Khan – advised him to calm down.

Meanwhile, an emergency meeting of available ad hoc committee members had decided that the act of gross indiscipline should not go unpunished. There was unanimous agreement that Younus Khan should be removed from the team for the Champions Trophy and disciplinary action taken for his conduct. The emergency committee decided to make Mohammad Yousuf (who was vice-captain for the Champions Trophy) captain and to promote Abdur Razzaq, the next player in order of seniority, as vice-captain.

At 1:00 pm, just as the orders of the disciplinary committee were being finalized, a message was received from Younus Khan stating that he was prepared to apologize to the Chairman (myself) in a one-on-one meeting and then express his regret to the press.

Younus Khan came to me at around 4:45pm. We had a one-on-one meeting in which I reminded him that I had made him vice-captain against much opposition (meaning Inzamam's coterie of senior players) and that I expected a smooth transfer of captaincy in his favour whenever Inzamam stepped down. I said his bizarre conduct that morning was inexcusable. For me it was 'Et tu, Brute'!

Younus Khan said that waiting a few minutes was not the reason for his outburst, which he now accepted was wrong. He regarded me almost like his father (a statement he repeated in India). He felt other forces were operating against him (meaning Inzamam and his close allies). He nevertheless deeply regretted his action and was ready to play under Yousuf as an ordinary player. He insisted that he would not proceed as captain.

We then addressed a press conference where Younus deeply regretted his action in the morning and agreed to play as an ordinary player in the team but declined to go as captain. Yousuf was announced as captain and Razzaq as vice-captain.

That night my resignation, that had already been conveyed to President Musharraf, was accepted and immediately my successor Dr Nasim Ashraf was announced as Chairman. He reinstated Younus Khan as captain but the Pakistan team did not get beyond the preliminary round of the Champions Trophy. Worse, Shoaib and Asif were found to have exceeded nandrolene limits by taking unauthorized drugs. Pakistan cricket had descended into a pit of humiliation.

So the demons unleashed by the Oval Test crisis came home to haunt Pakistan. The Pakistan public saw Darrell Hair as a representative of the hostile West. The ICC should never have appointed him so consistently to Pakistan series (probably true). It did so because the ICC establishment represented Western domination. After years of moderation and circumspection, Inzamam broke loose from his chains and organized a players' revolt. Even if he could be forgiven for having acted in the heat of the moment on the fateful afternoon at the slur on his team's (and therefore the nation's) honour (*izzat*), his subsequent refusal to play the ODIs against advice (even from the Patron) was a gross act of indiscipline. The Oval Test and its aftermath shattered the image that I, as Chairman of the PCB, had attempted to build – that of a disciplined team acting under the wise and mature leadership of Inzamam and Woolmer. A team that behaved responsibly, especially when playing against India and England. A team shorn of its usual propensity for tantrums and silly incidents. Though we won our case on the ball-tampering issue, the broken pieces were going to be difficult to glue together again. Besides, the confidence between the management and players had broken down. With only three months to go before the end of my contract, I felt that it was time to bow out.

WOOLMER'S DEATH

On the night of my resignation, I was at once relieved and disappointed. I had sent my written resignation to the President much earlier and asked him to keep it in his drawer to be accepted at the appropriate time. I indicated to the President that the moment had arrived. Younus Khan's bizarre behaviour had confirmed in my mind that it was time to quit. I had left the timing of its acceptance to the Patron. A telephone call from the President's Chief of Staff informed me that my resignation was being accepted. Later, during the call, the President came on the line and was gracious in his fulsome praise of my tenure. Subsequently he sent me a warm letter praising my contribution to cricket in Pakistan, which I decided not to make public.

Bob Woolmer visited me that night, red-eyed and distraught. He reminded me that he had several times told me that the day I left the PCB he would resign. He said there was no way he could continue as coach without my support. He knew that there were senior elements in the Board ranged against him and it would no longer be possible for him to carry on. I told Woolmer that he had done a superb job as national coach that had seen the team climb to near the top of the ICC ratings. I reassured him that my successor, Dr Nasim Ashraf, had been his strongest supporter in the ad hoc committee and that he could be certain of the new Chairman's full backing. I also reasoned that leaving the team four months before the World Cup would be deeply demoralizing and would see all his hard work go to waste. Woolmer was not sure but eventually accepted my advice, and paid me the rare compliment of stating that in his long years in cricket he had never come across a better and wiser cricket administrator.

Later that night Inzamam also arrived unannounced and seemed devastated at my resignation. He said he was prepared to motor up to Islamabad that night to persuade the Patron to reverse his decision, which he ascribed to various intrigues. I persuaded him not to take any such futile step. Inzamam felt the drastic change in the Board would seriously damage Pakistan's lead-up to the World Cup, as it would undermine team morale.

In the subsequent weeks, I deliberately withdrew from the public eye. I made no comment on our poor showing in the Champions Trophy and the shocking revelation that Shoaib Akhtar and Mohammad Asif stood accused of drug abuse. This led to huge controversy in the media and the final straw was Pakistan's ignominious exit after the preliminary round of the World Cup.

The night before the team left for the West Indies, Bob Woolmer came to see me again. He was in despair and sought my advice as a friend. He said that the team's morale was low and clear factions among the seniors had led to a deleterious effect on the team's performance. After the Champions Trophy exit, the tour of South Africa had been disastrous. Asif and Shoaib Akhtar, though exonerated by the Drugs Appeals Committee, still had enough nandrolone in their bodies to be penalized if they were tested under ICC regulations. The tribunal that found the two players guilty had its verdict overturned by the Appeals Committee on the grounds that the PCB had not formally warned them of the consequences of taking the banned drugs. The Appeals Committee's decision seemed to exacerbate the issue rather than resolve it, especially as the committee's drug expert had given a dissenting opinion.

Bob Woolmer told me that he had sent an email from South Africa after injuries to some players, requesting that the PCB and the selectors prepare reserve players (no names were mentioned) to be flown out in an emergency. The PCB hierarchy wrongly interpreted this as a request for Shoaib Akhtar, who was flown out only to break down again and fly back to Pakistan! Woolmer was accused of asking for Shoaib Akhtar behind Inzamam's back, which led to another regrettable face-off between the captain and the coach. Woolmer felt that this unfair criticism levelled at him was mainly due to his arch opponent, Salim Altaf, calling the shots in the PCB, especially as Dr Nasim Ashraf had only recently taken over and was obliged to spend time attending to his official responsibilities in Islamabad as Minister of State for Human Development. Bob Woolmer frankly admitted that with the steep decline in morale and performance, the team was unlikely to perform with credit in the World Cup. He obviously expected his reputation as a coach to be severely tarnished. Three months earlier, he had been full of hope and confidence. Bob Woolmer then put two questions to me. Firstly, he wanted to resign now as he had three months earlier. Should he do so? Secondly, in the unlikely event of a successful World Cup, should he continue as Pakistan's coach after his tenure came to an end in June 2007? To the first question I replied emphatically that despite problems, Bob should see Pakistan through the World Cup. A resignation now would be counterproductive from every angle. This was not the time to resign after all the dedicated work he had put into preparing the team.

As regards renewal of his contract, I told Bob that it was always preferable to go out with head held high. If the PCB wanted him to continue beyond his current tenure, he should quote his cricketing and financial terms, and if the PCB accepted, he could consider another year or two. He knew the vicious slings and arrows that a foreign coach faced in Pakistan, especially from the media and from frustrated cricketing icons. Having experienced the dilemma it was for him alone to decide whether or not to continue. For most genuine and neutral observers of cricket, Bob Woolmer's contribution to Pakistan cricket had been enormous. Bob thanked me for my counsel and resolved not to resign. As he left me, he gave me an un-English Pakistani bear-hug and gave my wife Minnoo a peck on the cheek. He was obviously emotional at this farewell call because of my friendship and support for him. Minnoo had also gone out of her way to make Bob's wife Gill and their two sons feel at home in Lahore during their occasional visits to Pakistan. It was my last meeting with Bob Woolmer.

On the day after our loss to Ireland in the 2007 World Cup, I was stunned by the news that Bob Woolmer had been found dead in his hotel room. My gut reaction about what had happened was that, shocked by Pakistan's ignominious exit from the World Cup, Bob had suffered a heart attack. Bob had been overweight and had an asthmatic condition, which required occasional use of an oxygen mask before he slept. Soon, however, news began filtering through that forensic reports indicated that Bob had been murdered, probably by strangulation and possibly after his drink had been spiked with poison. All the bottled-up demons relating to the Pakistan team's reputation and conduct were released after Woolmer's controversial death. No team in the world other than Pakistan would have the spectre of criminality hanging over its head, with wild speculations regarding excessive religiosity, hot-headed indiscipline and betting scandals doing the rounds of the information media.

The forensic expert confirmed the murder theory and predictably wild speculation was set afoot at possible motives for murder. It was suggested that one or more headstrong members of the team might have taken out their anger on Woolmer. There were also suggestions of a religious fanatic in or around the team perpetrating the crime, but the most common speculation was that Woolmer had unearthed a match-fixing syndrome and had been killed by agents of the mafia to silence him. There were suggestions that Bob was about to blow the whistle on such a match-fixing scandal and had recorded it in his forthcoming book. In all these speculative comments, members of the Pakistan team figured prominently. There were reports of a fracas in the team bus returning to the hotel that had led to a gash on Mushtaq Ahmed's cheek – later proved to be incorrect. Long ago, some members had been linked with match-fixing by the Malik Qayyum Report. The media, particularly in England, India and Pakistan, went berserk in speculating on the motive for Bob's murder. Meanwhile, in Kingston, team members were grilled by the Jamaican police, while video, forensic and eyewitness evidence was given headline coverage. The Pakistan team was not allowed to return home and was billeted for days in a separate hotel for more questioning by the Jamaican police. It was a harrowing experience for a team already demoralized by their early exit from the World Cup.

During these weeks, when outrageous rumours were swirling about the wires, I was convinced, first, that Woolmer would not himself be involved in any match-fixing scandal, and second, that no member of the Pakistan team would murder or conspire to murder Bob Woolmer. I had known Bob Woolmer for over two years and knew that character-wise he would have no truck with match-fixing. Moreover, if he had the slightest suspicion that any of his team had connections with the betting mafia, he would have shared his fears with me in the manner that he had with regard to players taking drugs. As for team members being involved in Bob's murder, I had got to know this team for three years and though there was justifiable criticism of their overt religiosity, it had given them a strong moral base that made any criminal act virtually impossible to contemplate. In any case, Bob Woolmer was a gentle human being who had established a relationship of respect and warmth with members of the team. Despite occasional skirmishes with Inzamam, both men respected each other and Inzamam was genuinely devastated by Woolmer's loss. For me the only possible motive for Bob's murder could be that he had discovered a match-fixing racket and before he could blow the whistle the mafia decided to silence him. Even this eventually seemed extremely remote, leaving me incredulous at the Jamaican coroner's conclusion that Woolmer had been strangled to death. In the months that followed it transpired that the initial conclusion that Woolmer had been strangled was not correct, as forensic experts from the UK, the USA and Canada concluded that Woolmer had died of natural causes.

Asad Mustafa, the assistant manager, who had stayed on in Jamaica throughout the investigation, returned to Pakistan after several months in Jamaica. I asked him to give me an account of what had happened during the fateful night. I have pieced together Asad Mustafa's account of the events.

After the loss to Ireland and Pakistan's exit from the World Cup, the atmosphere on the bus ride to the hotel was excessively gloomy. Woolmer, who had felt the loss as deeply as anyone, was the only person who had tried to rally the spirits of the players. Heartbroken himself, Woolmer still went up to each player in the bus in an effort to lift the team from its obvious gloom. It was typical of Woolmer's attitude that he should seek to lift his team after a disastrous World Cup, as he could easily have stayed in his seat and brooded like everyone else, but he chose to rally the boys into a more positive frame of mind. This account put paid to the rumour that a fracas between the players had occurred during the bus ride back to the hotel. Bob Woolmer then bid goodnight to Asad and his colleagues, saying that he would not come down to dinner and would take his meal in his room.

Next morning, Asad Mustafa came down to breakfast at 7:30 sharp with Murray Stevenson, the trainer. Woolmer, Stevenson and Mustafa regularly had breakfast together at 7:30 am to have a morning chat and plan out the day. On the fateful morning, Woolmer did not join his colleagues and they concluded that he must have overslept after a troubled night. After breakfast, Asad Mustafa went to a meeting at 10:30 am to organize departure details. At around 10:35 am Danish Kaneria, who occupied the room next to Woolmer's, entered the meeting in a state of agitation and told Asad that the manager, Talat Ali, wanted to see him. Asad told Kaneria that he would go over in a few minutes but Kaneria insisted that he was required urgently. Asad met Talat Ali outside Woolmer's room and was told that Woolmer had been found unconscious. They entered the room and found Woolmer stretched out on the bathroom floor. Soon, hotel security, the police and ambulance men arrived and carried a lifeless Woolmer to the hospital, where he was pronounced dead.

Asad told me that the hotel maid had entered Woolmer's room at 8 am and found him in bed 'asleep' (possibly unconscious). She had probably gone in early to make up his room as he normally went down to breakfast at 7:30 am. Seeing him in bed, she left the room and returned two hours later to find him unconscious in the bathroom surrounded by blood and vomit. This account suggests that the crisis that caused Woolmer's death occurred between 8 am and 10 am. If correct, it discounts the theory that Woolmer's 'killers' had gained access to Woolmer's room late at night or in the early hours of the morning. An email addressed to his wife before he turned in was a perfectly normal message carrying no hint of crisis or concern. Eventually, the Jamaican coroner reached an 'open' verdict. Now that the dust has settled, Bob Woolmer's soul can lie in peace and his family be reassured that there was no foul play in his death. He was too good a man to suffer the legacy of a controversial death.

After his death, Bob Woolmer received the most fulsome tributes from all quarters and especially from the players. They remembered him with genuine feeling for his coaching skills, his gentle persuasive demeanour and his humane and humble qualities. He proved that with a sensitive approach, a foreign coach could overcome the cultural and language gap.

May his soul rest in peace.

CHAPTER 12

CONCLUSIONS

The preceding chapters have dwelt on issues that ail Pakistan cricket. We have moved from general society-wide issues such as endemic corruption, lack of role models, accountability and education to how these factors are played out in a specific context as in the Oval Test and the spot-fixing saga.

There are no easy answers for some of these issues, particularly those that have roots in historical, social and political forces that prevail in Pakistan. There are others that are self-inflicted, for which short-term remedies are available if only they could be grasped.

Let us begin with the short-term measures that would help alleviate some of the problems that burden cricket in Pakistan. There is no better place for such a beginning than reference to the recently published Task Force Report compiled under the chairmanship of Giles Clarke, President of the ECB. The ICC had formed the Task Force with a view to assisting Pakistan at a time when its cricket was being seriously damaged and restricted by terrorism. The Task Force has, basically, addressed issues under three main headings:

1. A democratic workable constitution.
2. The importance of resuming bilateral series with India, which it considers to be at least on par with the Ashes.
3. Administrative and organizational changes.

All these recommendations should be taken in hand immediately and implemented. Most of the Task Force's recommendations touch issues that have been analysed in earlier chapters of this book. Now is the time to implement them for the benefit of Pakistan cricket.

As regards a constitution, the PCB is operating under an interim constitution whose permanent shape remains to be decided by the Presidency and the Ministry of Sports. This is symptomatic of the 'ad hocism' in Pakistan. Meanwhile, the ICC has announced that in the future, a board whose chairman/president is nominated and not democratically elected would lose its rights as a member of the Board of Directors. This measure affects Pakistan, Bangladesh, Sri Lanka and possibly Zimbabwe, and is obviously an attempt to curb political interference by governments in their respective cricketing boards. I have already referred to this issue in Chapter 5 and my suggestion was a halfway house between a democratically-elected and a nominated Chairman of the PCB.

The Task Force found it unacceptable that the Chairman of the PCB should be nominated by the Patron, who would also nominate 50 per cent of the Governing Council. The Chairman has the power to autocratically nominate the national selectors and has a final say in the teams selected by them. The Chairman is virtually the CEO of the Board and seems accountable to his nominator – the Patron – rather than to the game of cricket in Pakistan. Rightly, the Task Force has recommended that this process needs democratization.

I still have reservations about a completely democratic election for Chairman because, given access to the PCB's financial honeypot, the power and influence of the office, there is every likelihood of a free election throwing up unscrupulous politicians, mafiosi or feudal barons who would want to use the PCB as a stepping stone for further influence. In my time, as a director of the ICC, we saw this happen in the case of Sri Lanka, where various cabals had sought power, leading to ugly confrontations nationally and with the ICC. There is a need for a broadly representative constitution, which ensures that men of scrupulous integrity are at the helm of cricket affairs.

As regards the need for change in the PCB's administrative and organizational set-up, it is important to streamline the bureaucracy, which is far too large and flabby. All appointments need to be advertised and made through due process. In financial matters, integrity and transparency have to be ensured through checks and balances, deriving their authority from a revised constitution. Organizationally, the first-class programme needs careful reassessment. There are too many teams and too many players participating in first-class cricket, lowering the quality of cricket. The rich corporations (departments) should not be allowed to siphon away talent from the relatively poor regional teams that must form the bedrock of a restricted competition, as is the case in every other part of the cricketing world. Regional cricket must receive sponsorship and financial support from the PCB with a strong helping hand from the government.

It needs to be stated that the PCB's efforts have not been entirely bleak. There are some areas in which the PCB has been successful, such as training of umpires, curators and lower-level coaches. Tours by visiting teams have been efficiently organized and a programme for identifying talent at a young level put in place. Women's cricket has also taken off. Much needs to be done in other domains, however, like club and schools cricket that provide the main feeder belt to representative cricket. The selection process needs, as far as possible, to be corruption-free. In these domains the PCB requires the help of the government and its institutions so that grounds are made available for cricket at all levels. The government needs also to encourage sponsorship that only requires a directive from the top for it to become a reality in a short span of time. It is surely in the government's own interest to promote and encourage the game from the grass roots to the top of the pyramid as cricket, in Sir John Major's words, can lift a nation when its team succeeds or plunge it into despair when it fails. Need it be repeated that cricket affects the morale of a country, especially in the subcontinent? Government must therefore play a much more proactive and focused role in the development and promotion of cricket in Pakistan.

Already, some measures recommended by the Task Force have been implemented. There is now a strict code of honour that players have to sign. Players are made aware of the punishments that are prescribed in case they fail to meet standards. An integrity committee has been appointed. Drugs, spot-fixing and interaction with the betting mafia form part of the no-go area in the code of honour. However, more needs to be done to educate budding cricketers, given the fact that many of them are likely to be a product of *maidaan* cricket. All young cricketers would have to be taught basic spoken English and social graces on and off the cricket field. Primarily, more playing grounds need to be made available for grass-roots cricket.

There is a danger that with a drought of international cricket in Pakistan a diminishing of public interest could occur. Opportunities for cricketers to play against foreign teams would be limited and, certainly, financial income would be reduced. There are no signs, however, that the inability to host international cricket at home is affecting the public's enthusiasm for the game. The challenge for Pakistan is to gradually restore faith in security for visiting teams.

I anticipate the shadow of terrorism to be part of Pakistan's political scene for some time – perhaps ten to twenty years. Some teams from friendly Asian countries like Bangladesh, Sri Lanka and even India may be able to visit Pakistan sooner – perhaps in two to three years' time. Other non-Test-playing countries like Afghanistan, Nepal and Ireland could be persuaded to tour Pakistan – so could Zimbabwe and the West Indies. Their example would be useful to break the ice and encourage Australia, New Zealand, South Africa and England eventually to send their cricket teams to Pakistan. However, before such time as cricket teams begin visiting Pakistan, it would be practical where possible to develop five-star hotels on or adjacent to Test stadiums. This would eliminate the danger-prone coach journeys between hotel and stadium and would enable the security agencies to throw a secure cordon around the playing area. Finally, while these secure zones are planned, Pakistan should play its home series either in a third country like the UAE, Sri Lanka, Bangladesh or Malaysia or make special financial arrangements to play home series in the host country. This has been experimented with in New Zealand and England and though it is not ideal, it is better than not playing at all.

The Oval Test fiasco led to a number of lessons being drawn. Most of them were deep-seated, buried in the psychological complexes of a nation. The players' lack of education was obvious in their not understanding the significance of laws, and also in their not being able to assess and respond to a critical situation. Finally, a deep sense of persecution and insecurity that led to wild conspiracy theories and a feeling that the Western world was out to damage Pakistan permeated the team's psyche. Long after the immediate Ovel Test crisis, Inzamam refused to play the ODIs until ordered by the President and persuaded to see the light by his fellow Tableeghi sympathizer Mushtaq Ahmed (see Chapter 11).

There is one short-term lesson, however, that needs to be heeded by the ICC. This relates to the importance of treating every ICC member in an equal manner. The heavyweights like India or Australia must be measured with the same yardstick as the less important countries like Zimbabwe or Pakistan. Contrast their role with Pakistan's persistent pleas to the ICC not to appoint Darrell Hair to Pakistan series (and the ICC's refusal to heed these entreaties) with the ICC's immediate withdrawal of respected umpire Bucknor in the Australia–India series of 2010 after a poor decision against Tendulkar. Contrast also the ICC's legitimate sensitivity towards Sri Lanka by not appointing Hair for eight years after the Muralitharan incident with the fact that Hair was appointed five times in Pakistan series over three years. It was a time bomb waiting to explode, which it did at the Oval in 2006. Much of the blame for this disservice to cricket must be placed at the ICC's door. Equal and sensitive treatment to all ICC members would have prevented this cricketing shipwreck.

I agree entirely with the Task Force recommendation that the Pakistan–India series needs to be revived immediately. According to the ICC calendar Pakistan was scheduled to visit India in February/March 2012. I felt this opportunity should not be missed and even though it was Pakistan's turn to visit India, the BCCI was ready to give a written undertaking that Pakistan's 'missed' hosting would be made up later, possibly by having the home series in South Africa (where the Indians are prepared to go) as they will not play in the UAE for understandable reasons. This re-scheduling required advance planning and diplomacy, but the basic objective should be to start our bilateral series with India as early as possible. During an informal visit to India at the instance of the then Chairman Ijaz Butt, I obtained in principle the BCCI's agreement to host the Pakistan–India series on schedule (that is, February/March 2012). This opportunity was missed but I am glad that a short Pakistan–India series took place in India in December/January 2012–13. Most recent reports have highlighted the fact that the Pakistan Ministry of Foreign Affairs has been pushing for the resumption of ties as a way of kickstarting stalled bilateral relations.

When the resumption of an India–Pakistan series is discussed there are some people on both sides of the border who fear that the matches would reflect the deep political hostility between the two neighbours. This hostility is revived periodically by incidents like the Mumbai terrorist attack, the Kargil venture and the attack on the Indian Parliament. In Pakistan, a deep sense of resentment is felt by the killings on the Samjhauta Express, the Babri Masjid demolition and the anti-Muslim riots in Gujarat. These incidents open up existing wounds and sharpen the mutual hostility fanned by extremists on both sides. Some people become fearful that a cricket series would exacerbate this hostility that has its deep roots in history and in the aftermath of partition.

I do not share this concern and believe that cricket would act as a bridge of peace between Pakistan and India. The reason for this confidence is that I have seen Indian crowd behaviour when Pakistan visited India in 1999 and again in 2005. I have seen Pakistan crowds welcome the Indian team and 20,000 fans in 2004 and again in 2006. A new younger generation in both countries sees its cricket matches as a sporting contest rather than a battle. In Chennai in 1999, 15,000 Indian fans stayed on long after the match had been completed and India had narrowly lost the Test. I vividly recall captain Wasim Akram asking me after the presentation ceremony if he could lead his team on a victory lap, to which I readily agreed. The Chennai crowd then gave the Pakistan team a memorable send-off. In the same year I was witness to the Mohali crowd giving the 5,000 visiting Pakistani supporters a day to remember. The fans that came in buses were first treated to a free Indian film show. They were then invited at the ODI to a *langar* (buffet) hosted by the Chief Minister of Punjab. Once again, Pakistan won the match, but there were loud slogans from both sets of fans of 'Pak–India dosti zindabad' (long live Pak–India friendship). In the VIP enclosure I had seen a large number of attractive Sikh girls with the Indian flag painted on one cheek and the Pakistan flag on the other.[1]

The Pakistan public has been similarly welcoming to the Indian team in 2004 and 2006, events that I have described earlier in Chapter 3. My sense and judgement of the public mood is that whenever an Indo-Pakistan series begins, this mature mood will dominate. Of course, extremists on both sides would agitate, but I am sure that the general public will be welcoming. Deep political issues remain unresolved; incidents like the Mumbai attack (sponsored by extremists) will poison the atmosphere, but the new generation craves peace, development, good neighbourly relations, and wants the hostility and terrorism of the past behind them. Cricket should be allowed to play a healing role in that direction, which is vital for peace and well-being in both countries.

Figure 17 (left to right) Governor General Khalid Maqbool; Inzamam-ul-Haq; Dr Nasim Ashraf, then Chairman of the PCB; Shaharyar M. Khan, former Chairman of the PCB; and Talat Ali, Team Manager, attend Bob Woolmer's memorial service at the Anglican Cathedral Church of Resurrection, Lahore. Shoaib Malik and Mohammad Asif can be glimpsed in the background.

Having reached the upper levels of the international ladder under Bob Woolmer, Pakistan now languishes near the bottom in the company of Zimbabwe, Bangladesh and the West Indies. Occasionally there are flashes of success like topping the pool in the recent World Cup or winning the T20 tournament, but generally the results have been disappointing for the Pakistan public compared to the heady days of the 1990s and, more recently, when Pakistan defeated India in seven games out of nine. One of the factors in this decline is the absence of leadership on and off the field. The spate of controversies has cast a pall over the team as has constant changes in captaincy. This has in turn led to player factionalism, intrigue and lack of focus. Allied to these failings is the fact that except for Inzamam, Pakistan has not produced a world-class player in the past decade. Before the turn of the century, Pakistan had Imran Khan, Wasim Akram, Waqar Younis, Javed Miandad, Zaheer Abbas and Abdul Qadir. A few others were near that class and saw Pakistan win the World Cup in 1996 and several bilateral series. The reason for this dearth is that though abundant talent is available it is not being tapped to optimum advantage because of corruption and biased selection at lower levels. Nevertheless, Pakistan has unearthed some gems like Mohammad Amir and Mohammad Asif from unfashionable townships only to see them engulfed in a mudslide of corruption. I believe talent surfaces in cycles. All great cricketing countries have known their doldrums, including Australia, the West Indies, England and India, but decisive leadership and the turn of the wheel in unearthing talent revives them. I am sure Pakistan will also turn the corner as there is no shortage of talent, but it needs to be spotted and groomed.

Healthy finance is a fundamental requirement for the PCB. When I left the Board, the PCB had managed to increase its reserves from Pak Rs 730 million to Pak Rs 5.75 billion – over five times the initial figure. With a solid financial base the Board can sustain development at all levels. These reserves have to be husbanded diligently and development expenditure budgeted and planned by financial specialists. The National Academy has superb facilities. We need to develop regional coaching academies on a priority basis. Cricket in Pakistan is a lucrative business as our sponsors (ABN AMRO) calculated that for every rupee invested they gained a return of 11 rupees in a year, which is a significant profit. These figures need to be publicized in order to gain sponsorship and financial support from the private sector. I have a feeling that the PCB has never been able to project this potential profitability in an effective manner, as is the case in India. It is not too late to do so now.

My reservations on the increased use of technology may suggest that I am against its introduction. This is not the case. I would welcome it with the following provisos. The ICC should insist on the DRS being applied across the board and not, as at present, in a piecemeal manner. We have recently seen India reject the DRS system in its series against England and then agreeing to it without affecting lbws. In most other series lbws have been included in the

DRS. This is unsatisfactory and a uniform system, with or without lbws, is required. Secondly, I maintain that an umpire's general authority over the game is diminished when a player appeals over the heads of the field umpires to a third umpire against the original decision. This goes against the very principle of cricket and indeed, of life, that the umpire's decision is final. Surely a solution can be found when the appeal by the player against a doubtful decision is addressed to the umpire himself, who then decides to refer it upwards, except when he is absolutely sure of his decision, in which case no such referral is made. I know the umpires have welcomed, on the surface, the DRS, but deep down I am sure they do not like players going over their heads and questioning their judgement. Surely the ICC can devise a referral system that does not diminish an umpire's standing and authority while utilizing available technology.

The issue of excessive religiosity, which affected Pakistan cricket during the Inzamam years, can be put in perspective summarily. This phase was neither typical nor reflective of Pakistan society. It was a passing phase and the result of the religious inclinations of one man – Inzamam-ul-Haq. As I had anticipated, this phase ended immediately after Inzamam's retirement. There were no signs of excessive religiosity under the captaincy of Shoaib Malik, Younus Khan, Salman Butt and Misbah-ul-Haq, who succeeded Inzamam. Even his fellow Tableeghi comrades – Mohammad Yousuf and Shahid Afridi – did not invoke Inzamam's religious aura while they were briefly at the helm. The religious atmosphere has since reverted to normal with some players saying their prayers regularly but not in public, while others are left to decide their own religious practices without pressure or direction from the top. I consider the current atmosphere to be typical of 'middle' Pakistan attitudes towards religion.

Finally, let us analyse the long-term malaise that blights Pakistan cricket. Prominent in this spectrum are the issues of corruption, non-accountability, lack of education, economic wastage, political instability, absence of law and order, and social mayhem. All these ailments affect Pakistan cricket as described in Chapters 8 and 9. Their remedies do not, of course, lie in the hands of the PCB. They go much deeper to the national level. Who will bring us the security against terrorism and attacks against cricket teams, as was the case with Sri Lanka? Who will redress the plague of corruption, nepotism and patronage? Who can make up for the education drought when most of Pakistan's reserves have been diverted towards buying military hardware like tanks, F-16s, submarines, missiles and, of course, its nuclear programme? Our education budget stands far below the required UN quota for all developing countries. Moreover, lack of development in constructing health centres, schools, market-to-town roads, power and gas facilities and drinking water outlets have brought a deep sense of deprivation which has been a factor in promoting religious extremism and terrorism. Only responsible leadership can address these issues.

Yet there are some measures that the PCB could take in its own domain to address these problems. As mentioned earlier, in this sea of corruption there are a few islands that are recognized as efficient, disciplined and incorruptible. The Motorway Police and the Supreme Court are recognized as two beacons of integrity. The PCB should aim to create such an island of its own by ensuring discipline, integrity, financial probity and general transparency in its work. There are outstanding officers in the PCB like CEO Subhan Ahmed, who can deliver in creating such an island. It requires a head of the PCB with impeccable credentials and with the will to clean the swamp and to provide the necessary leadership.

And to the question of whether political, social and economic change in Pakistan is reflected in its cricket, the answer is evident, as we have traced our way through the book. Pakistan's broken education system is manifest in the cricket team. Its lack of accountability is evident, as are its insecurities and patronage structures. Even the phenomenal growth of its towns is reflected in the changing demographics of the Pakistan team. But while these traits do come out in the character of the team, so too do more positive qualities. Pakistan is defined by its youthful exuberance, its brilliant unpredictability and its unfettered and unharnessed natural talent.

What also of cricket's impact on society? Despite all the scandals and setbacks, cricket in Pakistan has brought more national joy and pride than anything else. Cricket has represented the one area in which Pakistan could compete and vanquish the very best. In the midst of the economic and political upheavals, victory in cricket could unite rich and poor, urban and rural, old and young, ethnic and religious sects. Differing backgrounds, ethnicities and religions were set aside for Pakistan's common joy and passion. It could lift the nation in a way nothing else could. The loss of international cricket in Pakistan is therefore a hammer blow to the heart and soul of an already troubled nation.

Recently, the cricket cauldron in Pakistan has been vigorously stirred. Many unsavoury contents have surfaced to the top. Yet a lot of golden nuggets lie at the bottom that can, and if properly primed, bring benefit and even glory to Pakistan cricket, lifting the morale of its devoted followers.

NOTES

INTRODUCTION

1. Marsden, Magnus, *Living Islam: Muslim Religious Experience in Pakistan's North-West Frontier* (Cambridge University Press, 2005); Jalal, Ayesha, 'The Sole Spokesman: Jinnah, the Muslim League and the Demand for Pakistan', *Cambridge South Asian Studies*, Cambridge University Press, reprint edition (28 April 1994); Khan, Naveeda (ed.), *Crisis and Beyond* (Critical Asian Studies) (Routledge India; 1st edition 2010); Shaikh, Farzana, *Making Sense of Pakistan* (C. Hurst & Co. Publishers Ltd, 2009); Lieven, Anatol, *Pakistan: A Hard Country* (Allen Lane, 2011); *Secularizing Islamists?: Jama'at-e-Islami and Jama'at-ud-Da'wa in Urban Pakistan* (South Asia Across the Disciplines) (University of Chicago Press, 2011).

2. Hamid, Mohsin, *Moth Smoke* (Penguin, 2011); Mueenuddin, Daniyal, *In Other Rooms, Other Wonders* (Bloomsbury Publishing PLC, 2010); Hanif, Mohammad, *A Case of Exploding Mangoes* (Vintage, 2009); Shamsie, Kamila, *In the City by the Sea* (Bloomsbury Publishing PLC, new edition, 2004).

3. James, Cyril Lionel Robert, *Beyond A Boundary* (Yellow Jersey, new edition, 2005).

4. Major, John, *More Than a Game* (London: Harper Collins, 2007), p. 7.

CHAPTER 1 CRICKET'S ROLE IN THE BIRTH OF PAKISTAN

1. It is suggested that polo was derived from the mountain sport of buzhkashi, played by the tribal people living in the high mountain

ranges of Central Asia. Buzhkashi comprises two teams of horsemen who wrestle on horseback to snatch the prize of a goat or calf carcass. There are practically no rules to the game, but it is still played in the Karakoram ranges in the north of Pakistan.

2. Gymkhana is the Indian equivalent of a sports and social club.
3. Jalal, Ayesha, *The Sole Spokesman* (Cambridge: Cambridge University Press, 1985).
4. Mahatma Gandhi as quoted in Shashi Tharoor & Shaharyar Khan, *Shadows Across the Playing Field* (New Delhi: Roli Books, 2009), p. 100.
5. Ibid, p. 152.

CHAPTER 2   THE CALL

1. Muhajirs are Urdu-speaking people from India who crossed over to Pakistan at Partition.
2. A hilltop village on the Kashmir Line of Control that was occupied by 'freedom fighters' supported by the Pakistan army. The incursion led to a violent skirmish between India and Pakistan.
3. Now named Khyber Pakhtunkhwa.
4. Khan, Shaharyar M., *Cricket – A Bridge of Peace* (Karachi: Oxford Unversity Press, 2005).
5. Saeed Anwar, a computer science graduate, was the only graduate of the 1999 Pakistan team that I managed. He was briefly appointed stop-gap captain.

CHAPTER 3   INDIA'S PATH-BREAKING TOUR OF PAKISTAN – MARCH/APRIL 2004

1. Jinnah's speech to the Pakistan Constituent Assembly on 11 August, 1947.
2. South Asian Association for Regional Cooperation.
3. MQM – Muttahida Quomi Mahaz – is a political party with an electoral base of Muhajirs living in Karachi and urban Sindh.
4. Until the record was broken by Australia and South Africa in the fifth ODI played in March 2006 at New Wanderers Stadium, Johannesburg. Australia scored 434 for four. South Africa replied with 438 to win by one wicket with one ball to spare.

CHAPTER 4   WOOLMER ENTERS THE FRAY

1. Described in greater detail in my book *Cricket – A Bridge of Peace* (Karachi: Oxford Unversity Press, 2005).

CHAPTER 5   URGENT ISSUES FACING THE PAKISTAN CRICKET BOARD

1. He later became Cabinet Minister for Privatization.
2. Subhan Ahmed was appointed the PCB's Chief Operating Officer in December 2010.
3. The Dutch banking chain.

CHAPTER 8   THE CONTROVERSIAL FACE OF PAKISTAN CRICKET

1. Khan, Imran, *All Round View* (London: Chatto and Windus, 1988), p. 195.
2. Ugra, Sharda, 'What makes sportsmen go corrupt?', 14 November 2010. Available at: http://www.espncricinfo.com/magazine/content/story/486782.html. Accessed 28 November 2010.
3. After the March hearing the Court decided to schedule the next hearing in October 2011.
4. International Cricket Council (ICC) v. Salman Butt, Mohammad Asif and Mohammad Amir. Determination (Redacted by the ICC Prior to Publication), p.12.
5. International Cricket Council (ICC) v. Salman Butt, Mohammad Asif and Mohammad Amir. Determination (Redacted by the ICC Prior to Publication), p.80.

CHAPTER 9   THE REASONS FOR PAKISTAN'S CONTROVERSIAL IMAGE

1. Ugra, Sharda, 'What makes sportsmen go corrupt?', 14 November 2010. Available at: http://www.espncricinfo.com/magazine/content/story/486782.html. Accessed 28 November 2010.
2. Ibid.
3. Excluding stand-in captains.

4. Webster, Rudi, 'Would a code of honour help?', 14 November 2010. Available at: http://www.espncricinfo.com/magazine/content/story/486861.html. Accessed 28 November 2010.

CHAPTER 10   2006 – THE FATEFUL YEAR

1. The match was originally awarded to England. This result was amended to an abandonment by the ICC in July 2008, although the change was disputed by the MCC, the custodians of the Laws of Cricket. In January 2009 the ICC voted to reverse their earlier decision and allow the original award of the Test to England to stand.

CHAPTER 11   THE OVAL TEST AND ITS AFTERMATH

1. *The Sunday Times*, 21 August 2006.
2. *Daily Mail*, 21 August 2006.
3. Full text on ICC Code of Conduct hearing involving Inzamam-ul Haq (ICC Media Release, London, 28 September 2006).

CHAPTER 12   CONCLUSIONS

1. These events are described in detail in my book *Cricket – A Bridge of Peace* (Karachi: Oxford Unversity Press, 2005).

INDEX

Bhopal, Nawab of, 55
Bhutan, 17
Bhutto, Benazir, 22, 51, 94, 122
Bhutto, Zulfiqar Ali, 21
Bird, Dickie, 271
Birmingham, 185
Bombay Hindu gymkhana, *see*
 gymkhana(s)
Bombay, Governor of, 2
Bombay, 1, 5, 7, 8, 11, 12, 39
Bombay Pentangular(s), 5–6, 7–8,
 9–11, 12, 13–15, 16
Bombay Quadrangular, 2, 4–5, 7, 9, 13
Bombay Triangular, 2, 4–5, 80, 129,
 130, 132
Botham, Ian, 151, 194, 260, 271
Boycott, Geoff, 282–83
Brabourne Stadium, 5, 12
Bracewell (John), 78
Bradman, Don, 37, 83, 131
Brearley, Mike, 221
Bridgetown, 147
Bristol, 185
Buchanan (John), 78
Bucknor, Steve, 159, 254, 302
Buddhists, 7, 138, 191
statues of Lord Buddha, 18
Bugti Stadium, 110
Bukhatir, Abdul Rahman, 170
Bunda, Naseer, 13
Burewala, 213
Burki, Javed, 33, 115, 183, 193, 213
Burney, Sami, 57
Bush, US President George W.,
 233–34, 235, 237–39
Butt, Ijaz, 93, 99, 303
Butt, Salman, 112, 130–31, 132, 141,
 151, 180, 190, 203, 206, 208, 209,
 218, 228, 230, 234, 237, 243, 246,
 255, 276, 307
Butt, Shujauddin, 115

Calcutta, 1, 7, 39, *see also* Kolkata
Canada, 39, 62, 170, 296
Canterbury, 244, 247
Cardiff, 185, 248
Carr, Donald, 151
Centurion, 59
Ceylon, 13, 129, *see also* Sri Lanka
Champions Trophy, 80, 110, 114, 160,
 195–96, 253, 287–88, 289, 290,
 292
Chanderpaul (Shivnarine), 147
Chandrashekhar, (B.S.), 54
Chappell brothers, 131
Chappell, Greg, 72, 75, 77, 78
Chappell, Ian, 32, 214
Cheema, Naveed, 49
Chenab formula, 22
Chennai, 55, 134, 304, *see also* Madras
China, 135, 170–71, 227
Chinese Cricket Association, 171
Chinese Taipei, 167
Chingoka, Peter, 158
Christchurch, 56–57, 58, 156
Christians, 7, 11, 12, 26, 138, 186, 187,
 188, 189, 191
chucker(s), 126–28
Clark, (Wayne), 128
Clarke, Giles, 114, 153, 298
Clive, Lloyd, 78, 130, 219, 268
Collector, K.R., 191
Collier, David, 265, 267
Collingwood, Paul, 149, 215, 245, 248,
 257, 264
Colombo, 117, 139, 239
Combined University team, 33,
 116
Commonwealth, 21, 37, 130, 170, 171,
 239
 British, 3
Compton, Denis, 12
Condon, Lord Paul, 200–01

West Indies (country & cricket), 13, 19,
36, 68, 77, 81, 101, 128, 132, 139,
140, 146, 147–48, 152, 158, 166–67,
175–76, 199, 206, 208, 219, 238,
251, 253, 255, 275, 279, 288, 292,
301, 305
West Pakistan, 29
Whatmore, Dav, 75, 77, 78
Wimbledon, 37
women's cricket, *see* IWCA; WCA;
PWCA
Woolmer, Bob, 72–87, 126, 130
World Cups, 19, 20, 24, 26, 30, 34,
51, 59, 72, 86–87, 110, 114, 123,
142, 143, 149, 153, 155, 158, 160,
164–65, 166, 167, 183, 184–85,
189, 190, 193, 194, 197, 199, 201,
202, 205, 221, 229, 238, 239, 240,
241, 249, 268, 279, 288, 292, 293,
294, 295, 296, 305
World War II, 10
Worrell, Frank, 219

Wright, John, 54, 66, 75, 77, 78

Yardy (Michael), 248
Yorkshire, 28, 106, 282
Younis, Waqar, 18, 31, 54, 74, 131,
185, 188, 193, 194, 198, 200, 213,
216, 218, 222–23, 241, 305
Yousuf Mohammad (Yousuf
Youhana), 149, 181, 184, 190, 218,
230, 245, 247, 249, 289, 307
Yousuf, Salim, 193
Yousuf, Shahid, 288

Zaman, Javed, 117
Zardari, Asif, 94
Zia, Lt. Gen. Tauqir, 20, 23–24, 26, 30,
35, 46, 47, 81, 90, 91, 97, 108, 110,
143, 144
Zia-ul-Haq, Gen. Muhammad, 21,
144, 182
Zimbabwe, 77–78, 88, 93, 114,
129–30, 158, 299, 301, 302, 305

ABOUT THE AUTHORS

Shaharyar M. Khan is an eminent international diplomat who served as Pakistan's High Commissioner in the United Kingdom, Ambassador to France and Jordan, Pakistan's Foreign Secretary and UN Secretary General's Special Representative in Rwanda. His cricket pedigree is impeccable. He distinguished himself at Cambridge University, played club cricket in Britain and Pakistan and was a playing member of the MCC. His family links him with the all-time 'greats' of cricket on the subcontinent including the Nawab of Pataudi, who played for England and captained India, and Mansur Ali Khan, a 'Blue' and Indian captain. He was Chairman of the Pakistan Cricket Board, 2003–6. Shaharyar Khan's previous publications include *The Begums of Bhopal: A Dynasty of Women Rulers in the Raj*, *The Shallow Graves of Rwanda* (both I.B.Tauris), and *Memoirs of a Rebel Princess*.

Ali Khan is Associate Professor of Anthropology and Department Chair at the Department of Humanities and Social Sciences at the Lahore University of Management Sciences (LUMS). His research interests vary from labour issues to popular culture in Pakistan, focusing particularly on cinema and sports. He has previously worked in Washington and in Islamabad for the World Bank and with the International Labour Organisation, primarily on projects related to child and bonded labour. He has an MPhil and a PhD in Social Anthropology from Cambridge University in England. He is the author of *Representing Children: Power, Policy and the Discourse on Child Labour in the Football Manufacturing Industry of Pakistan* (Oxford University Press, 2007). He is also the General Editor for a series of books on Sociology and Anthropology in Pakistan.